MuleSoft Integration Architectures

Definitive Reference for Developers and Engineers

Richard Johnson

Contents

4

Introduction

This book presents a comprehensive examination of MuleSoft integration architectures, aiming to equip architects, developers, and integration specialists with the in-depth knowledge required to design, implement, and govern sophisticated integration solutions. MuleSoft's Anypoint Platform serves as the foundation for modern enterprise connectivity, facilitating seamless communication between diverse applications, data sources, and devices in a secure, scalable, and manageable manner.

Beginning with an exploration of the MuleSoft platform's architecture and core concepts, the book lays out the essential components and runtime mechanisms that underpin the platform's robust operational capabilities. It details Mule Runtime's internal threading model, event processing strategies, and clustering approaches that ensure scalability and high availability. The principles of API-led connectivity are examined thoroughly, emphasizing strategic layering and modular flow construction patterns that promote reusability and maintainability.

Enterprise integration patterns form the backbone of effective system interoperability, and this work dedicates significant focus to these methodologies. It addresses advanced message routing, canonical data modeling, error handling, state management, and event-driven architecture patterns, underpinning reliable and flexible service orchestration. The treatment of batch processing and streaming patterns further underscores the platform's capabilities for handling large-scale and real-time data flows within complex environments.

Managing APIs effectively is critical to securing and optimizing enterprise interactions. This volume covers API management and governance extensively, discussing API specification standards such as RAML and OpenAPI, policy enforcement including custom security controls, metadata-driven governance, and runtime analytics. The creation of developer portals and the principles of zero trust security models highlight the book's emphasis on extending API security and improving the overall developer experience.

The evolving landscape of enterprise IT infrastructure demands hybrid, multicloud, and on-premises integration approaches. The book explores hybrid integration models, private connectivity via Anypoint VPC, and secure edge gateway patterns. It also addresses architecture considerations for disaster recovery, high availability, and federated platform management to support safe decentralization in distributed organizations.

Extensibility stands as a core principle within MuleSoft's platform strategy. Readers are guided through connector development using the Mule SDK, custom policy creation, integration with legacy systems, observability enhancements, and rigorous testing and certification of custom components. These aspects enable organizations to tailor the platform to specific business needs while maintaining reliability and governance.

Advanced data transformation and streaming techniques are vital for handling heterogeneous data in integration solutions. This book presents a deep dive into DataWeave transformations, batch processing patterns, reactive streaming APIs, and strategies for data validation, enrichment, and compliance. These capabilities ensure integrity and quality of data across integration touchpoints.

Performance, observability, and reliability engineering content focuses on capacity planning, tuning, caching strategies, distributed tracing, and resilience patterns. Such topics provide the foundation for building scalable, fault-tolerant integration solutions that maintain operational excellence in production environments. Centralized error handling and diagnostic frameworks are included to ensure swift issue resolution and system health monitoring.

DevOps and automation practices tailored for integration projects are discussed in detail, covering infrastructure as code, continuous integration and delivery pipelines, release orchestration, quality gates, and incident response. Emphasis is placed on automating deployments and managing integration lifecycle effectively while optimizing costs and resources.

Security, compliance, and data protection are critical considerations in enterprise integration. This volume examines identity federation, secure API design, encryption techniques, regulatory compliance automation, secure deployment topologies, and threat detection methodologies. These ensure that integration architectures adhere to stringent organizational and industry standards.

Finally, the book addresses emerging and future trends, including edge integration for IoT, AI and machine learning pipeline integration, blockchain and digital trust frameworks, composable microservice architectures, and the impact of no-code/low-code development paradigms. It concludes with guidance on architecting for extensibility and adaptability to meet changing business requirements over time.

This text provides an authoritative resource that aligns technical detail with strategic insight, enabling practitioners to master MuleSoft integration architectures and deliver resilient, scalable, and secure integration solutions that meet the demands of today's complex enterprise environments.

Chapter 1

MuleSoft Platform Overview and Core Concepts

Embark on a journey through the essential foundations of Mule-Soft, where powerful integration patterns, cloud-native principles, and modular design intersect to accelerate modern enterprise transformation. This chapter peels back the layers of the Anypoint Platform, revealing the architectural decisions and best practices that empower teams to connect applications, data, and devices—securely and at scale. Discover how foundational concepts and platform internals shape every robust, future-proof integration you design.

1.1. MuleSoft Anypoint Platform Architecture

The MuleSoft Anypoint Platform constitutes a comprehensive solution for API-led connectivity, integrating application development, deployment, and management within a unified framework. Its architecture is modular, facilitating the coordinated operation of distinct components that cover the full API and integration lifecycle. This system orchestrates the design, discovery, deployment, monitoring, and governance of APIs and integrations, spanning cloud-based and on-premises environments. The core architectural components—Design Center, Exchange, Management Center, API Manager, and Runtime Manager—form the backbone of this unified landscape, enabling seamless end-to-end integration lifecycle management.

Design Center

The Design Center serves as the cornerstone for integrated API and integration flow development. It provides a web-based, user-friendly environment for creating API specifications and integration applications using model-driven tools and visual editors. This component includes features such as the API Designer, which supports the creation and editing of RAML (RESTful API Modeling Language) or OAS (OpenAPI Specification) documents. The model API-first approach embedded in the Design Center facilitates the decoupling of API design from implementation, enabling reusable API contracts and consistent standards enforcement.

API and integration applications created within the Design Center are version-controlled and can be seamlessly exported for deployment. The environment encourages collaboration among developers, architects, and business analysts through shared workspaces and iterative design cycles. The Design Center integrates tightly with other platform components, especially the Exchange, for publishing assets and with the Runtime Manager for subsequent deployment phases.

Exchange

Exchange acts as the centralized repository and discovery hub for reusable assets, thereby promoting consistency, reusability, and

6

governance across enterprise integration projects. It hosts APIs, templates, connectors, policies, and other building blocks, all catalogued and searchable through metadata and tagging. These assets are versioned and documented comprehensively, simplifying their consumption in development scenarios.

The Exchange functions as a marketplace within the organization and across partner ecosystems, enabling teams to share and leverage prebuilt components. It fosters asset standardization and accelerates time-to-market by preventing redundant development. By connecting directly with the Design Center, Exchange allows developers to rapidly incorporate shared assets into new API or integration designs, maintaining alignment with architectural guidelines and compliance requirements. Furthermore, Exchange supports community engagement through feedback and rating mechanisms, which help surface high-quality components.

Management Center

Management Center encompasses the operational governance layer of the Anypoint Platform, providing advanced capabilities for policy enforcement, security, analytics, and lifecycle management. Often integrated with the API Manager and Runtime Manager, it offers comprehensive visibility and control over API consumption and runtime performance.

Its policy framework enables administrators to apply rate limiting, throttling, authentication, and OAuth scopes consistently across deployed APIs, regardless of their runtime environment. This uniform policy enforcement is critical for maintaining security postures and Service Level Agreements (SLAs) in hybrid deployment topologies. Management Center collects runtime metrics, logs, and events, thereby facilitating detailed analytics dashboards and custom reporting for capacity planning, fault detection, and compliance auditing.

Furthermore, Management Center supports automated

7

governance workflows, including approval chains and artifact promotion, bridging development and operations teams and enhancing DevSecOps practices. Integration with external identity providers via LDAP, SAML, or OpenID Connect protocols extends its security capabilities to align with enterprise standards.

API Manager

API Manager is a specialized component dedicated to the governance and lifecycle management of APIs throughout their entire existence. It acts as the interface for applying and managing policies, monitoring API usage, and controlling access. The API Manager supports the import of API specifications from the Design Center or directly from Exchange, enabling rapid onboarding of APIs into production environments.

This component allows fine-grained access control via role-based permissions, client ID enforcement, and throttling policies to protect backend services from abuse and failure. It also integrates with security appliances and API gateways to facilitate runtime enforcement of policies such as IP whitelisting, JWT validation, and threat protection.

The analytics capabilities within API Manager deliver real-time and historical insights into traffic patterns, error rates, response times, and API consumer behavior. Such data is critical for capacity management, anomaly detection, and business intelligence. By centralizing API operational governance, API Manager ensures compliance with industry regulations and internal policies, reducing compliance risk.

Runtime Manager

Runtime Manager is the deployment and operational control plane responsible for managing Mule runtime engines across diverse infrastructure landscapes, including cloud, on-premises, and hybrid environments. It supports multiple runtime fabric options such as CloudHub (MuleSoft's cloud-native integration platform), Mule runtime on virtual machines or containers, and Kubernetes cluster orchestration.

Through Runtime Manager, operators can deploy, monitor, scale, and troubleshoot Mule applications and APIs with granular control. It provides centralized dashboards for application health, resource utilization, and event logging. The management interface supports features such as blue-green deployments, rollback capabilities, and automated worker scaling based on runtime parameters.

Integration with continuous integration/continuous delivery (CI/CD) pipelines is facilitated via REST APIs and command-line interfaces, allowing programmatic deployment governance. Additionally, Runtime Manager integrates closely with API Manager and Management Center to propagate configuration, policies, and monitoring data, ensuring consistent operational states across the platform.

Intercomponent Integration and Lifecycle Orchestration

The structural design of the Anypoint Platform allows tight integration between the aforementioned components, enabling an uninterrupted workflow from API and integration design through to deployment and operational governance. For instance, API assets defined in the Design Center can be published directly to the Exchange, from where they are discoverable and reusable by other teams. Once an API is selected for deployment, Runtime Manager provisions and orchestrates the runtime environment, concurrently registering the API with API Manager to establish governance policies.

Such interplay ensures synchronization between version control, metadata, security policies, and operational insights, eliminating silos traditionally encountered in integration lifecycles. The platform's unified access and identity management reinforce secure collaboration across roles, while automated lifecycle management

9

through artifact promotion and environment migration streamlines release processes.

In hybrid cloud environments, this architecture supports decentralized deployment while maintaining centralized control, ensuring APIs and integrations comply with corporate standards across geographies. Monitoring data aggregated centrally enables proactive issue resolution and capacity forecasting, delivering high availability and resilience.

Consequently, the MuleSoft Anypoint Platform architecture's composition and synthesis effectively facilitate agile and governed integration practices. Through its componentized design, it provides enterprises with the flexibility to innovate rapidly without compromising security, compliance, or operational excellence.

1.2. Runtime Engine Internals

The Mule Runtime Engine (Mule) embodies a sophisticated architecture designed to address the demanding requirements of modern integration workloads. Its core capabilities revolve around delivering a high degree of scalability, resilience, and performance by leveraging an event-driven processing model, an optimized threading system, and a dynamic clustering mechanism. Complemented by robust persistence strategies and elasticity features, Mule ensures that integration deployments remain responsive and fault-tolerant in complex, distributed environments.

Threading Model

At the heart of Mule's runtime lies a finely tuned threading model centered on non-blocking, event-driven principles. Unlike traditional thread-per-request or thread-pooled execution models, Mule employs a reactor pattern where threads are assigned to dispatch and process events asynchronously, minimizing idle time and context switching overhead.

Each Mule runtime instance maintains a configurable set of worker threads organized within a thread pool, managed by the *Scheduler Service*. These threads are orchestrated to handle various stages in the message processing pipeline, including dispatching incoming events, executing processor logic, and managing outbound communications. The thread pool size can be adjusted according to workload characteristics and deployment environment, striking a balance between parallelism and resource contention.

Event processing tasks are typically partitioned into discrete units known as *processors*, which execute sequentially along a defined pipeline. Processors themselves are designed to be lightweight and stateless or maintain minimal state scoped to single event processing. Blocking operations within processors are discouraged; when necessary, Mule delegates these operations to specialized worker threads or offloads them to external systems, avoiding thread starvation scenarios.

Critical to the model is the separation between I/O-bound and CPU-bound work. The reactor threads primarily handle asynchronous I/O operations such as network reads and writes, while dedicated worker threads execute CPU-intensive processing. This separation allows Mule to handle thousands of concurrent connections and messages with minimal thread overhead, improving throughput and latency.

Event-Driven Processing Pipeline

Mule's event-driven pipeline architecture orchestrates message flow through a sequence of stages, where each stage corresponds to specific processing logic or routing decisions. The runtime represents each message as an immutable event object encapsulating inbound data, metadata, session information, and transactional context.

Processing within the pipeline is driven by *events* propagated through a directed graph of *message processors*. Each processor

11

subscribes to incoming events, applying transformations, routing logic, error handling, or protocol mediation as defined by the integration flow. Mule enforces a push-based model where events traverse synchronously or asynchronously depending on configured endpoint behavior.

Pipeline concurrency exploits the threading model by allowing parallel processing of independent events, leveraging thread pools and asynchronous connectors for network-bound operations. Moreover, processors that support asynchronous semantics are invoked without blocking the calling thread, enabling highly concurrent processing paths.

The runtime's event propagation mechanism supports sophisticated control constructs including scatter-gather patterns, parallel processing, and event aggregation. These constructs are realized by specialized processors coordinating multiple child events, synchronizing results, and managing error propagation transparently.

Error handling within the pipeline benefits from Mule's dual-layer event model, where *error events* encapsulate failure states, allowing error handlers to react contextually without disrupting unaffected parts of the flow. This mechanism enhances resilience by isolating fault domains and facilitating retries or compensating transactions.

Clustering and Distributed Coordination

Mule's runtime clustering capabilities address the challenges associated with distributed integration environments requiring fault tolerance and load balancing. Multiple runtime instances form a *cluster*, enabling workload distribution and state replication.

Clusters utilize an internal distributed coordination service based on algorithms like consensus and leader election to manage cluster membership and coordinate distributed transactions. The communication between cluster members employs a high-performance, low-latency messaging infrastructure that supports both unicast and multicast event dissemination.

Load balancing across cluster nodes occurs at the connection and event level, where the runtime transparently routes inbound events to available nodes based on criteria such as node capacity, endpoint affinity, and transaction context. This ensures horizontal scalability as new nodes can be added or removed without service degradation.

Stateful cluster members synchronize session and cache state using replication protocols designed for consistency and eventual convergence. Mule employs a variant of quorum-based replication for critical states to prevent data loss in the event of node failures.

The clustering layer integrates closely with the persistence mechanism to enable recovery of stateful flows and transactional contexts after failover, ensuring no event duplication or loss. Additionally, cluster-wide monitoring and management facilitate operational insights and dynamic configuration changes.

Persistence Strategies

Persistence forms a cornerstone for Mule's resilience and recovery semantics, enabling durable storage of message payloads, event metadata, and transaction states. Multiple persistence backends are supported, ranging from embedded lightweight databases to enterprise-grade transactional stores.

The runtime isolates the persistence layer behind well-defined interfaces, allowing seamless adaptation to different storage technologies depending on deployment needs. Persistent stores are utilized to checkpoint critical event stages, ensuring that in-flight messages can be reliably recovered after node crashes or planned restarts.

Mule employs write-ahead logging (WAL) and transactional commit protocols to guarantee data integrity and avoid inconsistencies arising from partial writes. This is particularly vital for transactional connectors and flows involving distributed transactions spanning multiple heterogeneous systems.

Persistent queues are extensively used to buffer events between processing stages and during error retries, decoupling producers and consumers to smooth out transient load spikes. Configurable retention policies, including time-to-live and maximum queue sizes, govern resource utilization without compromising durability.

The runtime supports both synchronous and asynchronous persistence modes, allowing flows to prioritize low latency or guaranteed delivery according to business requirements. Asynchronous persistence leverages batch commits and background threads to minimize the impact on critical path performance.

Elasticity and Dynamic Scaling

Elasticity mechanisms within Mule enable automatic adaptation to fluctuating workloads, crucial for cloud-native deployments and hybrid on-premises environments. The runtime exposes hooks and metrics essential for external orchestrators to make scaling decisions or trigger dynamic reconfiguration.

Horizontal scaling is achieved by adding or removing runtime instances within a cluster managed by container orchestration platforms like Kubernetes. The Mule engine supports graceful joining and leaving of cluster members, ensuring no disruption or event loss during scale operations.

At the runtime level, dynamic reallocation of thread pools and connector resources responds to changing load patterns. Thread pool parameters can be automatically tuned based on runtime metrics such as thread utilization, queue lengths, and event processing latencies, optimizing resource utilization.

Vertical elasticity is also supported through runtime introspection and adaptive resource management. For example, the engine monitors memory usage and garbage collection characteristics to dynamically adjust buffering strategies or trigger backpressure mechanisms in connectors.

Event prioritization and throttling capabilities form part of the elasticity toolkit, controlling event admission rates to prevent resource exhaustion during overload scenarios while maintaining throughput for critical flows.

The integration of elasticity features with Mule's clustering and persistence systems ensures that scalability enhancements do not compromise data consistency, fault tolerance, or transactional integrity.

Overall, the Mule Runtime Engine presents an architecture that harmonizes event-driven programming with sophisticated concurrency and distributed coordination models. Its threading model efficiently manages I/O and CPU-bound workloads, while the event pipeline offers a flexible and composable processing framework. Clustering delivers fault tolerance and scalable event distribution, persistence underpins durability and reliability, and elasticity enhances runtime adaptability.

Understanding these internals provides the technical foundation necessary to optimize integration deployments, troubleshoot performance bottlenecks, and design resilient integration patterns aligned with enterprise requirements. Practitioners can leverage this knowledge to fine-tune thread pools, configure persistence mechanisms, orchestrate clusters, and implement scaling strategies that uphold Mule's promise of seamless connectivity in heterogeneous environments.

1.3. API-led Connectivity Principles

API-led connectivity represents a methodological breakthrough in addressing the challenges of enterprise integration. Traditional monolithic integration approaches tend to create rigid, tightly coupled systems that hinder agility, slow down innovation, and complicate maintenance. By contrast, API-led connectivity strategically decomposes integration concerns into three distinct but interrelated layers: Experience APIs, Process APIs, and System APIs. This layered architecture underpins accelerated digital transformation initiatives through enhanced reusability, loose coupling, and modularity, enabling rapid iteration and scale even within complex technological ecosystems.

At the foundational level, *System APIs* abstract the underlying data sources and application systems. These APIs provide standardized, well-governed access to core enterprise assets such as ERP systems, databases, CRM platforms, and legacy applications. Rather than exposing the raw interfaces of these systems directly, System APIs serve as consistent interpolation points that encapsulate protocol translations, data model transformations, and system-specific authentication mechanisms. This encapsulation isolates systems from changes inside consuming applications or digital channels, allowing backend modifications without impacting external consumers. System APIs are crucial for maintaining stability and data integrity throughout evolving landscapes, enabling system modernization efforts without disruption.

Built atop the System APIs, *Process APIs* orchestrate and encapsulate business logic and data processing workflows. These middle-layer APIs combine and refine information retrieved from multiple system endpoints, applying validation, enrichment, aggregation, or decision logic to create canonical data representations suited for downstream consumption. The decoupling afforded by Process APIs facilitates the separation of business rules from interface specifics or channel considerations. This abstraction layer supports reuse across various digital initiatives and internal use cases by exposing business processes as modular, consumable services. It also embodies transaction control, exception handling, and state management centralized in one place, which simplifies compliance and auditing across distributed systems.

At the apex, *Experience APIs* tailor the exposure of data and functionality to the unique requirements of different user experiences or channels such as web applications, mobile apps, partner portals, or IoT devices. These APIs provide a focused, adaptive interface designed to optimize performance, usability, and security for a specific context. For instance, an Experience API serving a mobile application may aggregate and transform data differently from one serving a B2B portal, reducing payload size and adjusting data format to match client capabilities. Because Experience APIs do not interact directly with enterprise core systems but rely on Process APIs, they can evolve rapidly as user demands shift without affecting backend services. This separation enables agile, iterative delivery of front-end features while maintaining robust integration layers beneath.

The synergy among these layers fosters *loose coupling* across the technology stack. By clearly delineating responsibilities and contract boundaries, API-led connectivity minimizes dependencies between channel-specific implementations and underlying systems. Changes in one layer-whether system upgrades, business process modifications, or UI enhancements-can be managed independently. This characteristic significantly reduces the risk and complexity of digital transformation projects, leading to shorter release cycles and increased developer productivity.

An additional benefit lies in *accelerated reuse*. System APIs, once developed, become standardized interfaces to essential data, reducing duplication of effort across projects. Process APIs encapsulate common business logic that can serve multiple use cases without redundant coding. Experience APIs, by concentrating on particular experience patterns, enable rapid prototyping of new channels without backend rework. This reusability lowers total cost of ownership, improves consistency, and facilitates enterprise-wide governance.

Governance and security strategies integrate naturally within this layered approach. Because each API layer enforces distinct access controls and policies appropriate to its role, security is granular and aligned with business risk. System APIs can enforce strict identity and access management around sensitive systems, Process APIs manage usage monitoring and throttling of business services, and Experience APIs implement user authentication and data masking tailored by consumer type. Monitoring and analytics can also be applied at each tier to provide insights into performance and user behavior, enabling proactive optimization.

API-led connectivity also enhances *scalability* in complex environments. Each API layer can be independently scaled based on demand patterns. For example, Experience APIs facing external clients may require autoscaling during peak traffic, whereas System APIs might emphasize transaction throughput or data synchronization. This modular scalability reduces infrastructure costs and supports smooth handling of unexpected load, which is critical in digital business channels exposed to volatile consumer interactions.

The methodology facilitates continuous delivery and DevOps integration by promoting small, incremental API changes at appropriate layers rather than monolithic system rewrites. Through automated testing, versioning, and deployment pipelines, enterprise teams can release new features or fixes quickly with minimal risk. Furthermore, because APIs themselves define clear service contracts, automated mocks and simulations become possible, supporting parallel development and early quality validation. This alignment with modern software development practices enables enterprises to respond promptly to evolving market conditions.

From an architectural perspective, API-led connectivity harmonizes with other contemporary IT paradigms such as microservices, event-driven architectures, and hybrid cloud deployments. Its layered API model can serve as the backbone for microservices by defining coarse-grained service boundaries that encapsulate functionality and data within manageable domains. In event-driven systems, APIs represent the synchronous access points that complement asynchronous messaging. In hybrid cloud environments, APIs abstract heterogeneous systems running on-premises and in multiple clouds, presenting a unified integration surface.

A key strategic advantage is the facilitation of *business and IT alignment*. By mapping API layers to business capabilities and customer interactions, enterprises gain clearer visibility into how technology supports value streams. The Experience APIs directly correlate with customer journeys, Process APIs reflect operational processes, and System APIs represent technical assets. This traceability enables prioritization and funding decisions grounded in business impact, strengthening collaboration between stakeholders and improving overall governance.

In summary, the principles underpinning API-led connectivity emphasize decomposition, abstraction, reuse, security, governance, and agility. The explicit separation of concerns into Experience, Process, and System API layers transforms integration from a complex, rigid problem into a modular, manageable discipline. This paradigm fosters rapid innovation, scalable infrastructure, and resilient architectures-all essential in supporting digital business initiatives within dynamic and heterogeneous enterprise environments.

1.4. Flow Construction Patterns

Mule flows constitute the fundamental building blocks of MuleSoft integration applications, establishing a robust framework for processing, routing, and transforming data across heterogeneous systems. Understanding the anatomy of Mule flows, subflows, and private flows offers critical insight into designing integration solutions that are maintainable, modular, and scalable. Each flow construct embodies distinct behavior with respect to orchestration, transaction boundaries, and error propagation, which, when leveraged appropriately, facilitates clear separation of concerns, promotes reusability, and enhances fault tolerance.

A *Mule flow* typically represents a sequence of configured components that execute in response to inbound events or messages. The inherent orchestration capabilities provided by Mule flows enable the definition of a synchronous or asynchronous message pipeline, incorporating endpoints, transformers, routers, and connectors. Flows can be triggered by external events such as HTTP requests, JMS messages, or scheduler triggers, acting as entry points within the application. Crucially, a Mule flow defines its own transaction boundary; the transactional behavior applies to the entire flow and governs how propagated exceptions affect commit or rollback semantics.

Subflows constitute a subtype of Mule flows designed explicitly for modularization and reuse within the same Mule application. Unlike standard flows, subflows lack their own message sources and cannot initiate processing independently. Instead, they are invoked or referenced by a parent flow through the <flow-ref> component, enabling decomposition of complex logic into reusable units while maintaining a single transactional context with the invoking flow. Because subflows share the transaction and thread context of the parent flow, they are preferable for composing atomic operations that should execute within a singular, cohesive transaction boundary.

In contrast to subflows, *private flows* provide enhanced encapsulation by isolating execution contexts and transaction boundaries. Private flows can be invoked using asynchronous flow references, allowing concurrent and decoupled processing. This design facilitates segregation of transactional domains and error handling strategies. For example, a private flow may be configured to handle non-blocking, long-running processes or compensations without impacting the caller's transaction. The key distinction lies in private flows enabling autonomous execution with independent lifecycle control and error isolation, thereby improving scalability and resilience in complex integration scenarios.

Typical orchestration patterns involving these flow constructs illustrate the power of composition and separation. A common architectural pattern consists of an *orchestrator flow* acting as a coordinator that receives an inbound event, applies routing and transformation logic, then sequentially or conditionally delegates processing to multiple subflows and private flows. The orchestrator manages transactional boundaries by leveraging subflows to enforce atomic units of work, while private flows execute asynchronous or parallelizable steps. For example, interfacing with a legacy system to retrieve data might be encapsulated in a subflow, guaranteeing consistent rollback if subsequent operations fail, whereas logging, audit, or notification tasks might be delegated to private flows for eventual consistency.

Error handling patterns within Mule further illustrate the nuanced interplay between flow types. Since standard flows define transaction boundaries, exceptions thrown inside a flow propagate to its error handler, allowing rollback of transactional resources. Subflows propagate exceptions transparently to the caller, enabling centralized error management within the invoking flow's scope. By contrast, private flows may incorporate autonomous error handling strategies using local error handlers to prevent errors from affecting the main orchestration. This design reduces error propagation noise and permits implementing compensating transactions or retries without compromising the broader process flow. In scenarios requiring fine-grained error isolation, private flows enable fault-tolerant message processing, mitigating cascading failures.

Transaction boundary management is fundamental in integration logic, particularly in multi-resource distributed environments. Mule's transactional model supports *local transactions* bound to individual connectors and *distributed transactions* (e.g., XA transactions) that span multiple resource managers. Standard flows mark natural transaction scopes, frequently employing local or distributed transactions to ensure consistency. Invoking subflows within the same flow context retains the transactional state, allowing coherent commit or rollback semantics. Private flows, however, inherently define separate transaction boundaries, often paired with asynchronous messaging patterns such as Queue-Based Load Leveling or Event-Driven Architecture (EDA). This separation enables isolation of transactional concerns, reducing tight coupling and the risks of prolonged locks.

Reusability is a cardinal principle in flow construction patterns. Subflows serve as the primary mechanism to encapsulate reusable business logic or integration steps. By abstracting common functionality such as data transformations, protocol bridging, or validation logic into dedicated subflows, developers can achieve significant reductions in duplication, streamline maintenance, and ensure consistent behavior across diverse processing paths. Furthermore, private flows function effectively as reusable components when asynchronous or isolated execution semantics are desired. Leveraging `<flow-ref>` and asynchronous invocation patterns, private flows can process workloads independently, enhancing throughput and enabling horizontal scalability.

The combination of these flow constructs enables implementation of several well-established integration patterns. Consider the *Request-Reply* pattern: the primary flow handles the inbound request and synchronously calls a subflow responsible for invoking an external service, managing transactional rollback if the service call fails. For audit logging, the primary flow may dispatch messages to a private flow asynchronously to avoid impeding mainline processing. For *Scatter-Gather* scenarios, a flow may employ asynchronous references to multiple private flows performing parallel processing, aggregating results after completion. These patterns demonstrate how flow types can be orchestrated to optimize latency, reliability, and error recovery.

An illustrative snippet demonstrates the invocation of a reusable subflow and a private flow from an orchestrator flow:

```
<flow name="mainOrchestratorFlow" doc:name="Main Orchestrator
    Flow">
    <http:listener config-ref="HTTP_Listener" path="/process" doc
    :name="HTTP Listener"/>

    <flow-ref name="coreBusinessSubflow" doc:name="Subflow
    invocation"/>

    <async doc:name="Asynchronous Processing">
        <flow-ref name="auditPrivateFlow" doc:name="Private flow
    invocation"/>
    </async>

    <set-payload value="Process completed successfully" doc:name
    ="Set Response"/>
</flow>

<sub-flow name="coreBusinessSubflow" doc:name="Core Business
    Logic Subflow">
    <db:select config-ref="Database_Config" doc:name="Database
    Operation">
        <db:sql>#['SELECT * FROM orders WHERE id = ' + vars.
    orderId]</db:sql>
    </db:select>
    <!-- Additional business logic components -->
</sub-flow>

<flow name="auditPrivateFlow" processingStrategy="queued-
    asynchronous" doc:name="Audit Private Flow">
    <logger message="Audit record: #[payload]" level="INFO" doc:
    name="Audit Logger"/>
    <!-- Auditing or notification logic -->
</flow>
```

Error handler scope within Mule flows further refines fault isolation. Exception strategies defined in a parent flow envelop invoked subflows but do not automatically apply to private flows due to their asynchronous nature. Explicit configuration of error handlers within private flows ensures that faults do not propagate upstream, preserving the stability of the orchestrator. Patterns that integrate compensating transactions or message redelivery frequently rely on private flow-local error handling combined with dead letter queues or error notification channels.

Performance considerations similarly influence the choice between flow types. Synchronous subflow invocations incur the overhead of transactional locking and thread blocking, which may be untenable for long-running or non-deterministic tasks. Private flows, leveraging asynchronous processing strategies, decouple execution lifecycles and maximize resource utilization, enhancing throughput under load. Optimal design balances the need for strong consistency within a transaction boundary against latency requirements and failure isolation needs.

Effective flow construction patterns emphasize leveraging standard flows to define explicit transactional boundaries and event-driven entry points, subflows to encapsulate reusable, atomic processing units sharing transactional context, and private flows to provide isolated, asynchronous processing with autonomous error handling. Adopting these patterns yields integration applications capable of meeting stringent requirements for modularity, error resilience, scalability, and maintainability. Mastery of flow anatomy and invocation semantics is indispensable for architects and developers aiming to deliver robust MuleSoft-based integration solutions in complex enterprise environments.

1.5. Connector Architecture and Lifecycle

MuleSoft connectors serve as fundamental building blocks within the Mule runtime ecosystem, providing standardized, reusable modules that facilitate seamless integration across diverse applications, protocols, and SaaS platforms. By abstracting the complexities of protocol handling, authentication, and data transformation, connectors enable Mule applications to interact with external systems efficiently while maintaining consistency and reliability in integration flows.

At the core, a MuleSoft connector encapsulates the logic necessary to interact with a particular external resource or service. The architecture of a typical Mule connector is modular and extensible, designed to support a wide range of communication patterns and integration scenarios.

A connector generally consists of the following components:

- **Operations**: Declarative methods exposed to Mule applications that define discrete actions, such as querying data, sending messages, or invoking remote services. These operations map directly to API endpoints or protocol commands in the target system.

- **Connection Management**: A mechanism to establish, maintain, and terminate connections to external systems. This component handles authentication, session lifecycles, and resource pooling as necessary.

- **Configuration**: XML- or annotation-driven parameters defining how the connector behaves within the Mule runtime. Configuration elements include connection details (URLs, credentials), timeouts, and other system-specific settings.

- **Error Handling**: Strategies and constructs integrated with MuleSoft's error framework to capture, propagate, and resolve exceptions during connector operation.

Connectors in Mule leverage a declarative model augmented by the Mule SDK, enabling developers to define operations and configurations via annotations and supporting metadata. This approach facilitates automatic generation of schema, documentation, and tooling support, reducing boilerplate and easing maintenance.

The lifecycle of a MuleSoft connector instance closely aligns with the lifecycle of Mule applications and their constituent flows, encompassing phases from initialization through to disposal. The primary stages include:

- **Initialization**: Upon starting the Mule application, connectors initialize their configuration parameters and establish necessary resources. During this phase, connection pools may be created, authentication tokens refreshed, and any system-level setup executed.

- **Connection Establishment**: Prior to executing an operation, the connector ensures an active and valid connection to the target system exists. This may involve negotiating protocol handshakes, authenticating sessions, or retrieving connection-specific metadata.

- **Operation Execution**: The connector carries out the requested operation, handling input transformation, interacting with the external system, and producing a response. This phase aligns with the invocation semantics defined by Mule flows, supporting synchronous or asynchronous patterns as configured.

- **Error Handling**: If communication errors, timeouts, or data-related exceptions occur, the connector triggers MuleSoft's error handling framework. Fine-grained control over retries, fallback actions, or error propagation can be configured here.

- **Connection Release**: Following operation execution, the connector appropriately releases or retains connections based on pooling strategy and lifecycle policies to optimize resource utilization.

- **Disposal**: When the Mule application or connector is undeployed or stopped, any allocated resources are cleaned up, including closed connections, cleared caches, or halted background threads.

Proper lifecycle management is critical to maintaining runtime stability and avoiding resource leaks in long-running Mule applications.

The Mule SDK provides a comprehensive framework for developing custom connectors with rich extension capabilities. It modernizes connector development by replacing legacy DevKit-based approaches with a more maintainable, annotation-driven model that tightly integrates with Mule's ecosystem.

Key features enabled by the Mule SDK include:

- **Declarative Annotations**: Use of annotations such as @Configuration, @Connection, and @Operation to simplify binding of business logic to runtime metadata and configuration.

- **Lifecycle Hooks**: Methods annotated with lifecycle callbacks (e.g., @OnStart, @OnStop) allow precise control over setup and cleanup processes.

- **Connection Providers**: Interfaces and abstract classes to implement connection management policies, supporting varying scenarios like single connections, pooled connections, or caching strategies.

- **Parameter Types and Validation**: Built-in support for parameter constraints, default values, and expression language evaluation to enhance runtime configurability.

- **Metadata Generation**: Automatic generation of connector metadata used by Studio and Runtime Manager, enabling visual editing, validation, and improved documentation.

An example of a minimal Mule SDK connection provider definition is presented below:

```
@ConnectionProvider(friendlyName = "Sample Connection",
    configElementName = "connection")
public class SampleConnectionProvider implements
    ConnectionProvider<SampleConnection> {

  @Parameter
  private String host;
```

```
@Parameter
private int port;

@Override
public SampleConnection connect() throws ConnectionException
{
    try {
        return new SampleConnection(host, port);
    } catch (Exception e) {
        throw new ConnectionException(e);
    }
}

@Override
public void disconnect(SampleConnection connection) {
    connection.close();
}

@Override
public boolean validate(SampleConnection connection) {
    return connection.isValid();
}
}
```

This illustrates core lifecycle methods allowing controlled creation, validation, and release of connection resources.

Connector configuration in Mule employs a blend of XML descriptors and annotations, enabling declarative definition of necessary parameters and their schemas. Configuration properties encompass connection information (e.g., credentials, endpoints), timeout settings, security credentials (such as OAuth tokens or certificates), and optional operational flags.

Configurations are organized hierarchically:

- **Global Configuration**: Shared across multiple flows or connectors, often defining connection pools or common authentication schemes.

- **Connector Instance Configuration**: Specific to a particular connector use, allowing diverse target systems or environments within the same application.

28

- **Operation-Level Configuration**: Overrides or augmentations applied directly to individual operations in the Mule flow.

The Mule runtime enforces stringent type validation, default values, and expression language evaluation for configuration properties, enabling dynamic resolution at runtime. This enhances flexibility and supports DevOps best practices such as environment-specific configurations externalized from the application archive.

Efficient management of external system connections underpins connector performance and resilience. Mule connectors implement connection management strategies tailored to protocol semantics and throughput requirements, including:

- **Single Connection**: One persistent connection object per connector instance. Suitable for low-latency or stateful protocols, but may limit scalability.

- **Connection Pooling**: Maintain a configurable pool of reusable connections to support concurrent requests and reduce connection setup overhead.

- **Lazy Connection**: Delay connection establishment until the first operation executes, reducing resource usage during idle periods.

- **Automatic Reconnection and Failover**: Support for retry policies and fallback targets in the event of connection failure.

These strategies are implemented in the connection provider classes of Mule SDK connectors and are configurable at runtime. Additionally, Mule's non-blocking architecture allows asynchronous connection management, improving throughput and latency under heavy loads.

Effective development and deployment of custom or third-party connectors hinge upon adherence to MuleSoft recommended practices:

- **Design for Idempotency**: Connectors should aim for idempotent operations where possible-especially when handling retries-to prevent duplicate side effects.

- **Leverage the Mule SDK**: Utilize the Mule SDK's annotations and lifecycle methods to maximize maintainability, reduce boilerplate, and unlock tooling benefits.

- **Robust Error Handling**: Implement comprehensive error categorization and propagate meaningful exceptions aligned with Mule's error infrastructure. Define retries, timeouts, and fallback scenarios explicitly.

- **Parameter Validation and Security**: Validate input parameters rigorously and handle sensitive data-such as credentials-securely, avoiding plaintext exposure.

- **Resource Cleanup**: Ensure all connections and allocated resources are properly closed during application shutdown or redeployment to avoid memory leaks.

- **Documentation and Metadata**: Provide exhaustive annotations and descriptive metadata to facilitate user understanding within Anypoint Studio and other management tools.

- **Versioning and Compatibility**: Follow semantic versioning guidelines for connector releases and maintain backward compatibility wherever feasible.

- **Testing**: Employ unit tests for business logic and integration tests against target systems to validate stable connectivity and operation consistency.

Deployment of connectors occurs through packaging them as Mule domain libraries or standalone .jar files integrated into Mule runtime environments. Leveraging MuleSoft Exchange allows distribution and version control of connectors within teams or across organizations securely.

The connector architecture acts as the conduit between Mule's event-driven runtime and the external environment. Connectors' modular design, combined with precise lifecycle handling, delivers high reliability and adaptability. Extensibility through the Mule SDK ensures that developers can tailor connectors to evolving requirements while fully exploiting MuleSoft's tooling and infrastructure. Careful connection management and configuration underpin connector robustness, enabling scalable integration solutions that bridge on-premises and cloud-based resources seamlessly.

1.6. Designing for Modularity and Reuse

Modularity and reuse stand as foundational principles for building scalable, maintainable, and efficient integration solutions within MuleSoft environments. Effective application of these principles enables development teams to maximize asset utility across projects, reduce redundancy, and accelerate delivery cycles. This section elaborates on practical strategies for creating reusable assets, focusing on shared libraries, template flows, and integration patterns, alongside key repository management techniques and collaborative practices.

A modular architecture decomposes a complex integration system into discrete, loosely coupled components. Each component encapsulates a specific piece of functionality, which can be independently developed, tested, and deployed. Within MuleSoft, this approach fosters separation of concerns, enhances readability, and facilitates parallel development efforts. By engineering modules designed for reuse, organizations can establish a library of integration building blocks, which serve as templates or service components across diverse scenarios.

Shared Libraries represent one of the primary means of enabling reuse. These libraries encapsulate common functionalities such as authentication, error handling, logging, transformation utilities, and connectors configurations. MuleSoft supports reusable libraries through Mule domains and external Maven artifacts that can be included as dependencies in multiple Mule applications. A well-structured shared library abstracts complexities and exposes configurations and operations through well-defined interfaces or global elements within the Mule runtime. The design of shared libraries must prioritize loose coupling and explicit contracts via XML schemas, API specifications, or runtime properties to ensure interoperability and adaptability across consuming applications.

Beyond functional encapsulation, shared libraries demand rigorous versioning and dependency management. Semantic versioning combined with automated CI/CD pipelines helps maintain backward compatibility while allowing incremental improvements. Additionally, applying conventions such as feature toggles and environment-agnostic design increases the flexibility of shared assets, facilitating deployments across different stages and target systems without extensive rework.

Template Flows constitute reusable integration frameworks designed to address recurring integration challenges. These templates encapsulate common integration patterns, including request-response, publish-subscribe, scatter-gather, and error handling flows, executed in a consistent manner. MuleSoft provides building blocks in Anypoint Exchange where such template flows can be stored, discovered, and consumed by multiple teams across an organization. Implementing template flows involves parameterization techniques, where configurable properties tune flow behavior without altering core logic. Examples include dynamically setting endpoints, schema validation rules, or retry strategies via property placeholders or externalized configuration files.

The reuse of template flows enforces consistency in integration design and operational behavior. By standardizing error handling, logging, security enforcement, and performance monitoring at the template level, organizations reduce technical debt and avoid fragmentation in enterprise systems. Template flows also serve as educational assets, accelerating onboarding and knowledge transfer for new team members through clear, documented patterns.

Integration Patterns underpin reusable and resilient architectures tailored to common enterprise scenarios. These patterns define best practices for solving particular integration problems, such as content-based routing, message filtering, batching, and orchestration. They provide a conceptual and technical blueprint that guides developers in structuring Mule flows coherently. Integrating patterns into reusable assets requires explicit separation of control flow from business logic, complemented by declarative configuration where feasible.

MuleSoft's DataWeave expression language facilitates transformation and routing logic within these patterns, enabling compact yet powerful implementations. Using design abstractions such as subflows, private flows, and flow references encapsulates pattern logic, making it accessible for reuse and extension. Patterns should be designed with idempotency, fault tolerance, and scalability in mind, adhering to principles like compensating transactions and queue-based load leveling for asynchronous interactions.

Repository management plays a critical role in supporting modularity and reuse across large-scale programs. Centralized version control systems (e.g., Git) integrated with MuleSoft development tools enable systematic management of reusable assets. Branching strategies such as GitFlow or trunk-based development minimize merge conflicts and synchronize parallel feature developments. Repositories should structure assets hierarchically by separating domain projects, shared libraries, template flows, and application-specific code into distinct modules or repositories to prevent unnecessary coupling.

Anypoint Exchange acts as a governance platform for distributed reuse, providing a curated catalog with metadata, version histories, and usage analytics for shared components. It facilitates discovery and encourages adherence to published APIs and integration contracts. Effective governance models enforce quality standards, including security reviews, compliance checks, and performance benchmarks, as preconditions for asset publication.

Collaborative practices are integral to maintaining reusable assets at scale. Cross-functional teams comprising developers, architects, and operations personnel establish shared ownership and accountability. Documentation, automated testing, and continuous integration pipelines underpin asset reliability and rapid feedback cycles. The use of functional and integration tests within shared libraries and template flows ensures that modifications do not introduce regressions. Contract testing validates that interfaces meet expectations from consumers, supporting confidence in ever-evolving modular components.

By embedding modular design and reuse into the development lifecycle, organizations realize significant benefits: reduced time-to-market, enhanced code quality, consistent integration behavior, and improved maintainability. These practices also facilitate the alignment of IT with evolving business requirements, as reusable assets can be swiftly adapted or composed into new solutions without reinventing foundational elements.

Careful application of shared libraries, template flows, and integration patterns within a disciplined repository and collaboration framework maximizes the value of MuleSoft integration initiatives. Such modular architectures enable not only the rapid delivery of

34

robust integrations but also establish a scalable foundation for continuous innovation and growth.

Chapter 2

Enterprise Integration Patterns with MuleSoft

Step beyond point-to-point connectivity and unlock the proven patterns that power modern, large-scale integration ecosystems. In this chapter, you will explore MuleSoft's toolkit for orchestrating complex enterprise integrations—covering strategies for reliable message routing, transformation, error recovery, and asynchronous event processing. Discover how industry-standard patterns come alive within MuleSoft, equipping you to build agile, future-proof architectures and solve real-world challenges with elegance and confidence.

2.1. Message Routing and Exchange Patterns

Enterprise integration demands sophisticated message routing and exchange mechanisms that facilitate the coordination and transformation of data streams flowing through heterogeneous systems. These routing patterns ensure intelligent control over message propagation, enabling adaptable, scalable, and maintainable integration architectures. Central to these patterns are content-based routing, message filtering, dynamic routing, and the application of correlation identifiers-each addressing specific requirements for message distribution and lifecycle management.

Content-based routing (CBR) directs messages to one or more destinations based on the evaluation of message content. Unlike static routing, CBR leverages message payload or metadata characteristics to make runtime decisions, thereby supporting conditional processing paths without hardcoding destination endpoints. Typically, a router component inspects message attributes using expressions or predicates that represent business rules. For example, messages with a particular customer region might route to regional processing centers, while those indicating error-related flags redirect to exception handling workflows.

MuleSoft's Anypoint Platform natively supports content-based routing through components such as the `Choice Router` and `Scatter-Gather`. The `Choice Router` permits defining multiple mutually exclusive routes, each guarded by conditional expressions implemented using DataWeave or MEL (Mule Expression Language). Conversely, the `Scatter-Gather` facilitates parallel message delivery to multiple endpoints, aggregating or selectively processing responses as required. This design pattern allows orchestration of heterogeneous service calls while preserving atomicity and consistency in results.

Message filtering refines routing decisions by excluding undesired or irrelevant messages from further processing. Filters are predicates that evaluate message attributes to determine pass or block actions. Effective filtering improves overall system efficiency by reducing processing overhead and preventing propagation of invalid

or non-actionable messages downstream. MuleSoft introduces the
`Filter` component and `Message Enricher` pattern to selectively
process messages or augment filtered information with additional
contextual data before routing.

Dynamic routing enhances system adaptability by determining
message routes at runtime, not through fixed configuration but by
querying a routing registry or leveraging business logic. This is indispensable in scenarios where endpoint availability, load, or business priorities vary dynamically. Dynamic routers typically maintain state about message correlation, enabling messages within a
sequence or transaction to follow consistent paths. The pattern
supports late-binding of routing information and allows seamless
integration with service discovery mechanisms.

MuleSoft's `Dynamic Router` component embodies this pattern by
iteratively querying routing metadata and re-evaluating outbound
endpoints until processing completes. Its extensibility permits custom routing resolvers that access databases, cache stores, or external services to decide the next route based on the evolving message
context or system state.

Correlation identifiers serve as unique markers that associate related messages within a conversation or transaction spanning multiple services and transport layers. These identifiers are critical
in asynchronous and loosely coupled architectures, enabling message tracking, aggregation, and the reconciliation of responses that
may arrive out of order. The consistent propagation of correlation
IDs ensures traceability, fault isolation, and analytical insight into
complex message flows.

In MuleSoft, correlation identifiers are commonly implemented
using custom or standard message properties such as
`correlationId`, `messageId`, and `correlationSequence`.
The platform facilitates automatic correlation management
through inbound connectors and propagates these properties
transparently across endpoints and flows. This consistency

enables integration architects to design workflows such as aggregator, resequencer, and scatter-gather patterns that rely on correlation metadata to maintain the integrity of multi-message transactions.

The synergy between these routing and exchange patterns allows the construction of robust integration solutions. For instance, combining content-based routing with correlation identifiers empowers conditional message distribution while maintaining traceability. Dynamic routing complements this by adapting routes based on runtime context and resource status, and filtering ensures that only pertinent messages consume downstream processing capacity.

Consider a complex order processing system that leverages MuleSoft's flow orchestration: incoming purchase orders are first subjected to content-based routing to separate high-priority clients or product types into dedicated fulfillment streams. Each stream applies message filtering to exclude incomplete orders, while the dynamic router assigns processing endpoints based on current regional warehouse availability. Correlation IDs track the entire order lifecycle from placement through shipment, enabling audit, monitoring, and exception handling.

MuleSoft's unified architecture integrates these patterns within its lightweight runtime engine, providing visual modeling and declarative configuration for ease of management, debugging, and maintenance. DataWeave's expressive power augments routing decisions, allowing complex transformations and evaluations against hierarchical or semi-structured data payloads. Furthermore, connectors abstract transport details, making message routing agnostic to protocols, which is essential for hybrid cloud and on-premises ecosystems.

In advanced use cases, integration pipelines exploit parallelized routing using the Scatter-Gather pattern, which simultaneously invokes multiple services to optimize latency and aggregate results.

Concurrently, message enrichment patterns append contextual information fetched from ancillary systems before routing to target endpoints. This orchestration is accomplished declaratively, supporting retry, timeout, and error-handling strategies aligned with enterprise service level agreements (SLAs).

```
<flow name="order-routing-flow">
    <http:listener doc:name="Listener" config-ref="
    HTTP_Listener_config" path="/orders"/>
    <choice doc:name="Choice Router">
        <when expression="#[payload.priority == 'high']">
            <flow-ref name="high-priority-order-flow"/>
        </when>
        <when expression="#[payload.region == 'EMEA']">
            <flow-ref name="emea-order-flow"/>
        </when>
        <otherwise>
            <flow-ref name="standard-order-flow"/>
        </otherwise>
    </choice>
</flow>
```

```
<flow name="dynamic-routing-flow">
    <set-variable variableName="correlationId" value="#[uuid()]"
    doc:name="Generate CorrelationId"/>
    <dynamic-router doc:name="Dynamic Router" maxRoutes="3" doc:
    id="dynamicRouter">
        <dynamic-router-router expression="#[routingTable[event.
        currentStep]]"/>
    </dynamic-router>
</flow>
```

```
Output example from dynamic-router logging:
Processing step 1 with correlationId: f47ac10b-58cc-4372-a567-0e02b2c3d479
Routing to endpoint: http://warehouse1.example.com/processOrder
Processing step 2 with correlationId: f47ac10b-58cc-4372-a567-0e02b2c3d479
Routing to endpoint: http://billing.example.com/invoice
All routing steps completed successfully for correlationId: f47ac10b-58cc-437
2-a567-0e02b2c3d479
```

Advanced message routing and exchange patterns such as content-based routing, message filtering, dynamic routing, and use of correlation identifiers form the backbone of enterprise integration architectures. MuleSoft's suite of built-in components and flow control primitives, combined with its expressive transformation language and modular connector ecosystem, equip integration professionals with the tools necessary to design and operate complex, resilient, and observable integration solutions. Mastery of these patterns enables scalable service orchestration, adaptive workflow management, and comprehensive message lifecycle governance within heterogeneous enterprise environments.

2.2. Canonical Data Models and Mediation

Enterprise integration architectures often confront the challenge of reconciling diverse data formats and schemas originating from heterogeneous systems. The proliferation of point-to-point interfaces exacerbates complexity, brittleness, and maintenance overhead, as each interface requires custom handling for data translation and protocol adaptation. Canonical Data Models (CDMs) serve as a robust architectural strategy to mitigate these issues by establishing a standardized, unified schema for data representation across an integration landscape. This approach enables loose coupling, streamlined transformations, and enhanced interoperability between disparate applications and services.

A canonical data model abstracts domain entities into a neutral, consistent form that all participating systems agree to exchange. Each system interacts only with the CDM, translating its native data representations into and out of this common model. This eliminates direct dependencies between every pair of systems, reducing the number of custom mappings from an order of $O(n^2)$ (where n is the number of systems) in point-to-point architectures to an order of $O(n)$, thereby simplifying integration complexity significantly.

In practice, creating and adopting a CDM involves rigorous analysis of domain concepts to capture the essential data elements and their semantics. The model must balance comprehensiveness with simplicity and extensibility. Overly granular models can incur transformation overhead and reduce agility, whereas overly simplified models risk losing critical information needed by end-points. An iterative, collaborative approach with domain experts often yields the optimal model, ensuring alignment with business semantics and technical feasibility.

Message transformation is the operational core that enables communication between heterogeneous systems through a canonical data model. This transformation typically occurs in two stages: normalization and denormalization. Normalization converts source data formats into the canonical form, while denormalization translates canonical data into target system schemas. Robust transformation logic must handle structural differences (such as hierarchical versus relational formats), semantic enrichments, data type conversions, and protocol-specific nuances.

MuleSoft's Anypoint Platform exemplifies comprehensive support for canonical data modeling and mediation. Its DataWeave language provides a powerful, expressive framework for defining data transformation pipelines. DataWeave scripts can read various input formats (JSON, XML, CSV, EDI, etc.) and produce outputs conforming to the canonical model or target schemas. The platform facilitates the encapsulation of transformation logic as reusable modules, promoting maintainability and consistency.

Mediation patterns in MuleSoft leverage canonical data models to enable seamless data flow and orchestration between systems. Mediators act as intermediaries that perform message translation, routing, enrichment, and protocol bridging while preserving the integrity of the canonical format within integration flows. These mediation components enforce loose coupling, enabling endpoints to evolve independently without cascading changes.

Normalization entails converting diverse input payloads into the canonical structure. Consider a legacy CRM system emitting customer information in a proprietary XML schema. Transformation logic extracts relevant elements, maps fields to canonical attributes, reconciles differing terminologies (e.g., `custID` versus `customer_id`), and applies data type coercion. Data validation and cleansing can also be integrated here to uphold data quality before dissemination.

Denormalization processes canonical data to match the target system's requirements. For example, when sending customer data to an ERP system using JSON, the mediator transforms the canonical message to the ERP's expected schema, formats, and namespaces, potentially enriching it with additional contextual data retrieved from other systems. This flexibility allows each endpoint to function with its preferred data model while leveraging the canonical model as an integration lingua franca.

The adoption of canonical data models reduces the dependency on brittle point-to-point mappings but does not inherently eliminate all transformation requirements. Instead, it promotes strategic reuse of transformation artifacts and centralizes data semantics, facilitating governance and coherence. MuleSoft's design center and integration templates support this modularization by enabling developers to compose, test, and deploy transformations incrementally.

Canonical data models also support extensibility in evolving integration landscapes. As new systems are introduced, only their mapping to and from the canonical model is required, avoiding widespread changes to existing interfaces. This modular approach accelerates onboarding and reduces rework, critical in agile environments where change is constant.

Interoperability benefits significantly from CDMs, particularly in organizations leveraging microservices, APIs, and hybrid cloud environments. The canonical representation enables transparent mediation between synchronous and asynchronous communication paradigms, legacy and modern applications, and internal and external partners. In MuleSoft, API-led connectivity builds on this principle by defining experience, process, and system layers

44

that interact through canonical messages, ensuring consistent data handling throughout the lifecycle.

The strategy of mediation via canonical data models also facilitates runtime transformation optimizations. By standardizing data constructs, MuleSoft runtime engines can apply schema-aware routing, content-based filtering, and conditional processing with greater precision. This enhances performance and reliability, especially under high throughput and complex integration scenarios.

Moreover, canonical data models underpin effective monitoring and troubleshooting. Consistent data semantics across the integration fabric simplify log correlation, error analysis, and audit trails. MuleSoft's Anypoint Monitoring leverages these common representations to provide consolidated insights into message flows, transformation outcomes, and system interactions, enabling proactive management and rapid incident resolution.

Adopting canonical data models coupled with robust mediation patterns is a cornerstone of scalable, maintainable enterprise integration. MuleSoft's tooling and runtime environments provide comprehensive capabilities for defining, implementing, and governing canonical schemas and transformations. This approach significantly reduces integration complexity, promotes data consistency, and accelerates digital transformation initiatives by harmonizing data exchange across diverse technical and organizational boundaries.

2.3. Error Handling and Compensation Mechanisms

MuleSoft's integration platform provides a comprehensive error handling framework designed to build resilient and fault-tolerant applications. Effective management of errors is critical to maintaining data consistency and service reliability, especially within complex, distributed architectures where failures may propagate rapidly. The framework supports granular exception detection, configurable recovery strategies, and compensation mechanisms that respect transactional boundaries. These components collectively enable developers to architect integrations robust enough to endure partial failures, system disruptions, and inconsistencies in external dependencies.

At the foundation of MuleSoft's error management lies the concept of *error types* and *error handlers*. Each component or connector defines a set of specific error types, extending from Mule's core error structure, facilitating precise categorization and handling of exceptional conditions. Errors propagate along the execution flows until intercepted by an appropriate error handler composed within the Mule event processor or flow configuration. Three main handlers are distinguished:

- On Error Continue, which consumes the error and allows the flow to proceed.

- On Error Propagate, which propagates the error downstream expecting further handling or termination.

- On Error Propagate with rollback capabilities for transactional scenarios.

Transactional boundaries constitute a pivotal consideration in error and compensation strategies. Mule supports both local and distributed transactions, enabling atomic execution of operations against transactional resources such as databases or JMS queues. Within a transaction scope, an error prompts rollback semantics, reverting changes to maintain consistency. However, transactions across multiple loosely coupled systems or microservices cannot rely solely on traditional rollback due to the absence of a global transaction coordinator. Thus, the platform advocates design patterns such as the saga for eventual consistency and compensation.

The *saga pattern* embodies a sequence of steps in a distributed workflow, each with an associated compensation action to undo partial results if subsequent steps fail. Within MuleSoft, sagas are implemented via the Saga scope, allowing developers to define pairs of forward actions and compensating actions. When an error occurs after one or more steps have succeeded, the corresponding compensation logic is triggered in reverse order, mitigating the risk of data inconsistencies without requiring distributed transaction protocols like XA.

Consider a multi-step order processing integration involving inventory allocation, payment authorization, and shipment creation. If shipment creation fails due to external system unavailability, the saga framework ensures that previously successful operations-such as payment authorization and inventory locks-are compensated by issuing refunds or releasing inventory, restoring system state coherently.

Exception handling strategies in MuleSoft combine fine-grained control and flexibility. Error handlers can be defined globally at the application level, per flow, or scoped to a particular component or processor. This tiered approach enables reusable, centralized handling policies and localized, context-specific intervention. Error handlers may implement constructs such as retries with exponential backoff, error notifications (e.g., via email or message queues), transformation of error payloads, and alternate routing paths to maintain business continuity.

The orchestration of retries is particularly important when integrating with intermittent or unreliable external systems. Mule's error handling supports configurable policies that specify the number of retry attempts, delay intervals, and criteria for retry eligibility based on error types. This capability reduces the likelihood of transient faults causing critical failures and enhances system resilience without overcomplicating the main integration logic.

Strategic logging is tightly integrated into the error handling framework. Detailed capturing of error metadata-including exception class, error description, stack trace, and contextual variables-helps normalize error monitoring and accelerates troubleshooting. Combined with alerting mechanisms, these logs support proactive maintenance and operational visibility.

Compensation actions demand careful idempotency considerations. Since compensating steps might be invoked multiple times due to retries or partial failures, ensuring idempotent behavior avoids cascading faults. MuleSoft enforces idempotency either programmatically-requiring developers to design compensations to be safely repeatable-or via idempotent connectors and APIs that inherently support such operations.

Integration with external transaction managers and resource coordinators extends MuleSoft's error handling capabilities to enterprise environments requiring strict transactional guarantees. Mule's support for distributed transactions via the Java Transaction API (JTA) enables coordinated commits or rollbacks across heterogeneous resource managers. This facility is particularly relevant for synchronous flows where atomicity over multiple databases or messaging systems is essential.

The distinction between synchronous and asynchronous error handling is also critical. While synchronous flows benefit directly from immediate rollback mechanisms, asynchronous flows require compensating actions and sagas to maintain eventual consistency. MuleSoft's event-driven architecture facilitates both modes by supporting asynchronous messaging patterns, publish-subscribe models, and durable queues, all integrated with the error handling framework to guarantee message integrity and reliable delivery.

A succinct example illustrates the implementation of a saga in a Mule flow:

```
<saga doc:name="Saga">
    <processor-chain>
        <flow-ref name="AllocateInventoryFlow"/>
```

```
        <flow-ref name="AuthorizePaymentFlow"/>
        <flow-ref name="CreateShipmentFlow"/>
    </processor-chain>
    <compensation-handler>
        <processor-chain>
            <flow-ref name="CancelShipmentFlow"/>
            <flow-ref name="RefundPaymentFlow"/>
            <flow-ref name="ReleaseInventoryFlow"/>
        </processor-chain>
    </compensation-handler>
</saga>
```

In this configuration, the saga ensures that if any step within the main processor chain fails, all prior successful steps invoke their corresponding compensations in reverse order, safeguarding system consistency even amidst failures.

Ultimately, MuleSoft's error handling framework is underpinned by a design philosophy combining precise error classification, flexible yet controlled recovery pathways, transactional integrity where feasible, and compensation-based eventual consistency when necessary. This approach not only mitigates data corruption and operational downtime but also enhances maintainability by decoupling error recovery concerns from primary business logic.

Effective adoption of MuleSoft's error handling and compensation mechanisms equips integration architects with the tools to manage complex, stateful, and distributed business processes under real-world conditions characterized by unpredictability and partial failures. This empowers the development of integrations that remain consistent, reliable, and performant, preserving trust in automated systems and underlying data integrity.

2.4. State Management and Idempotency

Integration scenarios inherently involve the handling of state across distributed systems, where message exchanges and service invocations must be carefully orchestrated to ensure consistency, reliability, and fault tolerance. In complex MuleSoft integrations, managing state effectively is vital to avoid unintended side effects such as duplicate processing, data corruption, or loss of critical context. The principles of idempotency, persistent and transient state management, as well as the conscious design of stateless and stateful services, are foundational to building robust integration flows.

Idempotent message processing is the cornerstone technique ensuring that repeated processing of the same message yields the same outcome without adverse effects. This is particularly important in asynchronous and retry-prone environments common in integration solutions. When a message arrives multiple times due to network failures, timeouts, or manual resubmissions, idempotency guarantees that side effects (e.g., database updates, triggering downstream events) are applied only once. MuleSoft enables this through message identifier correlation and state checkpoints, allowing integration developers to implement idempotency by tracking message receipts and processing outcomes.

At its core, idempotent processing requires a unique message correlation key-often derived from message metadata or business identifiers-that serves as an idempotency token. MuleSoft's Object Store provides a persistent key-value store to record keys of processed messages alongside the associated processing state. This persistent store forms the basis for detecting and suppressing duplicate message processing attempts. The implementation pattern typically involves:

```
String idempotencyKey = message.getInboundProperty("uniqueId");
if (objectStore.contains(idempotencyKey)) {
    // Message already processed; skip or return previous
    response
} else {
    // Process the message
    objectStore.store(idempotencyKey, processingResult);
}
```

Persistent state management extends beyond idempotency keys to the broader need for durable context storage throughout integration lifecycles. MuleSoft supports persistent state via Object Stores that survive application restarts, enabling long-running transactions and process state retention. These are crucial when coordinating asynchronous steps, managing saga or compensating transaction patterns, and orchestrating multi-stage business processes. Properly architected persistent stores prevent loss of intermediate states during failures and ensure process recoverability.

In contrast, transient state management pertains to temporary data maintained during the execution of an integration invocation or session. Data stored transiently within variables, properties, or in-memory caches exists only during the runtime of a flow or processing context. Transient state is lightweight and fast, but volatile-making it suitable for short-term information such as message headers, control flags, or temporary aggregations that do not require durability after the transaction completes.

The choice between persistent and transient state hinges on the nature and duration of data relevance, consistency requirements, and failure recovery needs. Persistent state is indispensable where idempotent message handling, audit trails, or recovery checkpoints exist. Transient state suffices for intermediate computations and ephemeral routing decisions.

Designing services with regard to state management principles entails clear identification of statelessness versus statefulness. Stateless services avoid retaining client-specific or transactional state between requests, enabling horizontal scalability, fault tolerance, and simplified load balancing. MuleSoft leverages stateless service design by encouraging flows that process each message independently without reliance on previous interactions. Stateless integrations minimize mutable shared state and use idempotent endpoints or transactional guarantees on downstream targets.

Conversely, stateful services maintain interaction context or transactional state across multiple message exchanges or sessions.

These are necessary when implementing complex orchestration patterns, multi-step business processes with compensation logic, or session-aware interactions. Stateful Mule applications must judiciously use persistent stores and synchronization techniques to maintain consistency, avoid race conditions, and ensure atomic state transitions across distributed components.

A typical strategy for reliable and repeatable MuleSoft integrations involves combining idempotency, persistent state tracking, and stateless design where feasible, resorting to explicit statefulness only when justified by business logic. For example, message sources can implement idempotency checks at the edge, while internal flows leverage transient state for processing context. When orchestration requires, persistent state can track process progression, compensations, or timeout management.

Idempotency also extends to outbound calls, where invoked systems may not inherently support duplicate suppression. MuleSoft can mediate idempotency by applying retry policies combined with unique correlators or sequence identifiers embedded in requests. This ensures side effects at downstream systems remain consistent even when MuleSoft retries operations due to network issues or service unavailability.

Failure handling further amplifies the importance of reliable state management. When errors occur, preserving state information in the persistent store facilitates automatic or manual recovery by replaying messages without duplicating effects. MuleSoft's error handling framework, combined with dead-letter queues and object store checkpoints, forms a resilient architecture for managing partial failures.

In advanced scenarios, distributed state management can be realized with external caching or database-backed stores to maintain coherence across multiple Mule instances or clusters. These external stores enable coordination patterns such as leader election, semaphore-like locks, or global counters required for fine-grained control over parallel processing and resource allocation.

The core tenets are:

- **Idempotent Processing**: Guarantee exactly-once side effects by enforcing message deduplication using unique keys and storing processing outcomes persistently.

- **Persistent State Management**: Use MuleSoft Object Stores or external durable stores to maintain process context, support recovery, and track idempotency keys across crashes and restarts.

- **Transient State Management**: Utilize in-memory variables and ephemeral caches for temporary data during single flow executions, optimizing performance without risking durability.

- **Stateless Service Design**: Prefer stateless interactions to enhance scalability and simplify failure handling, delegating state concerns to persistent stores or downstream services.

- **Stateful Service Design**: Implement stateful logic only when necessary, with explicit state tracking, compensating transactions, and well-defined boundaries for process coordination.

Implementing these principles within MuleSoft's integration platform involves a deliberate combination of design patterns and Mule components. Object Store connectors provide transparent APIs for state persistence. Idempotent repositories encapsulate deduplication logic. Routing and choice components handle transient flow state. Error handling strategies ensure state is consistent even under failure.

Mastering state management and idempotency in MuleSoft integrations enables delivery of systems that are more reliable, predictable, and maintainable. It reduces the risk of inconsistent data, duplicated actions, and manual intervention, thereby increasing operational efficiency and trustworthiness of integrated applications. The effectiveness of any integration solution rests heavily on its ability to handle state intricately, aligning with the underlying architecture and business requirements.

2.5. Event-Driven Architectures

Event-driven architectures (EDAs) represent a paradigm that enables systems to react to changes and occurrences in real time, promoting scalability, flexibility, and resilience. MuleSoft's Anypoint Platform provides robust frameworks and tooling to design, implement, and operate event-driven systems, leveraging fundamental concepts such as asynchronous messaging, publish-subscribe (pub/sub) mechanisms, event streaming, and reactive architecture patterns. This approach encourages the creation of loosely coupled integrations that dynamically respond to business events, optimizing system throughput and responsiveness.

At the core of an event-driven system lies the notion of an *event*, typically defined as a discrete occurrence or state change within a domain of interest. Events can be generated by user actions, system state transitions, external APIs, or device telemetry. They serve as notifications rather than direct requests, thus enabling decoupling between event producers (emitters) and consumers (subscribers).

Asynchronous Messaging

MuleSoft facilitates asynchronous communication patterns by employing message brokers and queues that act as intermediaries between producers and consumers. This form of messaging ensures that the components involved do not require simultaneous availability, thus enhancing scalability and fault tolerance.

In an asynchronous Mule integration, the event producer posts a message to a message queue (e.g., JMS, AMQP, or MuleSoft's Anypoint MQ) without needing to wait for an immediate response. The message broker persists the event and delivers it to consumers when they become available, enabling event replay, load balancing, and temporal decoupling. This design benefits use cases where high throughput and failure isolation are critical, such as order processing systems or fulfillment workflows.

The asynchronous nature of the messaging pattern also aligns with eventual consistency principles in distributed systems. Rather than enforcing immediate state synchronization, systems process events independently while converging to a consistent state over time.

Publish-Subscribe Model

The publish-subscribe model abstracts event distribution by allowing multiple consumers to subscribe to specific event channels or topics without the producer's direct knowledge. MuleSoft supports pub/sub through native connectors and Anypoint MQ topics, as well as integration with external brokers like Kafka.

In a pub/sub configuration, event producers publish messages to one or more topics. Subscribers express interest in these topics, receiving messages dynamically as events occur. This enables complex event routing, filtering, and multicast capabilities essential for event propagation to multiple processing units.

For example, a payment processing service can publish transaction events to a topic, with downstream systems such as fraud detection, accounting, and notification services subscribing independently. This isolation improves modularity and system maintainability.

From an implementation perspective, MuleSoft's Event-Driven Consumer scope and Listener components facilitate topic subscription, message transformation, and routing without blocking execution threads. Service orchestration can be orchestrated in flows reacting to specific event payloads, empowering flexible real-time workflows.

Event Streaming

Moving beyond discrete message exchange, event streaming treats event flows as continuous data streams, enabling high-throughput, low-latency data pipelines. Streaming platforms such as Apache Kafka integrate seamlessly with MuleSoft to provide distributed logs of immutable events, preserving event ordering and enabling replay and time-travel semantics.

By coupling MuleSoft Connectors (e.g., Kafka Connector) with DataWeave scripts, events can be enriched, transformed, and routed in near real time. Streaming supports both event sourcing and CQRS (Command Query Responsibility Segregation) architectural patterns by maintaining event logs as authoritative data sources.

A typical event streaming scenario involves Mule flows subscribing to Kafka topics, processing and transforming real-time data (e.g., IoT sensor streams or customer activity logs), and republishing enriched events. This pattern promotes scalability through partitioning and consumer groups, allowing parallel processing and fault tolerance.

Event streaming also supports the implementation of complex event processing (CEP), where event correlation, aggregation, and pattern detection occur across event windows to derive actionable insights or trigger subsequent processes.

Reactive Architecture Patterns

Reactive systems emphasize responsiveness, resilience, elasticity, and message-driven interaction. MuleSoft's platform, through its runtime engine and connectors, inherently supports reactive principles by enabling non-blocking I/O, backpressure handling, and asynchronous communication.

In designing reactive Mule applications, event handlers and processors react to incoming events without maintaining state between invocations, thus enhancing scalability. Backpressure is managed by controlling event consumption rates and buffering, preventing system overload during traffic spikes.

An essential pattern within reactive architectures is the *event loop* or *reactor pattern*, allowing the Mule runtime to multiplex I/O events on a small number of threads, thereby maximizing resource utilization and minimizing latency.

The reactive manifesto's guiding principles manifest in MuleSoft's support for resilience through failover configurations, circuit breaker components, and retry strategies within event-driven flows. Additionally, elasticity is achieved by deploying Mule runtimes in container orchestrators or cloud environments that scale dynamically according to event load metrics.

Design Considerations for Scalable Event-Driven Integrations

Designing event-driven systems with MuleSoft involves critical thinking around idempotency, event schema evolution, and fault management:

- **Idempotency:** Given the asynchronous and potentially at-least-once delivery semantics of messaging systems, Mule applications must implement idempotent event processing to avoid side effects due to duplicate events. Techniques include event deduplication, transactional message consumption, and leveraging business keys.

- **Event Schema Management:** Schemas serve as contracts between event producers and consumers. Employing schema registries (e.g., Confluent Schema Registry) and versioning enables backward and forward compatibility, preventing integration failures due to data format changes.

57

- **Error Handling and Dead Letter Queues:** Events that cannot be processed successfully should be routed to dead letter queues or error handling flows to enable diagnostics, manual correction, or replay without disrupting the event pipeline.

- **Monitoring and Observability:** Real-time event processing demands comprehensive observability. MuleSoft's monitoring tools, combined with distributed tracing frameworks (e.g., OpenTelemetry), enable tracking event flows, latencies, and error rates, facilitating proactive maintenance.

Practical Integration Patterns and Examples

An event-driven Mule integration often employs the *Event-Driven Consumer* pattern, where flows listen on messaging queues or topics. Consider a Mule flow that consumes order creation events from Anypoint MQ and triggers inventory allocation services asynchronously. The design ensures loose coupling, as the inventory system need not be synchronously invoked at order placement.

```
<flow name="orderEventConsumerFlow">
    <amqp:listener config-ref="AMQP_Config" queueName="order.
    events" doc:name="Receive Order Event"/>
    <logger level="INFO" doc:name="Log Event" message="Processing
    order #[payload.orderId]"/>
    <flow-ref name="inventoryAllocationFlow" doc:name="Invoke
    Inventory Allocation"/>
</flow>
```

Alternatively, employing a pub/sub design, multiple Mule applications can independently subscribe to topics broadcasting product updates. Each ensures eventual consistency by reacting to product modification events and updating their local caches or views.

Event streaming use cases emerge prominently in telemetry ingestion scenarios. For example, MuleSoft connects to Kafka topics streaming IoT sensor data where streams are filtered, aggregated, and then persisted into analytics data stores. DataWeave's streaming mode facilitates transformation without materializing the entire dataset in memory, promoting efficiency.

Summary of Architectural Benefits

Event-driven architectures developed with MuleSoft deliver measurable benefits in several dimensions:

- **Decoupling and Scalability:** By separating event producers from consumers through asynchronous messaging and pub/sub models, integrations scale independently and tolerate component downtimes.

- **Real-time Responsiveness:** Event streaming and reactive patterns enable systems to respond immediately to business changes and external signals.

- **Fault Isolation and Resilience:** Message brokers and retry mechanisms localize failures without cascading effects, enabling system stability.

- **Extensibility:** New event subscribers or stream processors can be added with minimal impact on producers, facilitating continuous evolution.

Leveraging MuleSoft's rich tooling, connectors, and runtime capabilities enables enterprise-grade event-driven ecosystems that align tightly with modern agile and DevOps delivery processes while supporting complex integration scenarios across heterogeneous environments.

2.6. Batch Processing and Streaming

Handling high-volume data integration demands architectures that balance throughput, latency, and fault tolerance. MuleSoft provides robust capabilities to address these requirements through its batch and streaming processing features. These features enable efficient processing of large datasets by leveraging chunking, partitioning, parallel execution, and checkpointing, thereby ensuring scalability and reliability across demanding workloads.

Batch processing in MuleSoft orchestrates the execution of batch jobs that divide large datasets into manageable chunks, each processed independently across multiple execution threads. The batch job is composed of distinct phases: input, batch step(s), and on-complete, enabling structured and isolated processing of data segments. Initially, the input phase ingests the entire dataset and divides it into batch blocks, facilitating the efficient distribution of the processing load. Subsequently, batch steps perform transformations or integrations on these blocks, utilizing parallelism to enhance throughput. The on-complete phase enables final aggregation or cleanup activities once all batch blocks have been processed.

Central to batch processing is the concept of chunking. Chunking refers to breaking a voluminous dataset into smaller blocks or chunks that can be processed independently. Chunk sizes directly influence performance and resource utilization; smaller chunks minimize memory impact per thread but may increase overhead due to more frequent context switching, while larger chunks reduce overhead but consume more memory. Optimal chunk sizing depends on data characteristics, connector limitations, and system resource constraints, and often requires empirical tuning.

Partitioning advances the efficiency and scalability of batch processing by dividing each chunk further into partitions that execute concurrently on multiple threads or nodes. Partitioning is especially valuable when datasets exhibit natural segmentation (e.g., by customer ID or geographic region) that can be isolated without cross-dependencies. By distributing load across partitions, MuleSoft achieves horizontal scalability, improving throughput and reducing latency. Partitioning also facilitates fault isolation; the failure or retry of a single partition does not necessitate reprocessing of unrelated data segments.

Parallel processing in MuleSoft's batch framework is realized via configurable thread pools that allow concurrent processing of batch blocks and partitions. The concurrency level is adjustable, allowing tuning based on hardware resources and target service limits. Careful management of concurrency is essential to prevent contention or bottlenecks, particularly when interacting with external systems that have API rate limits or resource constraints. Parallelism must be balanced with idempotency and transaction management to ensure consistent data state when multiple threads perform simultaneous updates.

Checkpointing is an integral mechanism for fault tolerance within batch jobs. MuleSoft supports automatic checkpoint creation at logical points in the batch workflow, recording the state and progress of chunk or partition processing. In the event of failure, checkpoints allow the batch job to restart from the last successful point, avoiding reprocessing of completed data and reducing recovery time. Checkpoints are typically persisted to durable storage, protecting against node failures or application restarts. Proper checkpointing also facilitates transactional guarantees, ensuring that partial updates are either fully committed or rolled back to maintain data integrity.

Streaming complements batch processing by enabling near-real-time processing of continuous data flows. MuleSoft streaming connectors ingest, transform, and route events or messages sequentially, minimizing latency while still processing large volumes of data. Unlike batch jobs that operate on fixed datasets, streaming pipelines support ongoing ingestion with backpressure and flow control to maintain stability under fluctuating load conditions. Streams can be windowed into segments to apply batch-like operations such as aggregation and filtering over time intervals or count-based windows.

Efficient processing of large datasets requires careful consideration of data partition boundaries and the idempotency of operations. Records must be distributed such that cross-partition dependencies do not introduce inconsistent states. MuleSoft's batch
processing supports key-based partitioning, where records sharing a common key are guaranteed to appear in the same partition, simplifying stateful processing and avoiding concurrency conflicts. Idempotency patterns, such as unique transaction identifiers or upsert operations, ensure that repeated execution of the
same batch block or partition does not produce erroneous dupli-
cates or partial updates.

The choice between batch and streaming processing is dictated by
integration requirements. Batch processing is ideal for bulk data
migration, nightly loads, or workflows tolerant of latency where
throughput is prioritized. Streaming processing suits use cases requiring low latency, event-driven integration, or continuous synchronization between systems. Architectures often combine both
approaches, utilizing streaming for real-time updates and batch for
periodic reconciliation or processing of historical data.

Example configurations for batch jobs demonstrate the explicit
declaration of chunk size, partition strategy, and concurrency settings. The following batch:job configuration fragment illustrates
these principles:

```
<batch:job name="LargeDatasetBatchJob">
    <batch:input>
        <dw:transform-message>
            <dw:set-payload><![CDATA[
                payload.records
            ]]></dw:set-payload>
        </dw:transform-message>
    </batch:input>
    <batch:process-records batchSize="500" partitionSize="100">
        <batch:partition on="#[payload.customerId]"
    maxConcurrency="10"/>
        <batch:step name="ProcessPartition">
            <logger message="Processing record #[payload.recordId
    ] in partition #[batch.partition]" level="INFO"/>
            <!-- Transformation and integration logic -->
        </batch:step>
```

```
    </batch:process-records>
    <batch:on-complete>
        <logger message="Batch job completed successfully." level
    ="INFO"/>
    </batch:on-complete>
</batch:job>
```

In this configuration, the dataset is divided into chunks of 500 records, with each chunk partitioned by customer ID into partitions of size 100. The partition concurrency is limited to 10 threads, balancing parallelism and resource consumption. Such parameterization ensures scalability while maintaining control over system load.

Fault tolerance through checkpointing is evident in MuleSoft batch jobs' ability to resume processing from the last checkpointed position. When failures occur-such as network outages or service unavailability-MuleSoft relies on durable storage to record batch job state, minimizing data loss and processing repetition. Developers can customize checkpoint frequency, balancing overhead with recovery granularity.

Streaming processing, by contrast, utilizes constructs such as the streaming scope or streaming connectors like Kafka or HTTP streaming sources. They inherently process data record-by-record with minimal buffering. The processing pipeline supports operators for windowing, filtering, and aggregation, enabling complex event processing gateways capable of scaling with demand.

Integration of batch and streaming modalities with MuleSoft's management policies enhances operational visibility and control. Administrators monitor throughput metrics, thread utilization, and error rates to optimize performance. Advanced retry and error handling policies enable reprocessing of failed records without disrupting entire workflows.

Mastery of batch and streaming processing within MuleSoft involves understanding and applying chunking, partitioning, and parallelism specific to the volume and velocity of data. By leveraging checkpointing mechanisms, executions gain resilience and transactional consistency. The careful orchestration of these features affords integration solutions the capacity to scale gracefully and process large datasets efficiently under demanding conditions.

Chapter 3

API Management and Governance

Unlock the full value of your enterprise APIs by learning how to manage, secure, and govern their lifecycle with precision and confidence. This chapter takes you behind the scenes of effective API management using MuleSoft, guiding you through design-first practices, policy automation, compliance, and analytics to cultivate platforms your developers trust and your business can scale safely. Explore how robust governance transforms APIs from simple interfaces into powerful products that drive innovation, resilience, and organizational agility.

3.1. API Specification with RAML and OAS

Robust API design necessitates clear, standardized, and comprehensive specifications that facilitate seamless communication among architects, developers, and stakeholders. RESTful API Modeling Language (RAML) and OpenAPI Specification (OAS) represent two prominent frameworks for defining

API contracts with precision. Both approaches enable the explicit representation of API resources, methods, data models, and workflows, emphasizing interoperability and productive collaboration.

API specifications serve as living documents that capture the structure and behavior of a service interface. The design must balance expressiveness and simplicity, promoting discoverability and clarity. Both RAML and OAS adopt key modeling principles:

- **Resource-Oriented Representation**: APIs are described in terms of resources (entities or collections), each identified by unique URIs. This encapsulates domain-oriented semantics and aligns tightly with RESTful principles.

- **Uniform Interface Constraints**: Standard HTTP methods—GET, POST, PUT, DELETE, PATCH—define resource interactions. Specifications enumerate allowable methods per resource, expected parameters, headers, request bodies, and response payloads.

- **Explicit Data Typing**: Using JSON Schema or built-in primitives, both YAML-based specifications specify request and response bodies' structure, facilitating validation, code generation, and automated testing.

- **Reusability and Modularity**: Components such as data types, security schemes, and response definitions are abstracted into reusable fragments, promoting maintainability and reducing redundancy.

RAML introduces decorators like `traits` and `resourceTypes`, enabling semantic reuse and DRY (Don't Repeat Yourself) design. OAS similarly supports `components` for schemas and parameters, yielding modular and version-resilient definitions.

66

Although sharing similar aims, RAML and OAS differ syntactically and conceptually in representing APIs:

- **RAML** uses a top-down YAML structure with explicit keys such as `title`, `version`, `baseUri`, and `resources`. Resources are nested under path keys with attached methods, request/response definitions, and annotations. RAML focuses strongly on readability and composability, which benefits architects iterating on high-level API models.

```
#%RAML 1.0
title: User Management API
version: v1
baseUri: https://api.example.com/{version}
types:
  User:
    type: object
    properties:
      id: integer
      name: string
/users:
  get:
    description: Retrieve list of users
    responses:
      200:
        body:
          application/json:
            type: User[]
```

- **OpenAPI Specification (OAS)** also employs YAML but organizes the API contract with `info`, `servers`, `paths`, and `components` sections. The granularity enables detailed specifications for operation-level parameters, security schemes, and callbacks. OAS 3.0+ expands support for advanced features such as content negotiation and webhooks.

```
openapi: 3.0.3
info:
  title: User Management API
  version: v1
servers:
  - url: https://api.example.com/v1
paths:
  /users:
    get:
      summary: Retrieve list of users
```

67

```
responses:
  '200':
    description: A JSON array of user objects
    content:
      application/json:
        schema:
          type: array
          items:
            $ref: '#/components/schemas/User'
components:
  schemas:
    User:
      type: object
      properties:
        id:
          type: integer
        name:
          type: string
```

API versioning maintains backward compatibility and supports iterative enhancement. Both RAML and OAS accommodate versioning strategies; the choice must align with organizational policies and developer expectations.

- **URI Versioning**: Including the version number as a segment in the base URI path, e.g., /v1/users, is straightforward and widely adopted. Specifications declare the base URI parameterized with version identifiers in RAML, or declare multiple server URLs in OAS for distinct versions.

- **Header-Based Versioning**: Using custom HTTP headers for versioning allows cleaner URIs but reduces discoverability. Specifications specify expected headers at the request level and document their semantics clearly.

- **Content Negotiation Versioning**: Leveraging the Accept header to distinguish versions enables fine-grained control but increases client complexity. Both RAML and OAS support encoding versioning information in media type parameters.

68

Version management in RAML can utilize traits or resourceTypes to encapsulate version-specific variations, minimizing duplication. In OAS, leveraging `allOf` and `oneOf` schema composition supports incremental changes between versions.

API designs require active participation from multiple roles. Specifications act as a single source of truth accessible to architects, developers, testers, and business stakeholders. Effective collaboration involves the following considerations:

- **Human-Readable and Machine-Readable Documentation**: Both RAML and OAS enable generation of interactive documentation, making specifications actionable for non-technical stakeholders.

- **Iterative Design with Live Feedback**: Modeling tools supporting RAML and OAS allow real-time validation and preview of API behaviors, enabling rapid iteration and early discovery of design flaws or inconsistencies.

- **Standardized Terminology and Definitions**: Consistency in naming, data types, and error handling conventions is enforced by shared specification documents, reducing ambiguity and integration errors.

- **Code Generation and Testing Automation**: Specification-driven development pipelines facilitate generation of client SDKs, server stubs, mocks, and test cases, fostering parallel workflows between development and testing teams.

RAML and OAS do not exist in isolation but integrate into broader API management ecosystems. Their uptake in continuous integration/continuous deployment (CI/CD) pipelines accelerates API deployment, monitoring, and evolution.

Advanced modeling includes:

- **Security Schemes**: Authentication and authorization methods (e.g., OAuth 2.0, API keys) are declaratively modeled to enforce uniform security policies.

- **Error Modeling**: Well-defined error response schemas improve client error handling and diagnostic capabilities.

- **Extensibility**: Vendor extensions add domain-specific metadata without breaking compatibility, allowing bespoke tooling support.

Collaboration between architects and developers is enhanced when API specifications serve as contractual blueprints for both front-end and back-end teams, orchestrating integration with message brokers, databases, or microservices. Stakeholders gain confidence through transparent requirement traceability and change management enabled by version-controlled RAML or OAS definitions.

The choice between RAML and OAS often hinges on organizational context and tooling preferences:

- RAML's explicit modularity and clear separation of concerns suit organizations emphasizing API design-first methodologies with strong architectural supervision.

- OAS's widespread adoption and robust ecosystem, including extensive tooling for documentation, mocking, and code generation, provide broad compatibility with existing development workflows.

Both specifications interoperate with transformation tools that convert RAML to OAS and vice versa, enabling migration or mixed environments. Emphasizing standards compliance and rigorous documentation ensures APIs remain maintainable and future-proof regardless of the specification format chosen.

Ultimately, mastery of RAML and OpenAPI Specification as design artifacts elevates API quality, accelerates development cycles, and fosters transparent collaboration across all stakeholders involved in modern service-oriented architectures.

3.2. Policy Enforcement and Security

Effective policy enforcement and robust security are fundamental to safeguarding APIs in modern integration architectures. Mule-Soft's API Manager enables comprehensive control over authentication, authorization, rate limiting, and custom policy implementation, providing automated governance capabilities that protect APIs from malicious activity, ensure regulatory compliance, and adapt security postures dynamically based on contextual risk assessments.

Authentication forms the first line of defense by verifying the identity of clients accessing the API. MuleSoft supports a range of authentication schemes, including OAuth 2.0, JWT validation, Basic Authentication, and Mutual TLS (mTLS). OAuth 2.0 implementation, for example, leverages access tokens issued by an authorization server to securely delegate user credentials without exposing them to service endpoints. Enforcement of these mechanisms occurs transparently through API Manager policies, which intercept requests and validate credentials before routing to backend services. JWT validation policies inspect tokens for integrity, signature, issuer claims, and expiration times, preventing forgery and replay attacks.

Authorization complements authentication by controlling client permissions and resource access scopes. Role-based access control (RBAC) and fine-grained permissions can be enforced using MuleSoft policies that evaluate claims embedded within tokens or external LDAP/AD groups. These controls ensure users and applications have only the minimal privileges required, reducing the attack surface and complying with the principle of least privilege. Custom assertion policies can inspect additional request attributes or payload data to execute domain-specific authorization logic, dynamically allowing or denying actions based on business rules.

Rate limiting is a critical countermeasure against abusive usage patterns such as denial-of-service (DoS) attacks, credential stuffing, and scraping. API Manager provides built-in policies to limit the volume of API requests over specified time windows for each client, IP, or application. These thresholds can be configured globally or scoped per resource path, enabling granular protection tailored to anticipated usage patterns and SLAs. By rejecting excessive requests with standard HTTP status codes (e.g., 429 Too Many Requests), these policies preserve API availability and performance under high load or attack scenarios.

Custom policies extend API Manager's security toolbox by allowing bespoke enforcement rules encapsulated in DataWeave or Java code. These policies can execute additional validations such as payload schema verification, content inspection for injection attacks, or integration with third-party security services like web application firewalls (WAFs) and threat intelligence feeds. The ability to chain custom policies enables complex adaptive security models that dynamically adjust enforcement based on real-time telemetry, user behavior analytics, or geolocation data. This adaptive security pattern balances rigorous protection with usability and performance by modulating controls proportionate to assessed risk.

Automated governance leverages policy enforcement to standardize security practices consistently across the entire API ecosystem. By centrally managing policies through API Manager, organizations eliminate configuration drift and enable rapid remediation of vulnerabilities following security advisories or compliance updates. Policy execution is enforced at runtime on the API gateway layer, decoupling security concerns from business logic implemented in backend services. This separation allows rapid iteration of security policies without impacting API contracts or service implementations.

Threat protection policies vital to MuleSoft API security include XML External Entity (XXE) attack prevention, SQL injection detection, and cross-site scripting (XSS) mitigation. These are implemented by inspecting incoming payloads for known exploit patterns or malformed constructs. When anomalies are detected, the policies can block, sanitize, or quarantine suspicious requests, effectively reducing the risk of data breaches and service disruptions. Furthermore, built-in logging and alerting within API Manager provide auditors and security operations centers (SOCs) with comprehensive visibility into attempted intrusions and policy violations.

Ensuring compliance with regulatory frameworks such as GDPR, HIPAA, PCI-DSS, and others is achieved by leveraging policy-driven data masking, encryption, and access auditing capabilities. MuleSoft policies can redact sensitive fields in API responses or mask personally identifiable information (PII) during transit. Encryption policies enforce end-to-end confidentiality using standards like TLS 1.3 and facilitate tokenization or encryption of sensitive data at rest or in motion. Audit trails maintained by API Manager record every access attempt, policy decision, and security event, supporting forensic investigations and compliance reporting.

A practical approach in MuleSoft involves layering standard policies with organizational customizations to form comprehensive security stacks. The sequence of application often begins with authentication, followed by authorization, then threat detection/prevention, and finally rate limiting. Considerations for ordering policies are critical because early enforcement of identity verification prevents unnecessary processing of unauthorized traffic, while rate limiting as the terminal layer avoids prematurely blocking legitimate requests during complex validation steps.

Adaptive security techniques supported by MuleSoft's runtime collect contextual metadata such as device fingerprinting, anomalous timing patterns, geographic origin, and previous interaction history to continuously assess risk scores. Policies can dynamically escalate security requirements by invoking multi-factor authentication (MFA), issuing more restrictive tokens, or restricting access to specific API subsets. This continuous assessment and contextual response improve resilience against sophisticated threats, such as credential compromise or insider abuse, while maintaining fluid user experiences for low-risk scenarios.

The policy enforcement lifecycle also integrates tightly with CI/CD pipelines and governance workflows. Policies managed through the API Manager UI or via MuleSoft's REST APIs can be versioned, reviewed, and deployed systematically alongside API specifications and implementation artifacts. Automated testing frameworks validate policy responses prior to production rollout, ensuring stability and reducing human error. Incorporating policy lifecycle management into DevOps practices accelerates secure API delivery and proactively detects regressions or configuration drift.

```
<oauth-2.0-token-introspection
    name="OAuth 2.0 Token Introspection"
    enabled="true"
    introspectionUri="https://auth.example.com/oauth2/introspect"
    clientId="api-client"
    clientSecret="secret"
    audience="api-resource"
    requiredScopes="read,write"
/>
```

```
<rate-limiting
    maxRequests="#[1000]"
    timePeriod="#[3600]"
    unit="seconds"
    limitType="clientId"
    onLimitExceeded="reject"
/>
```

```
HTTP/1.1 429 Too Many Requests
Retry-After: 120
Content-Type: application/json
```

74

```
{
  "error": "rate_limit_exceeded",
  "message": "You have exceeded your request quota. Please try again later."
}
```

Extensive logging, monitoring, and alerting are integral to maintaining security posture and validating policy effectiveness. MuleSoft embeds rich runtime metrics and integrates with monitoring platforms via APIs and connectors, facilitating anomaly detection and incident response workflows. Metrics include policy hit counts, authentication failures, request latency, and throughput, providing actionable insights to API managers and security teams.

MuleSoft's API Manager establishes a robust, extensible framework for policy enforcement and security that aligns with enterprise-grade governance needs. By combining standardized authentication and authorization models with adaptive, contextual controls and comprehensive threat protection, organizations can defend APIs from evolving threats while maintaining compliance and operational agility. This balance of security, usability, and automation forms the cornerstone of resilient API ecosystems.

3.3. Metadata-driven API Governance

Automated API lifecycle management fundamentally relies on systematically capturing and utilizing metadata to enforce contracts, manage versioning and deprecation, and generate documentation. Metadata serves as the foundational element that enables governance policies to be applied consistently and automatically across diverse APIs, reducing manual intervention and mitigating risks of divergence. MuleSoft's approach encapsulates this principle by embedding metadata at every stage of the API lifecycle, thereby reinforcing governance while maintaining agility and developer productivity.

API contracts, encompassing specifications such as RAML, OpenAPI, or proprietary formats, act as authoritative metadata sources that delineate expected interface behaviors, data schemas, and operational constraints. Leveraging these metadata artifacts, MuleSoft automates contract enforcement by validating API implementations against defined specifications during both design-time and run-time. This dual-phase validation ensures that APIs remain compliant with prescribed behaviors before deployment and continue operating in adherence to contracts post-deployment. Contract enforcement mechanisms include schema validation for request and response payloads, policy execution to restrict or manipulate traffic, and monitoring to detect deviations from the contract in live environments. These capabilities minimize integration failures and elevate consumer confidence.

Versioning management is intricately linked to metadata, as changes in API contracts signal the necessity for new versions. MuleSoft supports versioning metadata at multiple granularity levels, including API specifications, endpoints, and resource operations. Automated workflows parse version identifiers embedded within the contract definitions, enabling the platform to orchestrate parallel version lifecycles. These workflows handle branching, merging, and compatibility checks by comparing metadata elements such as path structures, parameter types, and response schemas. Metadata annotations also facilitate semantic versioning, guiding decisions on backward-compatible versus breaking changes. Consequently, teams can deploy new API versions with controlled impact, while clients can migrate smoothly through explicit deprecation timelines.

Deprecation processes are similarly metadata-driven. Metadata fields included within the API specifications indicate deprecation statuses, sunset dates, replacement alternatives, and impact scopes. MuleSoft's automation interprets these metadata cues to enforce deprecation policies, which can trigger custom notifications to consumers, apply throttling or blocking policies on deprecated endpoints, and update internal dashboards to reflect the API portfolio's evolution. Metadata enables visualization of deprecated versus active APIs, aiding governance bodies in maintaining a sustainable API ecosystem. By automating deprecation management, organizations reduce technical debt accumulation and enhance forward compatibility.

Comprehensive API documentation generation tightly couples with metadata richness and accuracy. Automated tools within MuleSoft extract contract metadata elements such as endpoint definitions, parameter descriptions, response codes, and example payloads to produce unified, consumable documentation artifacts. Documentation is dynamically synchronized with the source metadata, ensuring that published materials remain consistent with the actual API state. This automation mitigates documentation drift-a common source of integration errors-and empowers both internal developers and external partners with up-to-date references. Moreover, enhanced metadata annotations enable advanced documentation features, including interactive consoles, usage analytics, and security requirements, all generated programmatically.

Underlying these capabilities is a metadata-driven governance framework that orchestrates policies through declarative configurations and metadata-awareness. MuleSoft's governance engine interprets metadata to enforce policy compliance automatically, such as authentication requirements, rate limiting, data masking, and audit logging, without manual configuration for each API. This declarative metadata governance reduces administrative overhead, accelerates policy propagation across the API landscape, and strengthens security and compliance postures. Governance metadata is extensible, supporting organizational custom rules that can be embedded alongside standard contract metadata, thus harmonizing global compliance with local needs.

MuleSoft's architecture facilitates integration of metadata-driven governance into continuous integration/continuous deployment (CI/CD) pipelines, embedding automated checks and enforcement as part of the development workflow. Metadata extracted from API contracts are fed into pipeline stages where quality gates validate schema completeness, adherence to organizational standards, and compatibility with existing APIs before progression. Any violations yield immediate feedback, preventing flawed API artifacts from advancing to production. This integration streamlines policy adherence by embedding governance into developer processes rather than imposing external manual reviews, promoting scalability in large API organizations.

Visualization and analytics tools consume governance metadata to provide platform-wide insights into API health, usage patterns, compliance status, and lifecycle progression. Dashboards aggregate metadata across thousands of APIs, highlighting contract adherence metrics, version distribution, deprecation schedules, and policy enforcement statistics. These insights enable governance committees to monitor ecosystem stability, identify risks, prioritize remediation efforts, and justify governance investments with quantitative evidence. Metadata provenance tracking also supports audit compliance by recording API definition changes, policy alterations, and user actions, thus providing traceability and transparency.

Metadata-driven API governance as implemented by MuleSoft represents a sophisticated integration of specification data, declarative policies, and automated lifecycle management tools. This approach empowers organizations to maintain rigorous control over their APIs, minimize manual governance burdens, and enable adaptive evolution of the API platform aligned with strategic and operational requirements. The reliance on rich, structured metadata ensures that contract enforcement, version management, deprecation workflows, and documentation generation become repeatable, scalable, and auditable processes, thereby elevating the overall quality and reliability of API ecosystems.

3.4. API Analytics and Monitoring

Effective API management necessitates comprehensive analytics and monitoring capabilities, functioning as the cornerstone for maintaining operational excellence and meeting service commitments. API analytics provide insight into usage patterns, performance trends, and potential failure modes, while monitoring facilitates real-time detection and response to emergent issues. Both native platform tools and third-party solutions play pivotal roles in establishing a robust observability framework that supports continuous API improvement, SLA adherence, and anomaly detection.

Tracking SLA Compliance Through Metric Collection

Service Level Agreements (SLAs) specify the quantitative criteria relating to API availability, response time, throughput, and error rates. Continuous monitoring of these criteria demands the systematic collection of relevant runtime metrics, often categorized as follows:

- **Availability**: Percentage of successful API responses over a defined period.

- **Latency**: Time taken for the API to respond, including percentiles (p50, p95, p99) to capture distribution nuances.

- **Throughput**: Number of API calls processed per unit time, which indicates load and capacity utilization.

- **Error Rate**: Incidence of failed API calls, classified by HTTP status codes or custom error types.

Native API management platforms (such as Apigee, AWS API Gateway, or Azure API Management) feature built-in telemetry engines that automatically track these core metrics, providing baseline SLA monitoring without additional instrumentation. These platforms typically expose dashboards with aggregated views and enable alerting based on threshold breaches.

Beyond native solutions, exporting metrics to centralized observability stacks (e.g., Prometheus, Datadog, New Relic) enhances SLA tracking by integrating API data with broader infrastructure monitoring. APIs instrumented with OpenTelemetry SDKs enable collection of distributed traces and custom metrics, enriching SLA monitoring with contextual details such as API call paths and backend service dependencies.

Anomaly Detection and Predictive Alerting

Detecting anomalies early reduces mean time to resolution and prevents degraded API experiences. Anomalies may manifest as sudden spikes in latency, error rates, or drop in successful responses. Traditional threshold-based alerts, defined by static limits, often produce false positives in dynamic environments. More sophisticated approaches employ statistical and machine learning models to identify deviations from learned normal behavior patterns.

Several analytic tools integrate anomaly detection engines capable of real-time and historical analysis:

- **Time-Series Analysis**: Algorithms such as ARIMA or Holt–Winters smooth metric data and forecast expected values, flagging deviations beyond confidence intervals.

- **Clustering and Density Models**: Identify outliers by grouping similar metric patterns and isolating anomalous ones.

- **Supervised Learning**: Classification models trained on labeled incident data recognize specific failure signatures.

By leveraging APIs' continuous metric streams, anomaly detection integrates with alerting systems that can trigger automated mitigation workflows-circuit breakers, retries, or traffic rerouting-before SLA violations cascade into major incidents.

Runtime Metrics Collection: Best Practices and Instrumentation

Instrumentation for API runtime metrics collection constitutes the foundation upon which analytics and monitoring rely. Effective instrumentation balances richness of data with minimal performance overhead and avoidance of data deluge. Critical design considerations include:

- **Granularity**: Collect metrics at a level that supports actionable insights without unnecessary detail; aggregate when possible.

- **Correlation Identifiers**: Use trace or correlation IDs to connect distributed components, enabling root cause analysis across microservices.

- **Metadata Enrichment**: Capture contextual metadata such as client identity, request parameters, API version, and deployment environment.

- **Sampling Strategies**: Employ adaptive sampling to reduce load while preserving representativeness, especially for high-throughput APIs.

Instrumentation can be embedded via middleware or proxy layers, leveraging technologies such as Envoy, Istio, or built-in platform hooks. Open standards like OpenTelemetry facilitate vendor-neutral collection and federation of telemetry data, allowing seamless integration with analytics backends.

```
const { NodeTracerProvider } = require('@opentelemetry/sdk-trace-
    node');
```

81

```
const { registerInstrumentations } = require('@opentelemetry/
    instrumentation');
const { HttpInstrumentation } = require('@opentelemetry/
    instrumentation-http');

const provider = new NodeTracerProvider();
provider.register();

registerInstrumentations({
  instrumentations: [new HttpInstrumentation()],
});

// Application API code continues...
```

Output: Telemetry traces generated for each HTTP request,
including spans representing downstream calls and timings,
exported to configured collector endpoints.

Design and Implementation of Actionable Dashboards

Dashboards visualize key performance indicators, enabling stakeholders to monitor individual API behaviors and holistic system
health. Effective dashboard design pivots on clarity, relevance,
and real-time responsiveness to support operational decisions.

Core components of API dashboards include:

- **KPI Panels**: Highlight latency percentiles, request volume,
  error distribution, and uptime within defined time windows.

- **Trend Charts**: Visualize metric evolution, enabling identification of gradual degradation or improvement.

- **Top Consumers and Endpoints**: Showcase highest traffic APIs and client applications to prioritize optimization.

- **Alert Summaries**: Provide status of triggered alerts with
  drill-down links to diagnostic data.

- **Dependency Maps**: Graph downstream services
  consumed by the API, illuminating potential impact
  domains.

Tools such as Grafana or Kibana offer highly customizable interfaces with support for dynamic queries and annotations, facilitating correlation of incidents with deployment events or configuration changes. Integrating dashboard solutions with APIs' native analytics or external monitoring platforms consolidates visibility across heterogeneous environments.

Continuous Improvement Driven by Analytics

API analytics and monitoring data generate a feedback loop essential for iterative enhancement of API ecosystems. Key improvement areas informed by these insights include:

- **Performance Tuning**: Identification of latency bottlenecks focuses optimization efforts on problematic endpoints or backend calls.

- **Capacity Planning**: Usage trend analysis informs scaling strategies to preempt overload or under-provisioning.

- **Error Reduction**: Frequent failure modes expose design flaws or integration issues, guiding code fixes and client communication.

- **User Experience Optimization**: Behavioral metrics reveal adoption patterns and deviations, supporting enhancements aligned with consumer needs.

- **Security Posture**: Unusual access patterns or spikes may indicate potential attacks, informing threat mitigation and compliance activities.

Incorporating periodic analytic reviews into API management workflows fosters a culture of proactive governance. Automating metric-driven policy adjustments enables adaptive SLAs and dynamically tuned service quality aligned to evolving business requirements.

Consequently, the synergy between native and third-party analytics platforms underpins a comprehensive observability strategy-transforming raw telemetry into actionable intelligence that secures API reliability, efficiency, and user satisfaction at scale.

3.5. Marketplace Publishing and Developer Experience

The transformation of APIs into successful, widely adopted digital products hinges on their visibility, accessibility, and usability within developer ecosystems. Publishing APIs to marketplaces and developer portals is a critical step in this evolution, enabling organizations to convert technical interfaces into discoverable, self-service offerings. Such platforms serve as the primary interface between API providers and consumers, shaping perceptions, influencing adoption rates, and fostering ongoing engagement.

At the core of effective marketplace publishing lies the principle of discoverability. Unlike conventional software distribution, which benefits from established retail and download channels, APIs require specialized marketplaces or portals tailored to developer needs. These platforms must present rich API catalogs that enable developers to quickly identify relevant APIs based on functional capabilities, technical compatibility, and business value propositions. Catalogs are typically enhanced with metadata tags, category classifications, and search functionalities driven by semantic indexing. This structural organization empowers developers to filter and compare APIs efficiently, reducing the cognitive load during evaluation.

Beyond discoverability, seamless onboarding mechanisms constitute a pivotal factor in converting interest into active consumption. Traditional API exposure methods often rely on manual registration processes, fragmented documentation access, and cumbersome credential workflows that impede rapid experimentation.

84

Modern developer portals unify these stages through streamlined self-service registration, automatic API key provisioning, and integrated API consoles that permit interactive exploration without requiring local setup. These capabilities leverage underlying identity and access management systems to safeguard security while minimizing friction in initial developer engagement.

Comprehensive documentation plays an indispensable role in both discovery and onboarding phases. High-caliber documentation is multifaceted: it includes not only reference specifications such as OpenAPI definitions, but also contextual guides, tutorials, and use-case-driven walkthroughs that elucidate common integration patterns. Effective documentation also integrates sample code snippets in multiple programming languages and offers SDKs generated directly from API specifications. This code-first approach removes barriers for developers by lowering the effort needed to incorporate APIs into applications. Furthermore, documentation is often complemented by community forums, FAQs, and support channels embedded within the marketplace ecosystem, providing ongoing assistance and fostering peer-to-peer knowledge exchange.

Rich, interactive API catalogs within marketplaces increasingly incorporate live feedback mechanisms, including usage metrics, ratings, and review systems. These community-driven data points contribute to a transparent quality assurance process, enabling potential consumers to gauge reliability, performance, and feature completeness from existing user experiences. Visibility into versioning history, deprecation policies, and service-level agreements further informs developer decision-making, reinforcing confidence in API stability and vendor commitment.

Standardization in the publication process significantly enhances both the provider's efficiency and the developer's experience. Utilizing established description formats such as OpenAPI or AsyncAPI enables automated ingestion and rendering of API specifications in the portal, facilitating dynamic documentation generation, automatic endpoint testing, and real-time mock server provision. These standards also permit marketplaces to validate APIs against conformity rules and security best practices before listing, ensuring higher overall quality and reducing integration risks.

Marketplace platforms can improve developer engagement by implementing event-driven notifications and lifecycle management interfaces. For instance, developers benefit from alerts regarding API updates, deprecations, or outages, delivered via email, SMS, or in-portal notifications. Correspondingly, API providers can track consumer activity, usage patterns, and feedback within the portal analytics dashboards, informing iterative improvements and targeted marketing efforts. Integrating analytics with monetization frameworks allows for granular usage-based billing or tiered subscription plans, delivering economic incentives aligned with usage levels, thereby encouraging sustained adoption.

In addition to technical and operational facets, marketplace publishing influences API governance and compliance. Portals often enforce policy adherence regarding data privacy, security standards, and legal usage clauses through automated workflows embedded during the publishing phase. These controls ensure that accessible APIs meet organizational risk profiles and regulatory requirements, especially vital in industries subject to stringent compliance regimes such as healthcare and finance.

The user experience design of developer portals directly impacts the subjective quality of marketplace interactions. Intuitive navigation, responsive interfaces, and contextual search recommendations substantially reduce the time required to find and assess APIs. Embedding API playgrounds-browser-hosted sandboxes supporting live calls to real or simulated backend services-gives immediate feedback and demystifies technical complexity. Such experiential affordances convert passive browsing into active experimentation, thereby accelerating the decision to adopt.

86

Several technical patterns have crystallized as best practices in marketplace publishing workflows. First, continuous integration pipelines now routinely incorporate API specification publishing stages, enabling real-time synchronization between development repositories and public marketplaces. This continuous publishing ensures that the interface and documentation presented to developers remain current with backend implementations, mitigating the risk of integration errors. Second, role-based access control governs both the publication and consumption phases, allowing for granular management of developer entitlements, including trial periods, restricted beta tests, or enterprise client exclusives.

To illustrate, the following simplified example demonstrates automated publication of an OpenAPI-described REST API to a developer portal using a hypothetical command-line interface (CLI) utility:

```
# Authenticate with developer portal API
portal-cli authenticate --client-id=myclient --client-secret=
    mysecret

# Publish OpenAPI specification with metadata
portal-cli publish-api --spec=./petstore-openapi.yaml \
                --name="Pet Store API" \
                --category="Retail" \
                --visibility=public \
                --support-email=support@petstore.com

# Verify API listing
portal-cli list-apis | grep "Pet Store API"
```

API Name	Category	Visibility	Version
Pet Store API	Retail	public	v1.0.0

The immediate availability of the API listing, together with integrated documentation and self-service onboarding tools, exemplifies the core attributes essential for marketplace success.

Developer portals that embrace extensibility and integration capabilities evolve beyond static directories into comprehensive platforms. They may integrate with external identity providers using OAuth 2.0 or OpenID Connect protocols to facilitate single sign-on

(SSO), integrate with CI/CD pipelines for API lifecycle automation, and expose rich RESTful or GraphQL APIs themselves to allow automated querying, subscription management, and billing. By embedding webhooks and event streams, portals enable tight coupling with third-party developer experience (DX) tooling, further enriching engagement opportunities.

Scalability considerations must also be accounted for when designing marketplace environments. High developer traffic, concurrent API testing, and dynamic documentation rendering require optimized caching strategies, content delivery network (CDN) utilization, and backend service resilience. Additionally, internationalization support increases adoption scope by delivering localized content, documentation, and support assets that accommodate global audiences.

Ultimately, the success of marketplace publishing initiatives can be measured through quantitative and qualitative metrics. Adoption rates, developer retention, average API call volumes, and conversion ratios from trial to paid usage provide tangible performance indicators. Concurrently, developer satisfaction surveys, sentiment analysis from community forums, and direct feedback serve as qualitative inputs guiding iterative enhancements to both the APIs and the supporting marketplace ecosystem.

Elevating APIs to discoverable, self-service products through targeted publishing on developer portals and marketplaces demands a confluence of technical rigor, user-centric design, and strategic ecosystem management. By addressing discoverability, seamless onboarding, exhaustive and interactive documentation, enriched API catalogs, community feedback mechanisms, standardized publishing processes, and agile lifecycle management, organizations can accelerate developer engagement, reduce adoption friction, and maximize the business impact of their API programs.

3.6. Zero Trust and Integration Security Controls

The increasing complexity and scale of modern IT infrastructures demand a fundamental rethinking of traditional security paradigms. Classical perimeter-based defenses, relying heavily on implicit trust within network boundaries, no longer suffice in environments characterized by dynamic cloud services, distributed architectures, and pervasive API integration. The zero trust security model, network segmentation, and context-aware controls collectively constitute a robust strategy to defend against sophisticated adversaries by consistently enforcing strict access boundaries and continuously validating trust.

Zero trust architecture (ZTA) operates on the axiom that no entity, whether inside or outside the network perimeter, should be inherently trusted. It mandates explicit verification and continuous assessment of every access request based on identity, device health, location, and other contextual information. The foundational principle of zero trust is the establishment of well-defined, fine-grained trust boundaries that segment resources and enforce least-privilege access policies.

Network segmentation within zero trust leverages microsegmentation techniques to partition complex environments into isolated zones. This granular separation significantly reduces the lateral movement opportunities for attackers who breach a perimeter or compromise credentials. Segmentation boundaries may coincide with individual applications, functional domains, or sensitivity levels of data sets. Enforcing segmentation relies on software-defined networking policies combined with firewalls, identity-aware proxies, or service mesh controls in containerized deployments. Segments are not only network constructs but also logical access boundaries where policy enforcement platforms validate identity and context before granting access.

Implementing least-privilege access is critical to zero trust success. Access permissions are minimized to the absolute necessities required for a user or service to perform its authorized functions. This contrasts with traditional models that grant broad access rights based on role or network placement. Role-based access control (RBAC), attribute-based access control (ABAC), and policy-based access control (PBAC) paradigms each contribute frameworks for codifying least-privilege principles. By dynamically evaluating attributes such as user role, location, device posture, and time of request, systems can enforce adaptive access decisions rather than static allowances. The enforcement of least-privilege mitigates risks arising from credential compromise or insider threats by limiting resource exposure.

Context-aware controls enhance zero trust security by incorporating real-time environmental and behavioral data into trust evaluations. Contextual signals include device integrity metrics, user behavioral analytics, geolocation, network characteristics, and anomalous activity detection. These inputs feed into decision engines that dynamically adjust access rights or trigger risk mitigation procedures such as multi-factor authentication or session termination. For example, an access attempt from an unusual geographic location or unfamiliar device may prompt additional verification steps before access is granted. This adaptive control paradigm ensures trust is continuously validated rather than assumed at session initiation.

Defending API ecosystems within zero trust demands special consideration due to their ubiquitous role in integration and data exchange. APIs often expose critical backend services and sensitive data, making them prime targets for advanced persistent threats and exploitation. Establishing zero trust for APIs involves identifying trust boundaries for each API endpoint, authenticating and authorizing calling entities with precision, and applying granular rate limiting and anomaly detection controls. API gateways and service meshes equipped with zero trust policies can enforce mutual TLS, OAuth tokens, JWT validation, and integration of identity providers to safeguard access.

Network segmentation supports API security by isolating API tiers from frontend clients, internal services, and databases. This segmentation limits the blast radius of attacks such as injection or credential compromise. Additionally, context-aware controls applied to API transactions monitor request patterns and parameters to detect and block sophisticated abuse techniques like API fuzzing, parameter tampering, or credential stuffing.

Integrating zero trust controls into existing environments requires systematic identification of high-value assets and data flows, followed by modeling trust zones around them. Critical systems are encapsulated within isolated segments protected by multi-layered authentication and authorization proxies. Policy engines enforce least-privilege by continuously evaluating identity and context data originating from enterprise identity management, endpoint posture assessments, and network telemetry. The integration of endpoint detection and response (EDR) tools with zero trust controllers provides visibility into anomalous access attempts, enabling automated containment of threats.

Crucial to zero trust's effectiveness is the orchestration of security controls across heterogeneous infrastructures. Centralized policy management enables consistent enforcement across cloud workloads, on-premises data centers, and edge environments. Visibility into trust boundary interactions is accomplished via telemetry aggregation, including packet inspection, API call logging, and authentication event streams. Machine learning techniques applied to this data facilitate risk scoring and proactive threat hunting.

The following example demonstrates a simplified enforcement policy snippet for API access controls within a zero trust framework, utilizing a policy specification language:

```
{
  "policyId": "api-access-001",
  "description": "Allow access to payment API for authenticated
```

```
     finance users during business hours",
  "rules": [
    {
      "effect": "allow",
      "actions": ["invoke"],
      "resources": ["api://payment-service/*"],
      "conditions": {
        "subject": {
          "group": "finance-team",
          "isAuthenticated": true
        },
        "time": {
          "start": "08:00",
          "end": "18:00"
        },
        "device": {
          "complianceStatus": "healthy"
        }
      }
    },
    {
      "effect": "deny",
      "actions": ["invoke"],
      "resources": ["api://payment-service/*"]
    }
  ]
}
```

This policy exemplifies critical zero trust attributes: explicit
authentication requirements, group-based authorization, device
compliance verification, and temporal constraints. Deny rules
serve as safe defaults, ensuring access is refused unless explicitly
permitted.

Operationalizing zero trust requires continuous monitoring to detect policy violations and trust boundary breaches. Incident response mechanisms must integrate with zero trust platforms to
enable rapid isolation and remediation of compromised entities.
Automated enforcement via policy-as-code and infrastructure-as-
code tools facilitates timely updates as threat landscapes evolve.

Zero trust and integration security controls establish resilient
defense mechanisms by eliminating excessive trust assumptions.
Through precise network segmentation, rigorous least-privilege
enforcement, and context-aware adaptive controls, organizations

can effectively safeguard modern API-driven environments against advanced threats. Zero trust architectures transform security into a continuous, policy-driven process that adapts to emerging risks without undermining operational agility.

Chapter 4

Hybrid, Multicloud, and On-premises Integration

In a world where applications, data, and processes stretch across public clouds, private data centers, and everything in between, seamless integration is more critical—and more complex—than ever before. This chapter demystifies the strategies, topologies, and best practices for unifying hybrid and multicloud landscapes using MuleSoft. Whether bridging legacy on-premises systems with modern SaaS or architecting federated cloud platforms, you'll explore patterns and security models that drive resilient, high-performing integrations without boundaries.

4.1. Hybrid Integration Models

The convergence of on-premises and cloud-based systems within enterprise environments presents substantial integration challenges. Hybrid integration models have emerged as indispensable frameworks enabling seamless interoperability while retaining the strategic benefits of both deployment paradigms. These models typify architectures that bridge isolated environments, manage data flows securely, and maintain consistency and reliability amid distributed processing.

A fundamental challenge addressed by hybrid integration is the need for secure, reliable communication channels that traverse disparate network topologies and security domains. On-premises systems, often entrenched within protected network perimeters, must exchange information with cloud services hosted in public or private clouds. This exchange requires robust tunneling mechanisms that enforce confidentiality, integrity, and authentication without significantly compromising performance or scalability.

Secure tunneling technologies employed in hybrid architectures typically leverage Virtual Private Networks (VPNs) or dedicated connections such as AWS Direct Connect and Azure ExpressRoute. VPNs establish encrypted tunnels over public networks, authenticating endpoints via protocols such as IPsec or TLS to mitigate the risks of data interception or man-in-the-middle attacks. Dedicated connections offer enhanced throughput and reduced latency by provisioned physical links or logically isolated channels, albeit at increased operational expense.

Authentication and authorization mechanisms are integral to secure tunneling. Mutual Transport Layer Security (mTLS) facilitates bidirectional trust, verifying both client and server identities through digital certificates. Token-based systems, often implemented with OAuth 2.0 or Security Assertion Markup Language (SAML), enable granular access control reflective of corporate identity management policies. These controls ensure that only authorized workloads can initiate communication, while traffic segmentation techniques, including micro-segmentation and software-defined networking (SDN), curtail lateral movement of

96

threats once established.

Ensuring data consistency between on-premises and cloud systems involves overcoming heterogeneity in data models, latency variation, and transaction management limitations. Hybrid synchronization architectures are designed to reconcile eventual consistency requirements with traditional ACID (Atomicity, Consistency, Isolation, Durability) guarantees in relational databases or distributed storage systems.

One prevalent solution utilizes messaging middleware implementing reliable delivery semantics. Message brokers such as Apache Kafka, RabbitMQ, or cloud-native services like Amazon MQ and Azure Service Bus support exactly-once or at-least-once delivery guarantees. These intermediaries decouple producers and consumers, buffering data changes and orchestrating ordered message flows to preserve transactional integrity. Message expiration, dead-letter queues, and acknowledgement protocols further improve handling of transient failures and idempotency at scale.

Event-driven architectures in hybrid models promote near-real-time data synchronization. Events propagated from on-premises systems trigger actions in cloud services and vice versa. Such choreography provides low-latency responsiveness essential for operational continuity and accurate state replication. Techniques like Change Data Capture (CDC) extract granular data modifications from source systems and stream them reliably to target environments. CDC implementations leverage database logs or triggers to minimize performance impact and avoid full data scans.

Data pipeline orchestration and monitoring are crucial adjuncts to integration reliability. Workflow schedulers ensure execution dependency resolution and recovery from interruptions. Observability enhancements, including distributed tracing and centralized logging, facilitate anomaly detection and root cause analysis spanning complex hybrid landscapes.

Latency fundamentally constrains hybrid integration architectures. Network delays, bandwidth limitations, and protocol overheads generate variable round-trip times that affect transactional consistency and user experience. Architectural remedies include edge computing, which positions compute resources closer to data sources, and intelligent caching mechanisms that reduce repetitive data transfers. Preprocessing and filtering at the edge diminish bandwidth demands, while cache-coherence protocols maintain valid, coherent views despite asynchronous updates.

The architecture design phase must carefully consider fault tolerance. Network partitions are an inherent risk in hybrid deployments, requiring strategies such as circuit breakers and retry policies to prevent cascading failures. Multizone redundancy and failover configurations ensure continuity when one communication path becomes impaired. Idempotent operations and compensation transactions address partial failure scenarios by enabling rollback or corrective updates.

From a development perspective, API management plays a pivotal role in hybrid integration. Unified gateways abstract varying backend systems, exposing consistent interfaces for cloud and on-premises resources. API gateways offer built-in security policies, rate limiting, transformation, and analytics, simplifying the integration complexity. Service meshes further extend these capabilities by managing inter-service communication within hybrid Kubernetes clusters or service-oriented architectures, providing fine-grained control over routing, observability, and security policies.

Data privacy and regulatory compliance overlays critically influence hybrid integration design choices. Sensitive data transmitted across borders must adhere to jurisdictional constraints, necessitating selective encryption and anonymization methods. Hybrid models often accommodate localized data handling within on-premises segments while leveraging cloud elasticity for less sensitive workloads. Role-based access controls and audit trails implemented uniformly across hybrid boundaries ensure governance policies are enforced consistently.

Illustrative hybrid integration architectures usually coalesce around three principal topologies:

- **Cloud Bursting Model:** On-premises systems handle baseline workloads, offloading spikes to cloud resources dynamically, necessitating robust synchronizing middleware and secure tunneling to maintain application state and session persistence.

- **Data Replication Model:** Continuous replication of data sets from on-premises databases to cloud data lakes or warehouses enables analytic workloads while preserving transactional integrity in operational systems.

- **Distributed Microservices Model:** Microservices deployed across on-premises and cloud environments communicate via service mesh or API gateways, facilitating modular scalability and resilience, with emphasis on consistent configuration management and observability.

The choice among these topologies depends on use case priorities related to latency tolerance, data gravity, cost considerations, and organizational compliance mandates.

```
-- Enable CDC on the source database table
EXEC sys.sp_cdc_enable_table
    @source_schema = N'dbo',
    @source_name   = N'Orders',
    @role_name     = NULL;

-- Capture insert changes for replication
SELECT *
FROM cdc.fn_cdc_get_all_changes_dbo_Orders(
    @from_lsn, @to_lsn, 'all')
WHERE __$operation = 2; -- 2 indicates Insert operations
```

_$start_lsn	OrderID	CustomerID	OrderDate	_$operation
0x0000001A000110345	CUST789	2024-05-21	2
0x0000001A000210346	CUST123	2024-05-21	2

This CDC mechanism illustrates extraction of recent inserts from an on-premises transactional system. The captured changes are streamed asynchronously via message brokers into cloud databases or data lake environments, preserving temporal order and enabling downstream analytics or reporting.

The operational complexity of hybrid integration demands automation and orchestration practices. Infrastructure as Code (IaC) frameworks provision network tunnels, firewall rules, and cloud resources reproducibly. Continuous integration/continuous delivery (CI/CD) pipelines enable frequent, safe deployment of integration components while minimizing disruption.

In sum, hybrid integration models embody a multifaceted confluence of secure communications, data consistency strategies, and resilient fault-handling architectures. They reconcile on-premises stability and cloud agility by applying principled engineering approaches grounded in secure tunneling, messaging reliability, and distributed system best practices. Mastery of these elements enables organizations to construct robust, scalable hybrid infrastructures aligned with evolving business and technological imperatives.

4.2. Multicloud Integration Topologies

Modern enterprise architectures increasingly depend on multicloud environments that combine multiple public cloud providers and Software as a Service (SaaS) ecosystems. This diversification addresses concerns such as vendor lock-in, regional compliance, performance optimization, and resilience. However, it simultaneously introduces significant complexity to integration architectures, demanding careful orchestration of communication, data flow, and governance across disparate platforms. Robust multicloud integration topologies are thus essential to enable seamless interoperability, ensure operational continuity, and enforce consistent policies at scale.

Architectural Patterns for Multicloud Integration

Integration patterns in multicloud environments must accommodate heterogeneity in platforms, protocols, and service models. Three canonical topologies often emerge: hub-and-spoke, mesh, and hybrid, each with distinctive characteristics concerning coupling, scalability, and fault tolerance.

Hub-and-Spoke Architecture employs a central integration hub that mediates interactions between multiple cloud environments and SaaS applications. In this pattern, all communication transits through a centralized broker-often implemented via an API gateway or integration platform such as MuleSoft's Anypoint Platform. This architecture simplifies governance and policy enforcement by concentrating integration logic, transformation, and security control within the hub. However, it introduces a single point of failure and may create latency bottlenecks if not architected with sufficient resiliency and elasticity.

Mesh Architecture features direct, peer-to-peer connections between cloud-based applications and services. Integration logic is decentralized, with each node responsible for managing its own APIs, transformation, and security policies. While this approach optimizes latency and can enhance resilience through redundancy, it increases operational complexity, requiring distributed governance and sophisticated topology management. Mesh architectures are best suited for ecosystems demanding real-time communication and low coupling.

Hybrid Architecture merges hub-and-spoke and mesh characteristics, leveraging centralized control for critical integration flows and decentralized direct communications for latency-sensitive or high-throughput services. This approach balances governance and scalability, enabling differentiation based on use-case priorities and compliance regimes within the multicloud landscape.

Role of MuleSoft in Cross-Cloud Orchestration

MuleSoft offers a comprehensive integration platform that natively supports multicloud orchestration, enabling enterprises to harmonize integrations across cloud vendors and SaaS ecosystems with agility and control. The Anypoint Platform is designed to abstract the underlying heterogeneity of cloud providers, exposing uniform APIs and integration services that implement consistent connectivity, transformation, and security policies.

Key MuleSoft capabilities supporting multicloud topologies include:

- **API-Led Connectivity**: Promotes layered API abstractions separating experience, process, and system layers, allowing integration logic to be modular, reusable, and portable across clouds. This decoupling facilitates flexible deployment models-whether centralized in a dedicated cloud, distributed across multiple clouds, or embedded within SaaS connectors.

- **Runtime Fabric and Hybrid Deployment**: Provides a container-based infrastructure to deploy Mule runtimes consistently across on-premises data centers, public clouds (AWS, Azure, GCP), and private cloud environments. This uniform runtime enables seamless scaling and failover while preserving operational consistency and observability.

- **Unified Policy Enforcement**: Implements centralized governance using API Manager, allowing policies such as security (OAuth, JWT), rate limiting, throttling, and SLA enforcement to be uniformly applied regardless of underlying cloud or SaaS endpoint.

- **Event-Driven Architecture Support**: Facilitates asynchronous communication patterns and event streaming (via MuleSoft's Anypoint MQ or integrations with Kafka and Enterprise Service Buses), enabling decoupled and resilient interactions between multicloud services.

Portability and Failover Considerations

Portability of integration artifacts-APIs, connectors, and runtime configurations-is a fundamental requirement for multicloud strategies to avoid cloud lock-in and enable workload mobility driven by cost, compliance, or performance factors.

MuleSoft enforces artifact portability by adhering to container standards and declarative deployment descriptors. Integration projects are packaged as deployable archives that run identically on diverse runtime fabrics. This capability allows seamless migration and load redistribution among clouds.

Failover strategies in multicloud integration leverage geographical and service-level redundancy. MuleSoft architectures typically employ active-active or active-passive configurations. Active-active setups distribute load across multiple cloud regions or providers, using API gateways with global load balancing and health monitoring. In active-passive configurations, standby runtimes are maintained to assume control upon failure detection. MuleSoft's API gateway health checks and monitoring frameworks facilitate rapid failover, minimizing downtime.

Transactional integrity and state management during failover require careful design, often necessitating idempotency, compensation logic, and event sourcing. MuleSoft's support for robust error handling, retry policies, and durable queues assists in maintaining message reliability across cloud boundaries.

Policy Enforcement at Scale

A consistent and scalable policy enforcement mechanism is critical to secure multicloud integrations, ensure compliance, and maintain service quality. MuleSoft's API Manager provides a centralized governance plane that decouples policy definition from enforcement points.

Policies are defined declaratively and automatically propagated to runtime nodes irrespective of physical deployment topology. This approach prevents drift and ensures uniform application of:

- **Security Policies**: Authentication, authorization, encryption standards, and threat protection via built-in connectors and external identity providers.

- **Traffic Control**: Rate limiting, throttling, spike arrest, and quota management to safeguard backend services from overload.

- **Compliance Policies**: Data masking, logging, and auditing policies adapted to jurisdictional requirements inherent in multicloud deployments.

At scale, distributed enforcement is orchestrated with lightweight sidecars or embedded proxies that intercept API calls at ingress points. MuleSoft supports this model via Runtime Manager and the deployment of policy enforcement components close to the runtime, improving performance and reducing cloud egress costs.

Integration Patterns Illustrating Multicloud Topologies

To contextualize these concepts, consider the following patterns enabled by MuleSoft for multicloud integration:

- **Cloud-to-Cloud Mesh with Centralized Control**: Multiple cloud environments expose APIs managed centrally by MuleSoft API Manager. While APIs invoke services directly within each cloud, policy enforcement and monitoring happen via the centralized platform. This pattern supports distributed service meshes yet retains governance.

- **Hybrid Hub and Spoke with SaaS Connectors**: A centralized MuleSoft runtime hub integrates on-premises systems, several cloud platforms, and SaaS applications like Salesforce or Workday. The hub processes transformations, error handling, and enrichment, then routes requests to systems of origin or external clouds as required.

- **Data Streaming Across Clouds**: MuleSoft integrates event streams across clouds using Anypoint MQ or connectors to Apache Kafka. Microservices deployed in different clouds consume and emit events, providing decoupled communication and eventual consistency while enabling fault-tolerant asynchronous workflows.

Challenges and Best Practices

Despite advances, multicloud integration introduces challenges in latency variability, data sovereignty, evolving APIs, and complexity of monitoring distributed transactions. Effective design must carefully select integration topology to balance these factors.

Best practices include:

- **Design for Idempotency and Retry**: Ensures reliable processing despite network failures or partial outages.

- **Employ API Versioning and Contract Management**: Reduces disruption from SaaS and cloud API changes.

- **Leverage Observability and Distributed Tracing**: Essential for troubleshooting across multicloud paths.

- **Automate Configuration and Deployment**: Infrastructure as code eases portability and consistency.

- **Implement Security by Design**: Incorporate policy enforcement and zero-trust principles spanning all cloud boundaries.

Taken together, these considerations allow enterprises to exploit the benefits of multicloud architectures, orchestrate integrations at scale, and respond flexibly to evolving technology landscapes while safeguarding operational continuity and governance integrity.

4.3. Anypoint VPC and Private Connectivity

Deploying Mule applications within securely segmented environments relies fundamentally on robust virtual network architectures that isolate and protect sensitive workloads. Anypoint Virtual Private Cloud (VPC) provides a dedicated, logically isolated network within the cloud infrastructure, where Mule applications can operate with controlled access to resources and external networks. The architecture of Anypoint VPC enables enterprises to implement private network connectivity, direct network integration, and enforce secure routing policies essential for compliance, data sovereignty, and operational security.

The Anypoint VPC is constructed as a private overlay network hosting Mule runtime instances, connectors, and other integration components. It offers customers exclusive IP address space and configurable subnet boundaries facilitating network segmentation. This isolated environment supports deployment of Mule applications in a manner analogous to traditional on-premises private networks but leverages cloud scalability and resilience.

Within the Anypoint VPC, each Mule runtime engine can be assigned private IPs from defined CIDR (Classless Inter-Domain Routing) blocks, permitting internal service-to-service communication that is entirely shielded from public internet exposure. Access control lists (ACLs) and security groups provide granular access policies, governing ingress and egress traffic. This tightly controlled environment drastically diminishes attack surfaces and enables compliance with regulatory mandates on data isolation.

Connecting an Anypoint VPC with enterprise networks requires careful consideration of network topologies and security requirements. Two principal private connectivity options dominate:

- **VPN Connectivity:** Virtual Private Network (VPN) tunnels establish encrypted channels traversing public internet infrastructure, linking on-premises data centers or corporate networks with the Anypoint VPC. Site-to-site VPN is a common configuration enabling broad network-to-network connectivity. VPNs support various tunneling protocols such as IPSec and can incorporate mutual authentication via certificates or pre-shared keys.

- **Direct Connect:** Direct Connect offers a dedicated, private network link between the enterprise environment and the Anypoint VPC. By bypassing general internet routes, it minimizes latency and enhances bandwidth guarantees. Direct Connect often involves physical fiber circuits or Ethernet connections provisioned between the enterprise data center and cloud provider's point of presence (PoP). These links integrate with the cloud environment using virtual interfaces and VLAN tagging to maintain traffic separation.

Each method presents trade-offs balancing security, performance, reliability, and cost. VPN delivers lower upfront expense and flexibility but introduces variable latency and dependency on public infrastructure. In contrast, Direct Connect ensures a predictable network experience critical for latency-sensitive integration workloads, although it demands formal provisioning processes and associated capital expenditure.

Implementing VPN connectivity with Anypoint VPC entails designing topologies that align with operational goals. Single-site VPN is the simplest, bridging one enterprise location to the VPC. More complex multi-site VPNs employ hub-and-spoke or full mesh configurations to accommodate distributed enterprises or hybrid cloud models.

Key design considerations include:

- **Redundancy:** Multiple VPN tunnels with automated failover policies reduce risk of single points of failure. Leveraging dynamic routing protocols such as Border Gateway Protocol (BGP) with multipath capabilities enhances resiliency.

- **Encryption Strength and Authentication:** Utilizing robust cryptographic algorithms such as AES with 256-bit keys and strong authentication mechanisms ensures confidentiality and integrity of data in transit. Employing certificate-based mutual authentication reduces risks of unauthorized access.

- **Segmentation and Access Control:** VPN configurations should integrate with network ACLs and firewall rules on both ends to strictly limit traffic flows to authorized resources. Layered security controls prevent lateral movement in case of compromise.

Careful monitoring of VPN tunnel health and traffic patterns is essential for early detection of performance degradation or potential threats.

Direct Connect interfaces establish point-to-point connections, which entail several network engineering practices to maximize security and performance:

- **Virtual Interfaces and VLAN Tagging:** Depending on use case, multiple virtual interfaces (private, public, transit) can be configured on the physical connection, each with independent VLAN IDs. This enables segregation of management traffic, application data, and service endpoints.

- **BGP Peering and Route Management:** Dynamic routing via BGP permits automatic path recalculations and efficient utilization of multiple links. Route filtering policies define which prefixes are advertised and accepted, enforcing policy-based traffic steering.

- **Latency and Bandwidth Optimization:** Direct Connect connections are engineered for low latency and high throughput. This is vital for Mule applications demanding near real-time processing and synchronous service orchestration.

- **Physical Security and Compliance:** The physical infrastructure of Direct Connect is operated within secure data center facilities, often compliant with standards such as SOC 2, ISO 27001, or PCI DSS. Leveraging such controls forms part of an enterprise's overall security posture.

Combining Anypoint VPC with private connectivity mechanisms requires holistic architectural strategies:

Network Segmentation and Micro-Segmentation: Beyond defining VPC boundaries, segmentation inside the VPC isolates integration workloads based on sensitivity and function. Micro-segmentation, operationalized through software-defined networking (SDN) and firewall policies, restricts east-west traffic, controlling application-level communication. This limits blast radius in case of compromise.

Zero Trust Principles: Adopting a zero trust security model in private connectivity frameworks mandates continuous verification of every access request regardless of network origin. Mutual Transport Layer Security (mTLS) and identity-aware proxies enforce strict trust boundaries between Mule applications, APIs, and backend services.

Latency-Aware Deployment Topologies: For globally distributed enterprises, deploying Anypoint VPCs in geographically proximal cloud regions interconnected via private connectivity reduces round-trip times. Regional Direct Connect links and localized VPN gateways help ensure workload proximity aligns with user and system distribution.

High Availability and Disaster Recovery: Architectures employ multiple VPCs and direct connectivity links with automated failover and active-active configurations. Leveraging cloud-native health checks and routing adjustments reduce downtime risks without sacrificing latency targets.

Consider an enterprise integrating on-premises ERP systems with cloud-hosted Mule applications handling critical business processes. Deploying the Mule runtime in an Anypoint VPC allows utilization of private IP addressing, immune from public internet exposure. A Direct Connect link provides guaranteed 10 Gbps bandwidth between the data center and VPC with VLAN-separated interfaces for management and application traffic.

BGP peering manages route propagation between on-premises routers and the VPC gateway, maintaining dynamic failover paths. Additionally, a site-to-site VPN acts as a backup connectivity channel to enhance availability. Security groups restrict inbound traffic to Mule runtime instances, allowing only approved on-premises IP ranges.

This configuration results in low-latency, high-throughput communication paths essential for processing high volumes of integration transactions with stringent SLAs, all while maintaining compliance with internal security policies and regulatory frameworks.

- **Consistent Network Monitoring:** Utilize tools capturing flow logs, VPN tunnel state, and Direct Connect interface metrics to promptly identify anomalies or degradation.

- **Regular Security Auditing:** Conduct periodic reviews of ACLs, encryption protocols, and authentication mechanisms to accommodate evolving threat landscapes.

• **Automation of Provisioning and Configuration:**
Infrastructure-as-Code (IaC) pipelines reduce human error
in setting up Anypoint VPCs, VPNs, and Direct Connect
connections, fostering repeatability and version control.

• **Documentation and Change Management:** Maintain
comprehensive network diagrams and change logs ensuring
that connectivity topologies remain aligned with operational
requirements and security policies.

4.4. Secure Edge and Gateway Patterns

API gateways serve as critical control points at organizational
perimeters and between distinct trust zones, enabling secure mediation of traffic while enforcing policies that protect sensitive integrations. Their deployment patterns are pivotal in establishing
a robust security posture, particularly where ingress and egress
controls meet hybrid perimeter enforcement requirements. The
complexity of modern distributed architectures, comprising cloud-
native components, on-premises systems, and third-party integrations, mandates nuanced strategies for gateway placement, policy
enforcement, and traffic management.

At organizational perimeters, API gateways function as the primary ingress point, acting as reverse proxies that authenticate,
authorize, and throttle inbound requests before they reach internal services. Deploying gateways at this boundary layer allows
organizations to impose strict access controls and protocol validation, minimizing attack surfaces exposed to external entities. Commonly, these gateways integrate with identity providers supporting OAuth 2.0, OpenID Connect, or mutual TLS, thereby elevating
the level of trust assigned to caller credentials. API gateways here
also facilitate payload inspection and transformation, enabling the

application of data loss prevention (DLP) and encryption policies at the network edge.

Between trust zones-such as internal corporate networks, partner ecosystems, and cloud-based environments-API gateways orchestrate egress traffic controls and interzone policy enforcement. Unlike the primary perimeter gateway, these deployment patterns emphasize lateral protection and segmentation to prevent unauthorized lateral movement and data exfiltration. Deploying gateways at interzone boundaries enables the enforcement of context-aware policies that consider source and destination attributes alongside behavioral analytics. Techniques such as zero trust network access (ZTNA) and microsegmentation become integral, with gateways mediating communications only between authenticated and authorized entities. This approach reduces implicit trust and mitigates risks associated with compromised internal assets.

Secure ingress control patterns leverage the principle of defense-in-depth by incorporating multi-factor authentication, rate limiting, and IP reputation checks at the earliest point of contact. Integration patterns utilize binding of identity tokens to contextual metadata, such as device posture or geographic location, to dynamically adjust access permissions. Implementing Web Application Firewall (WAF) capabilities within API gateways adds an additional layer of protection by filtering common attack vectors such as injection attacks, cross-site scripting (XSS), and distributed denial-of-service (DDoS) attempts. Edge gateways frequently enforce TLS termination and mutual TLS to ensure secure channel establishment, while concealing internal infrastructure details from external clients.

Egress control patterns focus on preventing unintended data leakage and enforcing compliance when internal services interact with external endpoints or cross organizational boundaries. By positioning gateways as controlled outbound proxies, organizations can implement stringent outbound request validation, protocol normalization, and anomaly detection. Gateways enforce usage policies by inspecting request payloads, verifying subscription entitlements, and monitoring data exfiltration attempts. These controls are particularly relevant where APIs expose sensitive data or regulate access to critical functionality. Logging and audit capabilities embedded in the gateway enable forensic analysis and real-time alerting, thus enhancing operational awareness.

Hybrid perimeter enforcement emerges from the convergence of on-premises and cloud environments, where traditional network boundaries become blurred. In these cases, API gateways must operate seamlessly across heterogeneous infrastructures, maintaining unified policy enforcement while respecting the nuances and constraints of each deployment locale. Techniques such as distributed gateway architectures and service mesh integration facilitate consistent security postures regardless of physical or virtual boundaries. Gateways synchronize policies and telemetry data to central control planes, enabling consolidated governance and rapid incident response. Edge gateways may be complemented by sidecar proxies within service meshes to provide granular enforcement at the service level, forming a layered defense strategy.

Architectural considerations driving secure gateway deployment include high availability, scalability, and low latency. Redundancy and failover configurations ensure continuous availability of ingress and egress controls, which is especially critical when gateways enforce blocking policies. Horizontal scaling supports traffic bursts without compromising security inspection fidelity. Additionally, gateways must support encrypted traffic inspection without degrading performance, often achieved through hardware acceleration or optimized cryptographic libraries.

Design patterns emphasize policy abstraction and reuse, separating authentication, authorization, transformation, and logging concerns into discrete, composable modules within the gateway. This modularity enables rapid adaptation to evolving threats and regulatory requirements. Configurable policy engines allow for dynamic enforcement based on risk scoring, threat intelligence integration, and machine learning–driven anomaly detection. Furthermore, API gateways implement fine-grained rate-limiting and quota policies tailored per consumer identity, enhancing resilience against abuse and service degradation.

Integration with centralized identity and access management (IAM) systems fosters trust consistency across multiple trust zones, facilitating federated authentication and delegated authorization. Gateways leverage token introspection endpoints to validate and enrich user credentials dynamically. The delegation of authorization to external policy decision points (PDP), under the paradigm of Policy-Based Access Control (PBAC), decouples security logic from gateway infrastructure, improving maintainability and scalability.

Auditability and compliance remain paramount in secure gateway deployments. Capturing detailed, tamper-resistant logs of all authentication attempts, request metadata, and policy enforcement decisions enables compliance with regulatory frameworks such as GDPR, HIPAA, and PCI DSS. Gateways support integration with Security Information and Event Management (SIEM) platforms to correlate security events and automate response workflows.

Secure edge and gateway patterns encompass a blend of strategic placement, rigorous ingress and egress controls, and hybrid perimeter enforcement techniques to protect organizational assets across diverse network boundaries. Deploying API gateways with advanced authentication, authorization, and inspection capabilities under a modular and scalable architecture ensures robust protection for sensitive integrations while maintaining operational agility and compliance.

4.5. Disaster Recovery and High Availability

Architecting integration platforms with resilience at their core involves a comprehensive approach to disaster recovery (DR) and high availability (HA) to maintain uninterrupted service delivery and business continuity. Integration platforms often serve as critical middleware, orchestrating data flows and transactions across diverse systems. Consequently, any downtime or data loss can have cascading effects, impacting operational efficacy and organizational competitiveness. This section explores industry-best practices for embedding disaster recovery strategies, automated failover mechanisms, geo-redundancy configurations, and high availability deployment models tailored to integration platforms.

Disaster recovery planning for integration platforms must accommodate the unique dependencies, stateful data exchanges, and complex transaction management inherent to these systems. A mature DR strategy focuses on minimizing Recovery Time Objectives (RTO) and Recovery Point Objectives (RPO), thereby reducing downtime and data loss.

The initial step involves clearly identifying critical components and workloads, such as message brokers, data transformation engines, configuration repositories, and persistent queues. These must be replicated or restored rapidly under failure scenarios. Common disaster recovery methods include:

- **Cold Standby:** The backup environment is offline until a disaster occurs. While cost-effective, it involves longer recovery times unsuitable for stringent RTO demands.

- **Warm Standby:** The DR site runs a partial system copy, ready to assume load with moderate configuration, balancing cost and recovery speed.

- **Hot Standby (Active-Passive):** The DR environment continuously replicates data and configurations, enabling

115

near-instantaneous failover at elevated operational costs.

- **Active-Active Multi-Site:** Both production and DR sites actively process workloads in a synchronized manner, offering seamless failover and load distribution but requiring sophisticated consistency mechanisms.

Central to these strategies is continuous backup and replication of integration artifacts (e.g., process definitions, routing rules) alongside runtime state (e.g., in-flight messages, transactional states). Employing transactionally consistent replication technologies such as snapshot isolation or write-ahead logging ensures synchronous state synchronization.

Effective DR plans also incorporate comprehensive runbooks detailing failover procedures, notification chains, and validation tests. Regularly scheduled disaster recovery drills are critical to verify assumptions and train teams.

Automated failover is essential to reduce manual intervention and decrease system downtime when failures occur. Integration platforms must incorporate mechanisms for prompt detection and transparent recovery from faults in hardware, network, or software components.

Health monitoring is realized through aggressive heartbeat protocols, latency measurements, and error rate thresholds. When these metrics exceed predetermined limits, automated orchestrators trigger failover workflows. Typical components facilitating automated failover include:

- **Load Balancers and Proxy Servers:** Act as intermediaries that redirect requests seamlessly from failed nodes to healthy ones.

- **Cluster Management Tools:** Systems like Kubernetes, Apache Zookeeper, or proprietary clustering technologies manage node status and orchestrate failover.

116

- **State Synchronization Protocols:** Mechanisms such as distributed consensus algorithms (e.g., Paxos, Raft) ensure consistent state transitions between active and passive nodes.

Failover procedures must consider session persistence, transactional integrity, and message ordering. For example, in message-oriented middleware, committed messages cannot be lost or replayed erroneously post-failover. Implementing idempotency checks and exactly-once processing semantics helps mitigate duplication or data corruption.

Integration platforms often combine health-check callbacks with orchestration scripts to trigger stateful failover operations, enabling minimal human exposure and rapid recovery.

Geo-redundancy involves deploying integration platform instances across geographically distributed data centers or cloud regions to mitigate localized failure risks such as natural disasters, power outages, or network partitioning. This architectural choice enhances disaster resilience and supports regulatory compliance where data sovereignty is mandated.

Key considerations in geo-redundant architectures include:

- **Latency and Bandwidth Constraints:** Real-time synchronization of transactional state across regions demands high-throughput, low-latency links to prevent bottlenecks.

- **Consistency Models:** Depending on business requirements, the platform may adopt strong consistency, eventual consistency, or a hybrid approach to balance availability and correctness under the CAP theorem.

- **Data Replication Topology:** Active-active and active-passive topologies impact both performance and complexity. Active-active geodistributed clusters require conflict resolution mechanisms and consistent hashing for workload distribution.

- **Failover Granularity:** Application-level failover decisions may vary from component-specific rerouting to entire region switchovers, influenced by SLA targets and cost.

To maintain reliable geo-redundant synchronization, data replication tools frequently use Change Data Capture (CDC) techniques or log-based incremental replication to efficiently transmit only delta changes. Furthermore, integrating global traffic managers and DNS-based routing policies supports dynamic user redirection based on region health states.

Careful consideration must be given to data protection laws, backup data encryption in transit and at rest, and audit trails for cross-region data transfers.

High availability in integration platforms is achieved through architectural models that eliminate single points of failure and ensure continuous operational capacity. Typical HA deployment models include:

- **Clustered Deployments:** Multiple nodes operate in concert, sharing load and replicating critical state. Failures trigger automatic redistribution without service interruption.

- **Microservices and Containerization:** Modularization into independently deployable services orchestrated by container platforms enhances fault isolation and rapid scaling.

- **Stateless Frontends with Stateful Backends:** Most integration logic is decentralized, allowing rapid replacement of frontend services, while durable state is maintained in replicated backends such as databases or distributed message queues.

State persistence is a core design criterion. Durable queues, transactional databases, and distributed caches with replication protocols (e.g., Multi-Paxos, chain replication) underpin robust state management. Graceful shutdown and restart handling in components preserve in-flight data and transactional boundaries.

Additionally, employing circuit breakers, bulkheads, and health check APIs within platform components enhances fault tolerance by isolating failures and preventing cascading effects throughout the system.

Supplementing architectural designs, operational best practices foster resilience:

- **Comprehensive Monitoring and Alerting:** Integration platforms require end-to-end observability spanning infrastructure metrics, application logs, and business transaction traces.

- **Capacity Planning and Load Testing:** Systematic stress testing identifies bottlenecks and validates failover thresholds.

- **Blue-Green and Canary Deployments:** Controlled release automation reduces upgrade risks and supports rapid rollback.

- **Data Integrity Verification:** Periodic audits and checksums confirm the fidelity of replicated data.

- **Automated Backups and Retention Policies:** Routine backups and defined retention strategies safeguard against data corruption and support regulatory compliance.

Integration platforms deployed on Kubernetes clusters can leverage native primitives for HA and failover. Consider a microservice responsible for message transformation, deployed as a Deployment object with multiple replicas and backed by persistent volume claims for stateful storage. Kubernetes liveness and readiness probes enable health monitoring; if a pod fails, Kubernetes automatically replaces it.

An example Kubernetes Deployment manifest for a stateful component is:

```
apiVersion: apps/v1
kind: Deployment
metadata:
  name: transformer-service
spec:
  replicas: 3
  selector:
    matchLabels:
      app: transformer
  template:
    metadata:
      labels:
        app: transformer
    spec:
      containers:
      - name: transformer
        image: integration/transformer:latest
        ports:
        - containerPort: 8080
        readinessProbe:
          httpGet:
            path: /health
            port: 8080
          initialDelaySeconds: 10
          periodSeconds: 5
        livenessProbe:
          httpGet:
            path: /health
            port: 8080
          initialDelaySeconds: 15
          periodSeconds: 20
        volumeMounts:
        - name: state-storage
          mountPath: /var/lib/state
      volumes:
      - name: state-storage
        persistentVolumeClaim:
          claimName: transformer-pvc
```

Combined with StatefulSets and persistent volumes replicated across zones, this setup enables automatic failover, persistence, and resilience.

By integrating comprehensive disaster recovery methods, automated failover capabilities, geo-redundant deployments, and proven high availability patterns, integration platforms achieve the reliability required for mission-critical operations. These architectural and operational strategies collectively reduce downtime, guard against data loss, and uphold service-level agreements in complex, distributed environments.

4.6. Platform Federation and Safe Decentralization

Scaling integration platforms across large enterprises necessitates addressing complexities in federated runtime clusters, distributed teams, and decentralized asset governance. The challenge lies in fostering autonomy among diverse organizational units while maintaining centralized oversight to ensure security, compliance, and operational consistency. Platform federation emerges as a strategic approach enabling this balance by distributing execution and management while enforcing uniform governance and standards.

Federated runtime clusters consist of multiple independent clusters operating cohesively. Each cluster manages local integrations and services with autonomy over resource allocation, operational policies, and scaling. Meanwhile, the federation layer provides centralized monitoring, policy enforcement, and lifecycle management.

A key architectural pattern involves a multi-tiered control plane: a global control plane manages federation-wide policies and metadata, while local control planes host cluster-specific orchestration and runtime execution. This separation enables:

- **Decentralized fault tolerance**: Failures or maintenance in one cluster are isolated, preventing cascading outages.

- **Compliance boundaries**: Clusters can adhere to regional data sovereignty or regulatory requirements without sacrificing global visibility.

- **Resource optimization**: Workloads dynamically shift among clusters based on locality, load, or specialized capabilities.

Technologies such as Kubernetes Federation v2 (KubeFed) and service mesh federations exemplify this approach. These frameworks enable synchronization of custom resource definitions (CRDs), deployment rules, and traffic shaping while preserving cluster-specific configurations.

Operationally, federated clusters require a clear definition of autonomous versus shared responsibilities. For instance, clusters manage their node lifecycles and patching, but the federation layer sets baseline security policies, identity federation, and audit logging standards. The employment of consistent service discovery and global configuration stores (e.g., GitOps-based repositories) further enables convergence without imposing rigid uniformity.

Distributed teams present organizational-scale decentralization akin to technical federations. Teams span different geographies, departments, and time zones, each possessing distinct expertise, priorities, and operational tempos. Effective scale demands that team autonomy is enabled alongside governance and alignment to enterprise objectives.

Role-based access control (RBAC) and attribute-based access control (ABAC) models must be federated analogously to runtime clusters, allowing teams to govern assets they own while preventing unauthorized cross-team access. Integration assets such as API specifications, transformation templates, or event schemas should reside in shared or federated registries that provide visibility without edit privileges for non-owners.

Cross-team workflows depend on interfaces and contracts.

Service level objectives (SLOs), versioning schemas, and change control processes need agreement and enforcement through automated pipelines. Continuous integration/continuous deployment (CI/CD) toolchains must incorporate multi-branch or multi-repository setups with validation gates centered on shared standards.

Communication and knowledge capture are essential to prevent siloing. Employing platform-native collaboration tools integrated with asset registries and runtime telemetry encourages transparency. For example, embedding chat ops linked to deployment systems enables teams to monitor distributed integrations' health effectively and respond proactively.

A decentralized model of asset governance mitigates risks of single points of failure or delay in updating and sharing critical integration artifacts. Yet loose governance risks inconsistency, divergence, and security vulnerabilities. Therefore, governance frameworks adopt a "federated yet federative" posture, combining autonomy with policy-driven guardrails.

Asset classification and tagging constitute critical enablers. Each artifact-whether a connector, flow template, or security policy-carries metadata encoding ownership, lifecycle status, sensitivity level, and dependencies. This metadata feeds automated compliance audits and impact analysis.

A layered approval process differentiates change types:

- **Routine changes**: Minor bug fixes or format updates may require only team-level approval and automated testing.

- **Significant changes**: Schema evolution, interface modifications, or security patches mandate federation-level review and integration testing.

- **Critical changes**: Changes affecting sensitive data flows or regulatory compliance escalate to governance boards or security officers.

Blockchain or distributed ledger technologies (DLTs) are emerging as innovative enablers for decentralized asset provenance and auditability. Immutable logs of artifact versions, approvals, deployments, and runtime events enhance trust without relying on a centralized authority.

Centralized registries remain valuable as neutral marketplaces or catalogs of approved assets but are complemented by federated repositories at the team or domain level. Synchronizing these repositories via eventual consistency protocols or conflict-free replicated data types (CRDTs) mitigates latency and conflict issues inherent in distributed governance.

Policy as Code and Automation

Encoding governance policies as code embedded in CI/CD pipelines ensures consistent enforcement without manual bottlenecks. Policies controlling access, deployment targets, and runtime configurations automatically validate pull requests and updates across federated domains. This approach scales governance while preserving agility.

Observability and Auditability

Unified observability platforms aggregate telemetry from federated runtimes, exposing anomalies, compliance violations, or capacity constraints in a centralized dashboard. Correlating logs, metrics, and traces with asset metadata assists root-cause analysis and continuous improvement.

Identity and Access Management

Federated identity and single sign-on (SSO) systems span clusters and teams, supporting fine-grained access control tied to organizational identities and roles. APIs utilize mutual TLS and token-based authentication with scopes reflecting federated boundaries.

Interoperability Standards

Harmonizing data formats, event models, and protocol standards across federated clusters enhances portability. Open standards such as OpenAPI, AsyncAPI, and OAuth underpin consistent integration contracts, reducing friction.

Governance Metrics and Feedback Loops

Continuous measurement of governance effectiveness-through metrics like deployment failure rates, mean time to resolve, and audit discrepancies-guides policy calibration. Cross-team governance councils foster transparent dialogues and rapid resolution of policy conflicts.

Safe decentralization leverages platform federation to distribute complexity, while centralized oversight safeguards standards and risk management. This balance enables enterprises to:

- Rapidly onboard new teams and environments with well-defined guardrails.

- Manage heterogeneous technology stacks and regulatory regimes through federation boundaries.

- Promote innovation through local autonomy without fragmenting enterprise-wide consistency.

- Maintain security posture by embedding policy enforcement into federated control planes.

Implementing these principles requires mature DevOps practices, cross-functional collaboration, and investment in shared tooling. The resulting ecosystem supports dynamic scalability while preserving the integrity and reliability essential for enterprise digital transformation.

Chapter 5

Extending MuleSoft: Custom Modules, Connectors, and Policies

Go beyond out-of-the-box integration and unlock the true flexibility of MuleSoft by learning how to extend the platform with your own custom modules, connectors, and policy logic. This chapter is your guide to building tailored components that meet unique business demands, bridge legacy systems, and embed compliance directly into your integration flows. Discover hands-on techniques, tooling, and architecture patterns that transform MuleSoft from a platform you use to a platform you actively shape.

5.1. Connector Development Using Mule SDK

Building connectors with the Mule SDK involves a systematic approach to design, implementation, performance optimization, packaging, and version management-each stage critical to crafting robust, reusable integration components. Connectors serve as the interface between Mule applications and external systems or services, abstracting communication specifics and providing a consistent API to Mule flows.

Effective connector design begins with a thorough analysis of the target system's API and underlying protocols. The abstraction level should balance simplicity for the Mule user and sufficient flexibility to accommodate advanced scenarios. Key design objectives include:

- **Idempotency:** Operations exposed by the connector should exhibit predictable side effects. Idempotent actions facilitate error recovery and safe retries.

- **Configurability:** Connection parameters, authentication methods, and runtime flags must be parameterizable via annotations, allowing users to customize behavior without altering code.

- **Error Handling:** Define comprehensive error models leveraging Mule SDK's error enums. Map external system error codes to Mule error types for consistent error propagation and handling in flows.

- **Statelessness:** Whenever possible, design connector operations to remain stateless. If state management is necessary, ensure thread-safe implementations.

Applying these principles early prevents costly redesign and enhances the maintainability and interoperability of the connector.

The Mule SDK employs a rich set of annotations and conventions that simplify development while enforcing best practices. Custom connectors are Java-based and take advantage of the Mule SDK's runtime to integrate seamlessly with Mule runtime engine.

- @Connector identifies the main connector class, defining global connection configuration.

- @Operations groups discrete functions, with each operation represented by a method annotated with @Operation.

- Configurable parameters use @Parameter annotations and support validation via annotations like @NotNull, @Optional, and @Token.

- Connection factories derive from the ConnectionProvider interface, responsible for creating, validating, and disconnecting connection instances. Connections are annotated with @Connection.

An example code snippet illustrating a simple connector interface is shown below:

```
@Connector(name = "sampleConnector")
public class SampleConnector {

    @Connection
    private SampleConnection connection;

    @Operation
    public String fetchData(@Parameter String query) {
        // Use connection to interact with external API
        return connection.executeQuery(query);
    }
}

public class SampleConnection {
    public String executeQuery(String query) {
        // Implement protocol-specific communication
        return "result";
    }
}
```

This architecture cleanly separates connection management and operational logic, enabling reuse of connection instances across multiple operations.

Connector performance has a direct impact on overall integration throughput and responsiveness. Key strategies include:

- **Connection Pooling and Reuse:** Connection management should implement pooling or caching mechanisms to avoid costly creation and teardown of connections, especially for protocols with expensive handshakes.

- **Lazy Initialization:** Defer resource-intensive setup until the connection or operation is first invoked to minimize startup time.

- **Efficient Data Serialization:** Use streaming APIs and minimize unnecessary data transformations between Mule and the external system.

- **Timeouts and Retry Policies:** Implement configurable timeouts and retries using Mule SDK facilities and external libraries to improve resilience and avoid blocking threads.

- **Thread Safety:** Ensure that shared resources within connectors are thread-safe to prevent race conditions in concurrent Mule flow executions.

Profiling and benchmarking the connector under realistic load scenarios is essential. Tools such as JMH (Java Microbenchmark Harness) or JProfiler help identify JDK-level overhead. Additionally, enable Mule runtime's built-in monitoring to visualize bottlenecks during flow execution involving the connector.

Packaging Mule SDK connectors involves creating a deployable archive that Mule runtime can load as an extension. The packaging procedure includes:

- **Maven Build Configuration:** Leverage Maven with the Mule SDK plugin to compile, test, and package the connector. The `mule-plugin-maven-plugin` simplifies resource inclusion and manifest generation.

- **Descriptor Generation:** The SDK generates the connector metadata, including operation signatures, parameter types, and connection details, forming the basis of Mule Studio tooling integration.

- **Dependency Management:** Include only necessary dependencies to minimize artifact size and avoid classpath conflicts in Mule runtime.

- **Testing:** Unit tests written with JUnit and integration tests leveraging MUnit validate the connector's correctness in isolation and within Mule flows.

- **Artifact Publication:** Deploy to internal Maven repositories or public registries for consumption by Mule applications.

An example Maven configuration snippet for packaging a Mule SDK connector might look like:

```
<plugin>
    <groupId>org.mule.tools.maven</groupId>
    <artifactId>mule-plugin-maven-plugin</artifactId>
    <version>${mule.sdk.version}</version>
    <executions>
        <execution>
            <goals>
                <goal>package</goal>
            </goals>
        </execution>
    </executions>
</plugin>
```

Proper versioning and adherence to semantic versioning practices facilitate straightforward upgrades and compatibility management.

External systems evolve with new features, deprecated APIs, and
protocol changes. Upgrading connectors maintains compatibility
and leverages new capabilities.

- **Backward Compatibility:** Introduce new operations or
  parameters while preserving existing behavior. Use optional
  parameters rather than breaking changes to existing signatures.

- **Deprecation Strategies:** Mark outdated operations or parameters with deprecation annotations and provide migration pathways.

- **Versioning:** Maintain distinct artifact versions for major, minor, and patch updates. Embed version metadata in
  connector descriptors to assist Mule Studio's compatibility
  checks.

- **Testing Against Target System:** Establish automated regression tests exercising the connector against new versions
  of the target API.

- **Documentation Updates:** Reflect changes in operation
  behaviors, configuration options, and error models.

A disciplined upgrade process prevents disruptions in Mule applications relying on the connector and facilitates seamless adoption
of improvements.

The Mule SDK supports advanced connector features that enhance
capabilities and extendability:

- **Custom Transformers:** Extend data transformation capabilities within the connector for converting between Mule
  messages and domain-specific formats.

- **Schedulers and Listeners:** Implement event-driven connectors that react to external system events by extending
  @Scheduler or @Listener annotations.

- **Streaming Support:** Design operations to support reactive streaming models, improving memory efficiency and latency for large payloads.

- **Parameter Grouping and Complex Types:** Organize parameters hierarchically with nested POJOs and validation annotations to represent complex configurations elegantly.

Harnessing these SDK capabilities yields connectors that not only meet functional requirements but also integrate naturally within Mule domain-specific language and tooling ecosystems.

- Adhere to clean separation between connection lifecycle and operation logic to maximize reusability.

- Annotate all configurable fields and enforce validation constraints to improve runtime safety and user experience.

- Profile connector performance holistically, considering both Mule runtime and external system responsiveness.

- Use semantic versioning and deprecation policies deliberately to minimize upgrade disruptions.

- Leverage SDK extension points for reactive and event-driven patterns to broaden connector applicability.

Following these guidelines in the connector development lifecycle enables the delivery of resilient, maintainable, and performant integration components critical to enterprise-grade Mule applications.

5.2. Custom Policy and API Proxy Development

API-driven architectures require rigorous enforcement of organizational policies to maintain security, compliance, and operational consistency. Custom policies and API proxies serve as critical instruments for embedding business rules, security controls, and compliance checks directly into the API traffic flow. These assets afford granular control over API behavior, enabling a high-assurance environment that adapts dynamically to evolving requirements.

Custom policy development begins with defining precise, organization-specific controls that address unique operational parameters such as data handling regulations, authentication protocols, rate limiting, and detailed logging mandates. Policies typically codify these constraints as executable modules that interface seamlessly with existing API gateways or management platforms. Unlike generic, out-of-the-box policies, custom policies align strictly with an enterprise's legal frameworks, security posture, and operational conventions, thereby reducing compliance risks.

The policy creation lifecycle includes rigorous specification, implementation, and verification stages. Formal specification ensures that the policy encapsulates the intended controls without ambiguity. Expressing policies using domain-specific languages (DSLs) or policy definition frameworks enables clear articulation of constraints. For example, a DSL may explicitly state conditions such as mandatory JWT (JSON Web Token) validation, IP whitelisting, or payload inspection before request forwarding.

Implementation leverages the extensibility features of the chosen API management system, commonly involving scripting languages such as JavaScript, Python, or proprietary policy expression languages. An example policy enforcing an IP whitelist can be conceptualized as follows:

```
function enforceIPWhitelist(clientIP, allowedIPs) {
    if (!allowedIPs.includes(clientIP)) {
        throw new Error("Access denied: IP not authorized");
    }
}
```

Comprehensive testing is paramount and involves unit testing policy modules to validate individual rules and integration testing within API proxies to ensure end-to-end behavior under realistic traffic scenarios. Automated test suites simulate various request conditions, including normal operations, edge cases, and intentional violation attempts to confirm resilience and correct enforcement. Test results should show unequivocal compliance or insightful failure diagnostics for refinement.

Deployment to production environments requires a robust CI/CD pipeline with policy version control, rollback capabilities, and monitoring hooks. Managing different policy versions ensures traceability and regulatory audit readiness, allowing organizations to demonstrate consistent enforcement over time. Deployment strategies often include canary releases or staged rollouts, limiting exposure of unproven policy changes and facilitating gradual validation of real-world impact.

API proxy development complements custom policies by providing programmable intermediaries that augment traffic flows with additional logic. Proxies enrich API interactions by performing functions such as protocol translation, data masking, request enrichment, and adaptive routing. These proxies act as a control plane, intercepting requests and responses while applying embedded policy logic before forwarding traffic to backend services.

The architecture of an API proxy typically incorporates layers that include routing, authentication, rate limiting, transformation, and logging. For example, a proxy can rewrite request URIs dynamically based on deployment environment metadata or inject access tokens required by downstream services. This dynamic adaptation maintains decoupling between client and backend, easing maintenance and versioning.

A representative proxy snippet in a commonly used API management tool's policy language might resemble the following:

```
<Set>
```

```
<Headers>
    <Header name="X-Org-Compliance-Id">{complianceId}</Header
    >
</Headers>
</Set>
```

Such proxies also facilitate integration of external threat intelligence feeds or context-aware access controls, enhancing the API
security posture. For instance, an API proxy might consult a real-
time blacklist service to reject calls emanating from anomalous
IP addresses or geographic locations disallowed by organizational
policy.

Embedding intelligent decision-making within proxies enables advanced scenarios such as selective payload encryption or adaptive
throttling, informed by request parameters or user roles. Machine
learning models can be integrated at this layer to detect anomalous patterns and respond by enforcing stricter scrutiny or denial
of service, thereby proactively mitigating risks.

Performance considerations are integral during proxy development. Policies and proxies must introduce minimal latency to
maintain acceptable user experience and throughput. Efficient algorithms, caching of repetitive policy decisions, and asynchronous
logging mechanisms contribute to operational efficiency. Extensive monitoring and analytics instrumentation provide insights
into policy impact and proxy behavior, supporting ongoing tuning
and capacity planning.

Combining custom policies with sophisticated API proxies yields a
unified framework for end-to-end control of API ecosystems. This
fusion enables enterprises to enforce complex, multifaceted governance mandates while preserving agility and scalability. Organizations achieve a high-assurance posture where APIs not only
implement functional business logic but also embody compliance
and security as intrinsic attributes, delivering resilient, trustworthy service interactions.

Achieving seamless integration of custom policies and proxies within API infrastructures demands meticulous design, disciplined development, exhaustive testing, and vigilant operational oversight. This multifaceted effort ensures that every API transaction adheres rigorously to the defined legal, security, and operational boundaries, thereby safeguarding organizational assets and maintaining stakeholder confidence in a human- and machine-interactive digital environment.

5.3. Reusable Asset Design and Distribution

Reusable assets-including template flows, accelerators, and custom libraries-constitute foundational elements for achieving scalable and consistent software development across distributed teams. Their coherent packaging, versioning, and distribution are imperative to maximize benefits such as reduced redundancy, accelerated delivery, and improved maintainability. This section presents a detailed examination of best practices that guide the creation of repositories and asset catalogues, ensuring their effective management and adoption organization-wide.

Asset Packaging: Modularization and Encapsulation

Designing reusable assets requires a deliberate modularization strategy that encapsulates functionality into discrete, well-defined components. Each asset should represent a single responsibility or capability, minimizing dependencies on external components except those explicitly exposed as interfaces. Encapsulation promotes independent development, testing, and upgrading of assets without unintended side effects.

Structured packaging conventions must be established, typically aligning with the technology stack and ecosystem standards. For example:

- *Template Flows* are packaged as meta-descriptions or declarative configuration files combined with parameter schemas. They must include documentation templates describing their purpose, expected inputs/outputs, and constraints.

- *Accelerators* (prebuilt logic or processing sequences) should be packaged as deployable units or libraries with clear API boundaries and parameter injection capabilities for customization.

- *Custom Libraries* ought to comply with language- or framework-specific packaging norms (e.g., JAR files for Java, NPM packages for JavaScript) with version metadata and dependency manifests.

Static assets, such as icons or style templates, must also be included within the asset package to ensure consistent appearance and behavior across different consuming applications.

Versioning Strategies: Semantic Clarity and Compatibility

Robust versioning is critical to manage asset evolution while minimizing disruption. Semantic Versioning (SemVer) principles serve as industry gold standards: a version number formatted as `MAJOR.MINOR.PATCH` conveys the degree and impact of changes.

- **MAJOR** version increments indicate breaking changes, such as alterations in asset interfaces or removal of existing features.

- **MINOR** version increments introduce backward-compatible new functionality or enhancements.

- **PATCH** version increments address backward-compatible bug fixes.

Adherence to semantic versioning ensures consumers can make informed decisions on upgrading: patch releases can be adopted automatically, minor releases with moderate confidence, and major releases with planned validation. Additionally, asset packages should embed explicit metadata describing compatible runtime or platform versions to prevent integration errors.

Version tags and changelogs are essential components of asset repositories. They provide traceability and facilitate regression analysis when integrating new asset versions. Automated tooling can enforce versioning conventions and verify compatibility during continuous integration processes.

Distribution Channels: Repositories and Catalogues

Centralized repositories provide the backbone for asset distribution, enabling discovery, access control, and lifecycle management.

Repository Architecture: Distributed teams benefit from repositories that function either as artifact registries or source control repositories with automation layers for packaging and release. Best practice is to separate asset source code (for maintainers) from published artifact repositories (for consumers).

Asset Catalogue System: A searchable, indexed catalogue enhances visibility and drives reuse by categorizing assets based on key attributes:

- Functional domain (e.g., data ingestion, transformation, UI components)

- Asset type (template, accelerator, library)

- Technology platform and version compatibility

- Maturity and stability indicators (e.g., beta, stable, deprecated)

- Ownership and support information

Rich metadata enables filtering and ranking, improving discoverability in large-scale environments. Integration with organizational identity and access management ensures proper authorization for sensitive or proprietary assets.

Repository Structure and Governance

A reproducible and standard repository structure is foundational, combining organizational conventions and automation scripts to streamline usage. Typical layout may contain:

```
/<asset-name>
  /src
  /docs
  /tests
  /examples
  /build-scripts
README.md
LICENSE
VERSION
CHANGELOG.md
```

Repository governance enforces quality and consistency through pull request policies, automated validation, and coding standards. Defined roles (maintainers, contributors, reviewers) ensure accountability. Additionally, automated pipelines validate asset integrity, performing tasks such as static code analysis, dependency audit, packaging, and deployment into the distribution repository.

Dependency and Compatibility Management

Reusable assets seldom exist in isolation; managing dependencies is pivotal to avoid "dependency hell." Explicit declaration of dependencies with version ranges within package manifests facilitates conflict detection and resolution during asset consumption.

For complex dependency graphs, lock files or shrinkwrap mechanisms preserve exact dependency trees ensuring deterministic builds. Compatibility matrices outlining supported versions of dependent assets or platforms are also vital documentation elements. Furthermore, backward compatibility policies must be clearly articulated, allowing consumers to gauge risks when upgrading assets.

Automated Publishing and Continuous Delivery of Assets

Integrating asset packaging and distribution into automated CI/CD pipelines significantly improves reliability and efficiency. Typical pipelines perform:

- Code quality and security scans

- Unit and integration tests on assets

- Version increment validation according to repository policies

- Packaging and artifact signing for provenance

- Deployment to asset registries

- Updating asset catalogues and documentation sites

Automation reduces human error and accelerates feedback loops, fostering confidence in asset quality and ease of adoption.

Cross-Team Collaboration and Reuse Policy

To sustain reuse discipline across distributed teams, organizations must define and promote clear policies covering asset lifecycle stages, usage guidelines, and support models. Policies should enforce:

- Cataloging newly created assets before usage

- Mandatory documentation standards

- Deprecation and retirement procedures ensuring smooth transition away from obsolete assets

- Feedback channels to collect consumer experiences and improvement requests

Community-driven governance models, characterized by working groups or asset stewards, facilitate consensus and continuous improvement.

Case Study: Modular Template Flow Repository

Consider an organization implementing a modular template flow repository for data pipelines. Each template flow is packaged as a self-contained directory with:

```
/template-flow-name
  /config
    parameters.yaml
  /scripts
    main.py
  README.md
  VERSION
  CHANGELOG.md
```

The `parameters.yaml` defines configurable inputs, enabling customization without modifying source code. Semantic versioning guides updates: only non-breaking parameter additions increment the minor version. The team uses a private artifact repository (e.g., Artifactory) as the distribution channel, combined with an internal catalogue that presents metadata including supported runtime environment versions and intended use cases. Automated pipelines validate template flows on every commit, generate documentation, and publish validated versions.

Such an arrangement ensures that multiple business units can reuse standardized pipeline flows with confidence in compatibility and supportability, avoiding costly duplication.

Summary of Critical Success Factors

The convergence of rigorous asset design, semantic versioning, structured repositories, and disciplined governance forms the cornerstone for scalable reuse. Clarity in packaging conventions and comprehensive metadata, combined with automation and collaborative policy frameworks, reliably drives reuse and consistency across distributed teams. These practices reduce technical debt and accelerate delivery velocity, ultimately enabling organizations to harness the full potential of shared software assets.

5.4. Integration with Legacy and Proprietary Systems

The integration of contemporary platforms such as MuleSoft with legacy and proprietary systems presents unique challenges rooted in the diverse nature of protocols, data formats, and security models that these older or specialized systems employ. Standard connectors and out-of-the-box components frequently fall short when interfacing with non-standard or undocumented interfaces. Overcoming these limitations necessitates a deep understanding of adapter design, protocol bridging, and the custom extension capabilities provided by the Mule SDK.

Legacy systems often rely on communication protocols predating modern RESTful or event-driven paradigms, including but not limited to IBM MQ, file-based exchanges, FTP/SFTP, FTP-over-SSL, JDBC for direct database access, or even bespoke TCP/IP socket communications. Moreover, proprietary systems might expose APIs through non-standard mechanisms or custom messaging formats such as ASN.1, EDI (Electronic Data Interchange) variants, or encrypted payload structures.

Adapter and Protocol Bridge Construction

Adapters are intermediary software components that translate between distinct communication protocols, data formats, or API semantics, enabling seamless interoperability. Within MuleSoft, the architecture advocates for constructing adapters as reusable and

configurable templates that abstract protocol-level complexities
from integration flows.

Key patterns in adapter development include:

- **Protocol Translation:** Conversion between legacy messaging protocols and MuleSoft's event-based internal message structure. For example, transforming an IBM MQ message (which may be encoded in proprietary formats) into
  a Mule Event with normalized payload and metadata attributes.

- **Message Enrichment and Transformation:** Legacy
  systems may supply incomplete or differently structured
  data. Adapters can enrich, cleanse, or transform messages
  during transit, ensuring conformity with downstream
  systems.

- **Session and Transaction Handling:** Some legacy protocols maintain session state or enforce distributed transactions. Adapters must implement state management or transaction coordination to maintain data integrity across system
  boundaries.

Building a protocol bridge typically involves creating connector
components that:

1. Open and maintain a connection adhering to the legacy protocol (e.g., persistent TCP socket, FTP session).

2. Handle incoming and outgoing messages or commands using the legacy system's protocol specifications.

3. Translate raw or structured data into Mule-compatible message payloads and attributes.

4. Support error handling strategies, including retry, dead letter queues, and alerts for failure scenarios.

Because many legacy systems use asynchronous message exchange, event-driven triggers or scheduled polling Mule flows can be utilized to sustain connectivity. When communication is synchronous but protocol mismatches arise, synchronous request-response pattern implementations combined with timeouts and fallbacks become critical.

An example abstraction for an adapter connecting via a proprietary TCP socket could be conceived as follows:

```
public class TcpLegacyAdapter {

    private Socket socket;
    private BufferedReader reader;
    private BufferedWriter writer;

    public void connect(String host, int port) throws IOException
      {
        socket = new Socket(host, port);
        reader = new BufferedReader(new InputStreamReader(socket.
      getInputStream()));
        writer = new BufferedWriter(new OutputStreamWriter(socket
      .getOutputStream()));
    }

    public String receiveMessage() throws IOException {
        // Blocking call that waits for a message according to
      legacy framing rules
        return reader.readLine();
    }

    public void sendMessage(String message) throws IOException {
        writer.write(message);
        writer.newLine();
        writer.flush();
    }

    public void disconnect() throws IOException {
        reader.close();
        writer.close();
        socket.close();
    }
}
```

This construction can be wrapped as a Mule connector through the Mule SDK, allowing flows to invoke these methods as implicitly managed resource operations.

145

The Mule SDK for Custom and Proprietary Integrations

The Mule SDK empowers integration architects to create custom
connectors, modules, and extensions when existing connectors do
not support specialized or legacy systems. It facilitates the encapsulation of complex protocols, proprietary APIs, and bespoke data
processing logic into reusable and composable Mule artifacts.

The SDK supports:

- **Custom Connectors:** Define operations, configuration parameters, and lifecycle methods. For legacy systems, connectors can implement specialized connection pooling, custom
  authentication schemes, and unique error handling policies.

- **Sources and Listeners:** Mule SDK allows creation of
  event sources capable of triggering Mule flows in reaction
  to events from non-standard systems, such as polling legacy
  message queues or listening to bespoke event buses.

- **Processors and Transformers:** Complex data
  transformation and enrichment logic tailored to legacy
  message schemas and proprietary encoding standards may
  be encapsulated within SDK processors.

The integration process using the Mule SDK involves several key
steps:

1. **Define Connector Configuration:** Capture connectivity
   parameters, credentials, and protocol-specific options, ensuring they adhere to Mule's configuration system and support secure management.

2. **Implement Connection Providers:** Build efficient,
   thread-safe, and pooled connection mechanisms compatible
   with the legacy resource constraints.

146

3. **Model Operations:** Each legacy API call or messaging operation becomes an SDK operation with clearly defined inputs and outputs, leveraging custom POJOs and serialization strategies if necessary.

4. **Error Handling and Retries:** Integrate with Mule error handling paradigms allowing for granular control of exceptions and recovery flows.

An example Mule SDK operation stub to perform a proprietary data fetch might look like:

```
@Extension(name = "ProprietaryConnector")
public class ProprietaryConnector {

    @Connection
    private ProprietaryConnection connection;

    @Operation
    public Payload fetchData(@Optional String queryCriteria) {
        // Implementation-specific logic to query the legacy
    system
        String response = connection.sendRequest(formatQuery(
    queryCriteria));
        return deserializePayload(response);
    }

    private String formatQuery(String criteria) {
        // Format input into system-specific request format
        return "QUERY:" + criteria;
    }

    private Payload deserializePayload(String response) {
        // Convert raw response into Mule payload object
        return new Payload(response.getBytes(StandardCharsets.
    UTF_8));
    }
}
```

Handling Data Format Variability and Security Considerations

Legacy systems often impose strict requirements on message encoding and encryption. Common challenges include:

- **Non-Standard Encoding:** Encodings such as EBCDIC,

147

fixed-width fields, or packed decimal types require specialized parsers and serializers.

- **Encryption and Signing:** Messages may be encrypted or digitally signed using legacy cryptographic standards or hardware tokens. Integrators must incorporate decryption modules and verify signatures within adapters.

- **Character Set Conversions:** Differences in character encodings (e.g., Shift-JIS versus UTF-8) must be handled carefully to prevent data corruption.

Designing a robust integration solution mandates embedding these transformations seamlessly within adapter workflows or custom SDK processors, supported by reusable libraries when possible.

Security protocols must also consider legacy authentication methodologies like Kerberos, NTLM, or custom token exchanges. Mule SDK connectors can incorporate native Java or third-party security libraries to facilitate these mechanisms, while MuleSoft's policies enable layered API security enforcement.

Performance and Reliability Aspects

Integrations bridging MuleSoft and legacy or proprietary systems must address inherent performance and reliability constraints:

- **Throughput Limitations:** Legacy systems may throttle maximum concurrent sessions or impose bandwidth quotas. Connectors should implement rate limiting and backpressure handling.

- **Latency and Timeout Management:** Long-lived transactions or slow response times necessitate configurable timeouts and asynchronous processing patterns.

- **Error Isolation:** Given the fragility of legacy systems, isolating failures through circuit breakers or bulkheads within

Mule flows helps maintain overall system stability.

Logging, tracing, and metrics collection are essential to diagnosing issues within bridging components. MuleSoft's monitoring capabilities augmented with custom logging in adapters or SDK operations provide end-to-end visibility into legacy integration behavior.

Case Study: Integrating a Mainframe CICS System via MuleSoft

Consider the integration of a mainframe system running CICS (Customer Information Control System), which supports transaction-based messaging over proprietary SNA protocols. Direct connectivity is unavailable or insecure over modern networks, so the integration employs an intermediary protocol bridge adapter using IBM MQ as a transport layer.

The approach involves:

- Deploying an MQ adapter built with Mule SDK to poll and send messages.

- Creating adapter logic to translate CICS transaction formats (commonly COBOL copybooks) into JSON or XML for Mule flow processing.

- Utilizing Standard Data Format Transformations (such as DataWeave) downstream of the adapter for business logic integration.

- Employing retry and dead-letter management to address transactional message failures.

This methodology encapsulates legacy complexity within adapters while exposing standardized, modernized APIs for downstream processing and orchestration.

The integration of MuleSoft with legacy and proprietary systems
requires a blend of architectural foresight, meticulous adapter engineering, and advanced use of the Mule SDK. Successful adapters
and protocol bridges are those that not only facilitate bi-directional
communication but also encapsulate legacy idiosyncrasies, enforce
security best practices, and enable maintainable, scalable solutions
within the enterprise integration ecosystem.

5.5. Extending Platform Observability and Metrics

The effective integration of custom telemetry, diagnostics, and observability workflows fundamentally enhances platform visibility
beyond standard monitoring capabilities. Extending observability
requires deliberate design to capture and convey high-fidelity operational data, enabling deeper system insights, facilitating proactive operations, and ensuring rigorous compliance tracking. This
section details critical methods for exposing and exporting custom
metrics, traces, and logs, emphasizing the synergy among these
data types to form a robust observability infrastructure.

Custom metrics represent quantifiable measurements tailored to
the unique behavior and performance characteristics of the platform. These metrics encode system states, resource consumption,
business transactions, or user interactions that are not captured by
default instrumentation.

A proven approach to expose custom metrics is through instrumentation libraries compatible with standard monitoring frameworks,
such as OpenTelemetry or Prometheus client libraries. These libraries allow developers to programmatically define metrics types
including counters, gauges, histograms, and summaries. Counters
accumulate monotonically increasing values useful for events or
request counts. Gauges track instantaneous values such as CPU
utilization or queue lengths. Histograms and summaries enable

detailed latency and error rate distributions.

The following example illustrates exposing a custom histogram metric using Prometheus client libraries in a Go-based microservice:

```
var (
    requestLatency = prometheus.NewHistogramVec(
        prometheus.HistogramOpts{
            Namespace: "platform",
            Subsystem: "api_gateway",
            Name:      "request_latency_seconds",
            Help:      "Request latency distribution for API
    calls",
            Buckets:    prometheus.ExponentialBuckets(0.001, 2,
        15),
        },
        []string{"endpoint", "method", "status_code"},
    )
)

func init() {
    prometheus.MustRegister(requestLatency)
}

func instrumentedHandler(w http.ResponseWriter, r *http.Request)
    {
    timer := prometheus.NewTimer(requestLatency.WithLabelValues(r
    .URL.Path, r.Method, "200"))
    defer timer.ObserveDuration()

    // Business logic here
}
```

Instrumentation must attach relevant contextual labels to enable filtering and aggregation downstream. An effective labels design includes service identifiers, deployment environment, request provenance, and error classifications.

The metrics should be exposed via an HTTP endpoint (e.g., /metrics) providing a raw textual or protocol buffer exposition format consumable by scraping agents. OpenTelemetry also supports exporting metrics through protocols such as OTLP over gRPC, facilitating remote collection and aggregation.

To complement metrics, distributed tracing offers granular insight

into the causal flow of operations spanning multiple services or
components. It elucidates latency sources, bottlenecks, and error
propagation paths essential for debugging and compliance validation.

Extending observability with custom tracing begins with instrumenting critical request paths, including network boundaries, messaging queues, database interactions, and caching layers. Instrumentation libraries enable injection and propagation of trace context according to standards like W3C Trace Context.

A typical trace consists of a tree of spans, each representing a unit
of work with metadata such as operation name, timing, attributes,
and events. Custom attributes can be added to spans to record
domain-specific information critical to business or regulatory requirements.

The following demonstrates custom span creation and annotation
in a Python application using OpenTelemetry:

```python
from opentelemetry import trace
from opentelemetry.trace import SpanKind

tracer = trace.get_tracer(__name__)

def process_transaction(transaction_id):
    with tracer.start_as_current_span("process_transaction", kind
    =SpanKind.SERVER) as span:
        span.set_attribute("transaction.id", transaction_id)
        # Perform validation
        span.add_event("validation_started")
        validate(transaction_id)
        span.add_event("validation_completed")
        # Execute main business logic
        result = execute_business_logic(transaction_id)
        span.set_attribute("transaction.result", result.status)
        return result
```

Tracing data is commonly exported to centralized backends like
Jaeger, Zipkin, or commercial SaaS platforms supporting high cardinality query and analysis. For compliance tracking, trace data
retention policies and access controls must align with regulatory
frameworks such as GDPR or HIPAA.

Logs provide a detailed narrative of system events and contextual diagnostics indispensable for forensic investigations, audit trails, and anomaly detection. Extending observability requires logs with structured formats, rich context, and integration with telemetry systems.

Structured logging typically adheres to key-value JSON or protocol buffer encodings that maintain semantic consistency and machine-readability. Thus, each log entry may capture timestamp, severity level, service identifiers, trace and span correlation IDs, user IDs, and error codes. This enables correlation of logs with traces and metrics for comprehensive observability.

The following sample illustrates injecting trace context into structured logs in a Node.js environment using Pino logger and Open-Telemetry:

```
const pino = require('pino');
const { context, trace } = require('@opentelemetry/api');

const logger = pino();

function logTransactionStart(transactionId) {
    const span = trace.getSpan(context.active());
    const traceId = span ? span.spanContext().traceId : undefined
    ;

    logger.info({
        transactionId,
        traceId,
        event: "transaction_start",
        severity: "info",
    }, `Transaction ${transactionId} started`);
}
```

Log aggregation solutions such as the ELK stack (Elasticsearch, Logstash, Kibana) or Loki enable indexing, searching, and visualization of structured logs alongside metrics and traces. Integrating these systems within observability workflows optimizes alerting, root cause analysis, and compliance reporting.

The orchestration of telemetry types into coherent observability workflows addresses the requirements of proactive operations and stringent compliance. Effective workflows automate data collection, enrichment, storage, analysis, and alerting through integrated pipelines.

Export strategies typically involve push or pull models. Metrics are often scraped periodically by monitoring systems, whereas traces and logs usually employ push exporters sending data to backends with guaranteed delivery or batching mechanisms to balance latency and throughput.

An example workflow leverages OpenTelemetry Collector as an intermediary, responsible for receiving instrumented data from applications, enriching metadata, sampling traces, transforming formats, and forwarding to multiple destinations:

- **Collection**: Applications export metrics, traces, and logs in OTLP format to the Collector.

- **Processing**: Collector applies filtering, sampling, and attribute enrichment.

- **Export**: Data is forwarded concurrently to long-term storage (e.g., Prometheus for metrics, Jaeger for traces, and Elasticsearch for logs).

- **Consumption**: Alerting rules and dashboards query aggregated data sources to detect anomalies, SLA violations, or security events.

Ensuring observability platform scalability is crucial due to data volume growth. Strategies include adaptive sampling for traces, hierarchical metrics aggregation, and log retention policies governed by regulatory mandates.

Extending observability generates a large volume of sensitive telemetry data necessitating secure handling and compliance enforcement. Key considerations include:

- **Data Minimization**: Collect only the telemetry data required for monitoring and compliance to reduce exposure.

- **Access Control**: Implement role-based access control (RBAC) for observability data repositories to restrict sensitive information access.

- **Data Encryption**: Encrypt data in transit and at rest using industry-standard protocols such as TLS and AES encryption.

- **Audit Logging**: Maintain immutable audit logs for telemetry access and configuration changes supporting compliance audits.

- **Anonymization and Redaction**: Apply anonymization or redaction techniques especially for user-identifiable data within logs or traces.

Compliance frameworks often require demonstrable observability capabilities, including the ability to trace data flows, detect unauthorized access, and provide transparent reporting. Incorporating compliance tags and metadata within telemetry facilitates automated compliance validation.

Maximizing observability effectiveness demands interoperability with a breadth of tools and technologies across heterogeneous platform components. Adherence to open standards such as OpenTelemetry for telemetry data instrumentation and export fosters vendor-neutral data formats and APIs, facilitating integration.

Custom telemetry should align with established semantic conventions and naming conventions to ensure compatibility with ecosystem tools and enable meaningful cross-system analysis. For example, OpenTelemetry semantic conventions define standardized attribute names for common resource types, messaging systems, and HTTP operations.

Interoperability also benefits from adopting common data models and exporting telemetry using widely supported protocols like OTLP, Prometheus exposition format, or Fluentd forward protocol for logs. This facilitates seamless data ingestion into monitoring, analysis, and visualization platforms.

By integrating custom metrics, distributed tracing, and structured logging into a unified observability framework, platforms unlock unprecedented depth of visibility. This extended observability underpins proactive operational excellence and robust compliance tracking, enabling timely detection, diagnosis, and mitigation of issues before they impact service quality or breach regulatory obligations. The ensuing telemetry workflows and export strategies form a resilient foundation to support the ongoing evolution of increasingly complex technology ecosystems.

5.6. Testing and Certifying Custom Components

The assurance of reliability and robust performance in custom extensions hinges on comprehensive automated validation and rigorous certification workflows. Custom modules, connectors, and policies, as critical building blocks within an extended architecture, demand systematic verification methods to prevent faults, ensure compliance, and validate operational correctness across evolving environments.

Unit testing forms the foundational layer for validating the smallest functional elements of custom components. Each unit— defined as an atomic code segment or configurable parameter set—must be exercised independently from the system. This isolation enables rapid fault localization by verifying input-output behavior against expected results. Effective unit tests typically employ mocks or stubs to abstract dependencies, thus simulating interaction with external services or data sources. For custom modules, assertions verify core logic correctness, boundary cases, and error handling mechanisms. In connectors, unit tests validate protocol adherence, message format transformation, and security credential handling. Policies, given their declarative or procedural nature, require unit tests that confirm rule evaluation outcomes, conditional branching, and side effects under varying inputs.

Integration testing extends beyond unit scope to assess the interaction of multiple components in concert. These tests confirm that assembled units collaborate correctly, exchanging messages and state with consistency and efficiency. Integration tests for custom connectors may involve invoking real or simulated external APIs, validating end-to-end workflows and error propagation. For comprehensive coverage, integration scenarios include success paths, failure modes, latency handling, and security compliance checks such as authentication token exchange and encryption enforcement. Policies integrated within a runtime environment are tested for decision logic across composite triggers and chained conditions, ensuring that combined rules provide consistent authorization or transformation outcomes. Test environments must mimic production configurations closely, leveraging containerization or virtual machines to replicate dependencies, network conditions, and service orchestration.

Certification processes formalize the validation outcome, providing an auditable guarantee to stakeholders regarding component correctness and compliance. Automated certification pipelines integrate static code analysis, dynamic testing, and compliance scans within continuous integration/continuous deployment (CI/CD) workflows. Static analysis tools verify adherence to coding standards, detect security vulnerabilities, and identify potential performance bottlenecks. Dynamic code coverage metrics track the extent of exercised paths, including boundary and exception cases, ensuring thorough behavioral tests. For connectors and modules interfacing with external standards or protocols, certification includes conformance tests mapped to relevant industry specifications.

Compliance assurance is critical for long-term maintainability and regulatory adherence. This involves embedding compliance checks into the certification workflow, including license validation, encryption standards, data handling policies, and security best practices. Policy components must be verified against organizational governance frameworks, data privacy rules, and audit trails. Automated tools facilitate these validations by scanning for forbidden API calls, verifying cryptographic key lengths, or enforcing access control policies. Traceability matrices link test cases to compliance requirements, enabling transparent reporting for internal audits or third-party assessments.

An illustrative example of an automated workflow for a custom connector begins with pre-commit validations running unit tests on stubbed API interactions. Once committed, integration tests deploy the connector within an isolated environment, simulating backend systems and exercising full request-response cycles. Following successful testing, the connector undergoes static security analysis, checking for common vulnerabilities such as injection flaws or insecure transport usage. Finally, a certification job verifies compliance against protocol-specific conformance tests before marking the component as release-ready.

Over time, regression testing safeguards against the introduction of defects during iterative development or platform upgrades. Automated test suites must be adapted as extensions evolve, capturing new functionality and deprecated features. Code coverage tools facilitate periodic audits to identify insufficiently tested regions. Continuous feedback from monitoring data and error reports enables refinement of test cases and adaptive certification criteria.

```
import unittest
from my_custom_policy import evaluate_conditions

class TestPolicyEvaluation(unittest.TestCase):

    def test_basic_condition(self):
```

```
        input_data = {'user_role': 'admin', 'request_time':
    '14:00'}
        expected = True
        result = evaluate_conditions(input_data)
        self.assertEqual(result, expected)

    def test_failing_condition(self):
        input_data = {'user_role': 'guest', 'request_time':
    '02:00'}
        expected = False
        result = evaluate_conditions(input_data)
        self.assertEqual(result, expected)

    def test_edge_case_empty_input(self):
        input_data = {}
        with self.assertRaises(KeyError):
            evaluate_conditions(input_data)

if __name__ == '__main__':
    unittest.main()
```

```
Output:
...
---------------------------------------------------------------------
Ran 3 tests in 0.002s

OK
```

Key metrics influence the design and assessment of testing and certification strategies. These include test coverage percentage, mean time to detect failures, false negative rates in security scans, and compliance validation completeness. Tooling integration must accommodate usage patterns across development teams, supporting parallel execution, incremental builds, and artifact traceability. Emphasis on automation ensures reproducibility and minimizes human error, while visualization dashboards aid in timely issue detection and quality reporting.

Ultimately, embedding testing and certification within development lifecycles fosters a culture of quality and trustworthiness for custom extensions. This proactive diligence mitigates risk and delivers consistent behavior aligned with both technical specifications and regulatory mandates across deployment contexts.

Chapter 6

Advanced Data Transformation and Streaming

Data is the lifeblood of integration—and the ability to shape, stream, and validate it in real time separates leading platforms from the rest. This chapter dives into the advanced data transformation and streaming capabilities that make MuleSoft a power-house for both traditional and next-generation integration work-loads. From handling unstructured feeds to enforcing quality and compliance at scale, you'll learn how to deliver data wherever and however your enterprise demands.

6.1. DataWeave Deep Dive

DataWeave is the powerful, domain-specific language at the core of MuleSoft's data transformation capabilities. It enables pre-cise manipulation of complex data structures through a rich set of declarative constructs grounded in functional programming paradigms. Designed for seamless integration within Mule applications, DataWeave offers a resilient framework for data transformation across diverse formats such as JSON, XML, CSV, Java objects, and beyond. The language's expressive power and flexibility emerge from its core features: complex mappings, recursive transformations, functional programming constructs, and inherent optimizations tailored for high-throughput processing environments.

At its foundation, DataWeave expressions operate on immutable data structures, including arrays, objects, numbers, strings, booleans, and nulls. This immutability guarantees referential transparency and simplifies reasoning about transformations, enabling extensive reuse of expressions without side effects. The syntax's conciseness and composability allow developers to define intricate mappings declaratively while preserving readability.

Complex Mappings

The core mechanism for data transformation in DataWeave is the mapping of input data structures to output constructs. This mapping often involves deeply nested objects or arrays, requiring precise navigation and modification of elements. Key operators such as the object constructor {} and array constructor [] facilitate constructing the output with explicit control over key names and ordering.

Transform-aware functions such as map, filter, reduce, and pluck enable iterating over collections, filtering elements by predicates, accumulating values, and extracting subsets of data respectively. For instance, mapping over an array of user objects to extract email domains involves chaining these functions for clarity and brevity.

```
%dw 2.0
output application/json
var users = [
  { name: "Alice", email: "alice@example.com" },
```

```
  { name: "Bob", email: "bob@sample.org" }
]
---
users map ((user) ->
  user.email splitBy "@"[1]
)
```

```
[
  "example.com",
  "sample.org"
]
```

DataWeave supports conditional and optional key definitions within object constructors through ternary expressions or the use of the when keyword. This enables dynamic shaping of output data based on input values or external variables, enhancing transformation flexibility in heterogeneous environments.

Functional Programming Techniques

DataWeave leverages functional programming principles extensively, providing first-class functions, higher-order functions, and closures. Functions are declared using concise lambda syntax, supporting multiple parameters and implicit return values. This functional core permits encapsulating common transformation logic for reuse and composition.

Referential transparency enables function chaining without unintended side effects, improving maintainability in complex transformations. Built-in functions can be combined with user-defined functions to create modular, testable transformation pipelines.

For example, composing a data normalization function illustrates this pattern:

```
%dw 2.0
output application/json
fun normalizeEmail(email) = email lower() trim()
fun getEmailDomain(email) = email splitBy "@"[1]
var emails = [" Alice@example.com ", "Bob@Sample.org"]
---
emails map (email) -> normalizeEmail(email)
         map getEmailDomain
```

In the snippet above, chaining map with composed normalization and extraction functions abstractly separates concerns and fosters clean code.

Recursive Transformations

Handling deeply nested or arbitrarily structured data often necessitates recursive approaches, especially when the depth or shape of input documents is not fixed. DataWeave supports recursion by allowing functions to call themselves, subject to stack depth limitations.

Recursive transformations can traverse hierarchical trees, flatten nested arrays, or perform structural rearrangement. For example, recursively normalizing all string values within an arbitrarily nested object ensures consistent data hygiene before further processing.

```
%dw 2.0
output application/json
fun normalizeStrings(data) =
  if (data is String) then
    data lower() trim()
  else if (data is Array) then
    data map (item) -> normalizeStrings(item)
  else if (data is Object) then
    data mapObject ((value, key) -> (key): normalizeStrings(value
      ))
  else
    data
var input = {
  user: {
    name: " Alice ",
    contacts: [
      { email: "Bob@Org.com " },
      { phone: " 123-456-7890 " }
    ]
  }
}
---
normalizeStrings(input)
```

```
{
  "user": {
    "name": "alice",
    "contacts": [
```

```
    {
      "email": "bob@org.com"
    },
    {
      "phone": "123-456-7890"
    }
  ]
}
}
```

This recursive strategy elegantly traverses mixed-type data structures, applying transformations contextually and preserving non-string data intact.

Performance Optimization for High-Throughput

In scenarios demanding high throughput and low latency, such as real-time streaming or large batch processing, optimizing DataWeave transformations is critical. Several best practices and language features allow achieving efficient execution:

- *Lazy Evaluation and Streaming*: DataWeave processes input data streams lazily where possible, avoiding loading entire datasets into memory. Structuring transformations to leverage streaming by reducing intermediate array expansions and data copies enhances scalability.

- *Avoiding Nested Iterations*: Excessive nested `map` or `filter` operations exponentially increase computational complexity. Flattening transformations or combining filtering conditions reduces overhead.

- *Leveraging Native Functions*: Built-in functions implemented in optimized native code execute faster than equivalent user-defined functions. Favor functions such as `mapObject`, `filter`, and `reduce` for aggregation or transformation tasks.

- *Selective Key Extraction*: Using `pluck` and conditional key mappings avoids unnecessary traversal and allocation of outputs, saving cycles especially when output schemas are sparse subsets of inputs.

- *Immutable Data Structures*: Although immutability simplifies reasoning, excessive copying of large objects should be avoided by minimizing intermediate assignments and reusing expressions.

An example of performance-conscious transformation consolidates filtering and mapping in a single pass:

```
%dw 2.0
output application/json
var users = [
  { id: 1, active: true, email: "a@example.com" },
  { id: 2, active: false, email: "b@example.com" },
  { id: 3, active: true, email: "c@example.com" }
]
---
users reduce ((item, acc = []) ->
  if (item.active) acc ++ [item.email] else acc
)
```

This approach avoids scanning the array twice by combining filtering and projection into a single reduction pass, lowering CPU cycles and memory use.

Advanced Use Cases: Dynamic and Parametric Transformations

DataWeave's support for dynamic keys and parametric expressions facilitates adaptable mappings driven by external variables or metadata. Utilizing the ${...} syntax inside key names enables key name composition at runtime. Parameters passed via Mule flows or invoked APIs can direct the transformation logic dynamically without redeployment.

An example includes generating output with keys derived from input values, typical in pivot or transpose operations:

```
%dw 2.0
output application/json
var data = [
```

```
  { category: "A", value: 10 },
  { category: "B", value: 20 }
]
---
data reduce ((item, acc = {}) ->
  acc ++ { (item.category): item.value }
)
```

```
{
  "A": 10,
  "B": 20
}
```

This technique permits flexible reshaping while maintaining declarative clarity, crucial in data integration pipelines needing to adapt on the fly to source schema variations.

Error Handling and Validation

Robust data transformation requires proactive error handling and validation capabilities. DataWeave provides mechanisms to check data types, existence of keys, and apply guarded logic to prevent runtime failures. Operators such as is, default, and pattern matching with match expressions safeguard against unexpected input shapes.

Embedding validation steps within transformation scripts enables early detection of data inconsistencies or invalid formats, facilitating graceful degradation or error propagation. The ability to return custom error messages or partial outputs based on validation results bolsters reliability in production deployments.

Interoperability and Extensibility

DataWeave's language architecture integrates natively into Mule runtime, enabling seamless interaction with connectors, flow variables, and external services. This interoperability allows transformations to be embedded within larger orchestration processes, leveraging rich context and external data sources.

Extensibility is achieved through custom modules and scripting using Java interop, where domain-specific functions or utility libraries can be imported and invoked. While most transformation logic remains in declarative DataWeave, extension points permit addressing specialized requirements without compromising maintainability.

DataWeave thus epitomizes a sophisticated, expressive, and efficient language designed specifically for the challenges of modern, heterogeneous data transformation in API-led connectivity and integration paradigms. Mastery of its core constructs-complex mapping expressions, functional programming techniques, recursion, and performance optimizations-enables the architecting of robust, reusable, and scalable data pipelines tailored to demanding enterprise integration contexts.

6.2. Batch Integration Patterns

Within modern enterprise environments, processing large volumes of data efficiently and reliably is paramount. MuleSoft's batch processing architecture offers a robust framework designed to handle the complexities inherent in large-scale asynchronous integrations. This section elucidates core design principles, architectural considerations, and optimization strategies essential for mastering batch integration patterns using MuleSoft's framework.

The batch processing model in MuleSoft is fundamentally designed to address workloads that exceed the capacity or responsiveness expected from synchronous processing. It encapsulates a decoupled, asynchronous approach where data records are ingested, processed in discrete chunks, and aggregated to provide consistent and reliable results. A typical batch job in MuleSoft consists of three primary phases: *Input, Batch Step Processing*, and *On Complete* processing. Understanding the interplay among these stages is crucial for designing scalable solutions.

Batch Job Structure and Execution

The input phase is responsible for feeding data into the batch job, typically consuming and splitting large datasets into manageable records. This process can be triggered from various sources such as files, queues, or APIs. Batch steps execute defined processing logic against each record iteratively while maintaining fault tolerance and transactional integrity. The final *On Complete* phase serves for aggregation, reporting, or committing outcomes that require coordination across all processed records.

Partitioning for Scalability

Partitioning divides the batch workload into smaller, parallel-executable fragments, allowing the processing engine to make efficient use of system resources. In MuleSoft, partitioning is configurable per batch step, and each partition processes a subset of records independently. The degree of partitioning should align with the available hardware parallelism and the nature of the workload to strike a balance between throughput and resource contention.

Optimal partition size depends on factors such as the computational cost of processing each record, external system latency, and transaction boundaries. Excessive partitioning may increase overhead due to thread contention and synchronization, whereas insufficient partitioning underutilizes system capacity. Comprehensive profiling and load-testing are vital in determining the optimal parameters.

Parallel Processing Model

The batch framework leverages asynchronous threading to facilitate parallelism in processing individual records across partitions. Each batch step can be configured with a defined level of concurrency, dynamically allocating threads to process multiple records simultaneously. This parallelism dramatically reduces execution time for large datasets when external system calls or processing computations can be parallelized.

However, parallel processing introduces complexities around ordering guarantees and shared resource access. Batch steps must be designed to be idempotent and stateless or use MuleSoft's state management features to prevent inconsistencies or race conditions. When external systems have constraints on concurrent access, throttling mechanisms and error handling strategies must be implemented to accommodate these limitations.

State Management and Transaction Context

Maintaining state within batch integrations is necessary both at the per-record level and across batch job execution. MuleSoft provides batch variables, session variables, and record variables to persist data scopes with distinct lifetimes and visibility:

- **Record variables** are ephemeral, scoped only to individual record processing.

- **Batch step variables** retain data across all records in a batch step.

- **Session variables** persist throughout the entire batch job lifecycle.

These variable scopes enable complex data transformations, accumulation of intermediate results, and coordination of cross-record logic within batch steps. Additionally, MuleSoft supports transaction management encompassing JDBC databases and JMS messaging, ensuring atomic commit or rollback capabilities. It is critical to design batch operations such that transactions are scoped to manageable sizes to avoid long-running transactions that degrade performance or block resources.

Error Handling and Retry Strategies

Effective error handling is essential in batch integrations to maintain data integrity and facilitate recovery. MuleSoft batch jobs support granular handling of record-level exceptions using the `on-error-continue` and `on-error-propagate` constructs. Records that fail processing can be redirected to dead letter queues or persisted for manual review, preventing complete batch failure.

Retries can be orchestrated with policies that define retry counts, intervals, and exponential backoff to tackle transient issues, such as network timeouts or temporary service unavailability. Coupling retries with idempotent processing logic prevents duplicate side effects. Furthermore, job-level error handling allows for compensating transactions or alerts when batch execution experiences systemic failures.

Integration with External Systems: Throughput and Latency Considerations

When batch processing involves heterogeneous external systems-databases, RESTful APIs, messaging queues-the integration pattern must balance throughput with system limitations. Performing bulk operations (e.g., bulk database inserts or API calls) within batch steps is preferred to minimize network overhead and transaction time. MuleSoft provides built-in connectors optimized for batch operations, such as Bulk API connectors for Salesforce.

Latency-sensitive systems necessitate appropriate pacing and resource configuration to avoid saturating endpoints. Chunk size for input splitting and batch size for commits should be tunable parameters aligning with external system capacities. MuleSoft's batch framework supports throttling mechanisms and backpressure handling to prevent resource exhaustion or service degradation.

Monitoring, Auditing, and Reporting

Observability is critical in large-scale batch processing for operational insight and troubleshooting. MuleSoft furnishes detailed audit trails for batch job executions, including record counts, success/failure statistics, and processing duration per batch step. These metrics can be exposed through integration with monitoring tools or the Anypoint Monitoring platform to provide real-time dashboards.

Designing batch jobs to emit custom events or status updates allows fine-grained tracking of business-specific KPIs. Additionally, generating post-processing reports consolidating batch results informs decision-making and compliance audits. Incorporating idempotent checkpoints or persistent state markers improves resumability and fault recovery, facilitating automatic or administrative restarts from failure points.

Design Patterns and Best Practices

Certain recurring patterns emerge as best practices in the implementation of batch processing jobs within MuleSoft:

- **Chunked Input Processing**: Data sources that produce vast datasets should be partitioned into optimal chunk sizes upfront to reduce memory footprint and support incremental processing.

- **Idempotent Processing**: Ensuring that individual record processing fragments are idempotent secures robustness against retries and partial failures.

- **Decoupled Steps**: Modularizing batch logic into discrete steps facilitates parallel execution, simplifies error handling, and enhances maintainability.

- **Asynchronous Result Aggregation**: Deferring result aggregation until the *On Complete* phase allows individual record processing to remain stateless and performant.

- **Use of External State Stores**: Where necessary, integrating reliable external state stores like databases or distributed caches can offload state persistence and provide fault tolerance.

172

Architectural Considerations for Large-Scale Deployments

In enterprise-scale environments, batch job execution must be orchestrated with considerations for scalability, failover, and resource isolation. MuleSoft supports clustering and horizontal scaling of batch processes, enabling concurrent execution of batch jobs on multiple worker nodes. This distributed execution model requires coordination and shared state management typically achieved via external systems.

Load balancing across nodes and idempotent job definitions guarantee predictable execution regardless of the node performing the work. Additionally, scheduling and triggering mechanisms, whether cron-based or event-driven, integrate batch jobs seamlessly into broader integration workflows and process chains.

In scenarios where extremely large datasets are involved, adopting a micro-batch processing approach can mitigate resource spikes and smooth downstream system load. Employing data streaming techniques combined with batch-style checkpoints yields near-real-time processing with batch semantics.

MuleSoft's batch integration patterns offer a comprehensive framework tailored to the demands of large data volume processing by abstracting operational complexities such as threading, state management, and error recovery. The framework's design supports extensibility, combining partitioning and parallelism to exploit modern multi-core architectures and distributed environments. Integration with MuleSoft's ecosystem of connectors, monitoring tools, and management services further enhances operational visibility and governance.

By applying these architectural principles and patterns, solutions can achieve predictable performance, fault tolerance, and maintainability essential in mission-critical enterprise systems requiring reliable asynchronous data integration and transformation at scale.

6.3. Streaming APIs and Reactive Integrations

The increasing demand for real-time data processing in enterprise environments necessitates the adoption of advanced integration paradigms capable of handling continuous event streams with low latency and high throughput. MuleSoft's streaming APIs offer a robust platform for building such event-driven, non-blocking flows that leverage reactive programming models to process and route data streams efficiently. These capabilities enable integration architects to design systems that respond promptly to live data feeds, improving operational agility and decision-making accuracy.

At the heart of MuleSoft's streaming design lies the principle of backpressure-aware data handling. Backpressure is a critical mechanism in reactive systems, ensuring that consumers dictate the data flow rate to prevent overwhelming downstream components. MuleSoft's streaming APIs embody this principle through the use of reactive streams, a specification that standardizes asynchronous stream processing with non-blocking backpressure. By adhering to this model, MuleSoft guarantees seamless integration between diverse components and external systems, permitting smooth handling of unbounded data sequences without resource exhaustion.

The asynchronous, event-driven nature of these APIs fosters non-blocking executions. When utilizing MuleSoft's streaming connectors-such as the HTTP Connector configured for streaming mode or the Kafka Connector streaming Kafka topics-data is processed incrementally as it arrives, avoiding the latency typically introduced by batch processing or full message buffering. This architecture enables immediate reaction to incoming events, promoting enhanced throughput and reduced memory footprint.

Consider the processing pipeline for a continuous stream of sensor data routed from an IoT gateway. Data ingress through a streaming-enabled HTTP Listener, configured for event consumption, passes through a series of transformation and enrichment processors implemented as reactive operators. Each operator applies a distinct, non-blocking function, for example, filtering anomalous readings or enriching data with contextual metadata from external sources. The reactive operator chain reflects a declarative pipeline, where propagation of elements downstream respects backpressure signals, allowing graceful scaling in high-volume scenarios.

Reactive programming in MuleSoft employs constructs analogous to those in Project Reactor or RxJava, exposing primitives such as `Flux` and `Mono` for handling sequences of data asynchronously. A streaming flow thus often resembles a directed graph of reactive operators linked together, encapsulated inside Mule components. Reactive sources, such as event streams from JMS queues or database change logs, generate data asynchronously, which is processed through transformations and side-effect operations configured to execute when demanded by downstream subscribers.

The flexibility in integrating streaming APIs across heterogeneous data sources is a significant advantage. Streaming connectors support protocols and systems widely used in enterprise event buses and messaging platforms, including Kafka, JMS, AMQP, TCP, and WebSocket. This enables comprehensive reactive integration architectures that seamlessly fuse internal business events, third-party feeds, and legacy application notifications into consolidated, real-time pipelines.

A sample MuleSoft streaming flow illustrates these principles by connecting a Kafka topic subscribed to live transaction records with a downstream service that performs fraud detection in real time. The flow is designed to maintain a continuous fetch from Kafka using the reactive streaming API, with each incoming transaction event immediately fed into a fraud detection component implemented as a reactive processor. The processor applies stateless filtering and enrichment using asynchronous calls to external rating engines, returning a reactive stream of evaluated transaction events. This stream is then routed conditionally based on fraud scores to alerting services or archival storage, maintaining continuous flow without blocking or bottlenecks.

```
<flow name="realTimeFraudDetectionFlow">
    <kafka:consume config-ref="Kafka_Config" topic="transactions"
        streaming="true" doc:name="Kafka Stream"/>
    <ee:transform doc:name="Deserialize JSON">
        <ee:message>
            <ee:set-payload><![CDATA[%dw 2.0
output application/java
---
payload map (item) -> {
    transactionId: item.id,
    amount: item.amount,
    timestamp: item.timestamp,
    userId: item.user
}]]></ee:set-payload>
        </ee:message>
    </ee:transform>
    <custom:fraudDetectionProcessor doc:name="Fraud Detection"/>
    <choice doc:name="Route Based on Fraud Score">
        <when expression="#[payload.fraudScore > 0.8]">
            <http:request config-ref="Alert_Service" method="POST"
    " doc:name="Send Alert"/>
        </when>
        <otherwise>
            <file:write path="/data/processed/" doc:name="Archive
    Transaction"/>
        </otherwise>
    </choice>
</flow>
```

Reactive processing models emphasize the decoupling of producers and consumers with asynchronous event propagation. Mule-Soft streaming APIs utilize this decoupling to optimize throughput and latency by allowing streams to be consumed by multiple subscribers, enabling branching and merging of event streams without data duplication or unnecessary buffering. Flows remain responsive under load fluctuations, with backpressure mechanisms ensuring downstream slow consumers signal upstream to throttle data emission.

Another critical feature is the ability to apply windowing and batching strategies within streaming flows, supporting aggregation and stateful computations over event windows. This is particularly useful for scenarios such as real-time analytics, rate limiting, or complex event processing (CEP). MuleSoft APIs expose operators like groupBy, window, and buffer that facilitate temporal or count-based segmentation of streams while preserving backpressure-aware behavior.

Integration of reactive streams with MuleSoft's DataWeave transformation language further enhances data manipulation within streaming pipelines. DataWeave transformations operate declaratively over streaming payloads, allowing partial data processing without requiring full materialization in memory. This approach increases efficiency and scalability, especially when performing complex schema mappings on voluminous or infinite data streams.

Latency reduction is achieved by minimizing data serialization and deserialization overheads and avoiding blocking I/O. Streaming APIs commonly leverage non-blocking network I/O paradigms underpinned by frameworks such as Netty, enabling the handling of thousands of concurrent connections with minimal thread utilization. The event-loop model inherent in such frameworks complements the reactive stream specifications to optimize resource utilization while guaranteeing high responsiveness.

Error handling within streaming APIs requires specialized approaches distinct from traditional request-response integration. Failures can occur at multiple points in the reactive pipeline, from data transformation errors to connectivity disruptions with external systems. MuleSoft supports various error-handling strategies, including retries, fallback streams, and circuit breakers, implemented as reactive operators that handle error propagation and recovery asynchronously. This design enables building resilient streaming applications capable of maintaining service continuity and graceful degradation under adverse conditions.

Security considerations remain paramount in reactive integrations. Streaming APIs support integration with MuleSoft's security policies such as OAuth2, TLS encryption, and data masking, applied transparently across streaming connectors and processors. Ensuring authentication and authorization at stream ingress points safeguards against unauthorized access, while encryption protects stream contents in transit. Additionally, MuleSoft's observability features provide metrics and tracing tailored to streaming contexts, capturing throughput, latency, and error rates per stream for operational visibility.

From a deployment perspective, MuleSoft streaming integrators benefit from the runtime's support for horizontal scaling and cluster-based deployment. Streaming flows designed on reactive models can be distributed across multiple runtime instances, balancing load and improving fault tolerance. CloudHub and Kubernetes-based deployments facilitate elastic scaling, responding dynamically to variable event rates inherent to streaming sources.

MuleSoft's streaming APIs and reactive integrations form the back-bone of modern, real-time data processing architectures. By har-monizing event-driven, non-blocking programming models with flexible connector support and comprehensive data transforma-tion capabilities, these streaming constructs enable enterprises to harness continuous data flows with minimal latency and maximal throughput. They embody the principles of resilience, scalabil-ity, and responsiveness critical to real-time digital business ecosys-tems.

6.4. Data Validation and Enrichment

Ensuring robust data quality control is fundamental to any data-driven system, where both incoming and outgoing data must meet stringent business and regulatory requirements. Data validation and enrichment form the cornerstone of these controls, offering mechanisms to detect, correct, and augment data before it propagates through complex processing pipelines.

The implementation of validation frameworks primarily revolves around enforcing schema adherence and integrity constraints, executed in an automated manner to handle high-volume or real-time data flows. Schema validation verifies that data conforms to an expected format, type, and structure, commonly defined using formats such as JSON Schema, Avro, or Protocol Buffers. Automated schema validation serves as the first line of defense against malformed or corrupted data inputs, drastically reducing downstream processing errors and improving overall system reliability.

At its core, schema validation distinguishes between structural, syntactic, and semantic layers of data quality. Structural validation confirms that the data possesses the required fields with appropriate data types and hierarchical arrangements. Syntactic validation enforces constraints such as allowable value ranges, string patterns through regular expressions, and mandatory fields, while semantic validation examines logical consistency and inter-field dependencies. For example, a date field should not precede a creation timestamp or mandatory relational keys should not be null. These layered validation checks are often composed into pipelines with conditional branching paths, triggered based on business rules or compliance standards.

Implementation of validation frameworks typically integrates with modern ETL (Extract, Transform, Load) or ELT (Extract, Load, Transform) platforms, as well as message brokers and streaming engines such as Apache Kafka or Flink. Popular validation libraries

179

offer declarative syntax for schema definitions and provide APIs for embedding validations in data ingestion stages. In distributed systems, validation components are employed both at edge nodes for initial filtering and centralized data lakes for comprehensive audit and reconciliation.

Complementing validation, data enrichment processes enhance the value and completeness of datasets by appending relevant information or refining existing data elements. Enrichment strategies include reference data lookups, normalization, geocoding, and semantic annotation. They serve as critical enablers for improving data usability, enabling better analytics, and ensuring compliance with regulatory mandates such as GDPR or HIPAA.

Reference data enrichment involves augmenting datasets with authoritative information from external or internal registries, such as customer demographic data, classification codes, or product master data. This is often realized through synchronous API calls or asynchronous batch processing, depending on latency constraints. The enriched attributes can facilitate enhanced entity resolution, segmentation, or risk assessment.

Normalization techniques unify heterogeneous data representations into standardized formats. Examples include transforming address fields into canonical forms using postal service databases, standardizing date-time values to ISO 8601 formats, or harmonizing measurement units according to international standards. Data normalization is essential for eliminating ambiguity and ensuring data comparability across distributed systems.

Geospatial enrichment leverages geocoding and reverse geocoding services to translate physical addresses into latitude and longitude coordinates and vice versa. Geospatial metadata enables location-aware analytics, fraud detection, and compliance checks such as jurisdictional data access restrictions. Integration of geospatial enrichment into data pipelines typically requires high-performance spatial index structures and APIs capable of bulk geocoding with error handling strategies for ambiguous or incomplete inputs.

Semantic enrichment centers on the application of metadata and ontology-based annotations to improve data interpretability and machine-readability. This often involves linking data elements to standardized vocabularies, classification schemes, or domain taxonomies, enhancing capabilities such as intelligent search, automated reasoning, and regulatory reporting. Semantic enrichment can also identify sensitive data categories, aiding in data masking and anonymization policies for compliance.

To meet business and compliance standards, validation and enrichment processes must be tightly governed and auditable. Data quality frameworks often implement versioned schemas, ensuring backward and forward compatibility as data models evolve. Any deviations detected during validation trigger error handling workflows, including alerting, quarantining, or automated correction strategies, all logged with traceability metadata for audits.

In many regulated industries, validation includes compliance-specific checks such as ensuring Personally Identifiable Information (PII) is handled according to privacy laws or that financial transaction data adheres to Anti-Money Laundering (AML) rules. Embedding these domain-specific validation modules requires extensible architectures supporting pluggable validators that can be updated frequently without disrupting production workflows.

Error handling and data correction mechanisms associated with validation and enrichment can be categorized into reject, repair, or alert modes. Reject mode discards nonconforming records, which, while enhancing data integrity, may lead to loss of valuable data insights and thus requires balance with business tolerance. Repair mode attempts automated corrections driven by business heuristics or machine learning models, such as imputing missing values or correcting data format errors. Alert mode raises exceptions or notifications for human review, often employed in high-stakes environments where precision surpasses throughput priorities.

Architecturally, validation and enrichment workflows are implemented as modular, reusable components within data orchestration frameworks. This facilitates standardized quality control across heterogeneous data sources and sinks. Modern implementations favor declarative pipelines for easy maintainability and integration with CI/CD systems, enabling continuous validation schema testing and enrichment rule updates.

An example of schema validation using JSON Schema might define rules requiring a customer record to contain a non-null string customer_id, an email field matching a standard email pattern, and an age field with a minimum value of 18:

```
{
  "type": "object",
  "properties": {
    "customer_id": { "type": "string" },
    "email": { "type": "string", "format": "email" },
    "age": { "type": "integer", "minimum": 18 }
  },
  "required": ["customer_id", "email", "age"],
  "additionalProperties": false
}
```

In a streaming pipeline leveraging Apache Kafka and a schema registry, producers validate messages against registered schemas before publishing, while downstream consumers enforce the same validations prior to processing. This reduces data drift and maintains contractual data interfaces across services.

For enrichment, example pseudocode illustrates augmenting a dataset with geographic coordinates based on address fields:

```
def enrich_with_geocode(records, geocode_api):
    enriched = []
    for record in records:
        address = record.get('address')
        if address:
            coords = geocode_api.lookup(address)
            record['latitude'] = coords.latitude
            record['longitude'] = coords.longitude
        enriched.append(record)
```

```
return enriched
```

To enforce data quality policies continuously, integration of metrics and monitoring is essential. Data validation frameworks commonly emit metrics such as validation failure rates, enrichment success ratios, and latency per processing stage. These metrics feed into alerting dashboards supporting proactive remediation and capacity planning.

The confluence of automated schema validation, targeted enrichment flows, and comprehensive auditing establishes a defensible stance on data quality and compliance. These safeguards underpin reliable data-driven operations, facilitate interoperability across systems, and support adherence to evolving regulatory landscapes without compromising operational agility.

6.5. Dealing with Unstructured and Semi-structured Data

The growing heterogeneity of data sources in modern enterprise environments necessitates flexible and robust integration approaches capable of handling various data formats. MuleSoft's Anypoint Platform excels in orchestrating flows that consume and transform JSON, XML, CSV, and amorphous unstructured formats, leveraging dedicated connectors, transformers, and intelligent routing mechanisms. The challenges inherent in these integration scenarios arise from disparate syntaxes, schema variability, irregularities in field mappings, and the absence of rigid structural definitions in unstructured data.

Parsing Diverse Data Formats

Effective integration begins with the accurate parsing of incoming data streams. MuleSoft supports native handling of JSON and XML through its built-in json:transform and xml:transform modules, which rely on streaming parsers to maintain efficiency in processing large payloads. Streaming parsers are preferred over in-memory DOM-based parsers, especially for XML, as they consume less memory and enable partial document processing.

Parsing CSV data, while simpler syntactically, poses challenges when delimiter consistency and quoting conventions vary. MuleSoft's CSV module allows customization of delimiters, quoting characters, and escape sequences, enabling adaptation to diverse CSV specifications. Additionally, MuleSoft supports schema-aware CSV parsing by mapping CSV columns to fields, facilitating transformations into JSON or XML for downstream processing.

Unstructured data sources such as log files, plain text streams, or loosely formatted documents require more advanced parsing strategies. Regular expressions, grammar-based parsers, or custom transformers implemented with DataWeave scripts become essential to extract meaningful tokenized data elements. DataWeave's pattern matching and string manipulation functions provide powerful tools for capturing and structuring embedded entity relationships within unstructured inputs.

Normalization and Canonical Data Models

Once data is parsed into an intermediate representation, normalization is critical to unify heterogeneous schemas and ensure consistency across system boundaries. This process involves mapping source-specific fields to a canonical data model, often represented as a standardized JSON or XML schema. Employing canonical models reduces complexity within integration logic by centralizing field definitions and semantic interpretations.

DataWeave expressions can define transformation pipelines to normalize field names, data types, and hierarchical structures. For example, date fields may appear in diverse formats (ISO 8601, UNIX timestamps, locale-specific strings), requiring conversion into a uniform representation using DataWeave's date functions. Hierarchical flattening or nesting transformations can align data shapes to the canonical model's expectations.

In scenarios involving schema evolution or partially missing data, MuleSoft supports dynamic schema validation and conditional transformations. The use of DataWeave's `isEmpty()`, `match()`, and `default` operators enables graceful handling of optional or unforeseen fields, preventing runtime errors and ensuring resilient integration flows.

Intelligent Routing and Message Enrichment

Complex integration ecosystems routinely demand intelligent message routing based on content inspection or metadata, facilitating parallel processing paths or conditional transformations. MuleSoft implements content-based router patterns using the `choice` router combined with DataWeave expression evaluators to predicate routing decisions.

For instance, JSON messages containing certain field values can be routed to distinct processing queues, or XML payloads with particular namespace attributes may require specialized enrichment before transmission. Such conditional routing optimizes resource usage and enhances maintainability by encapsulating format-specific logic behind abstracted flow branches.

Message enrichment is often necessary to append supplementary data from external sources or compute derived attributes enhancing downstream utility. MuleSoft connectors to databases, REST APIs, or caching layers enable lookup and enrichment patterns. The enriched data is merged back into the canonical payload using atomic DataWeave merge operators, preserving consistency and traceability.

Handling Ambiguous and Mixed-Format Inputs

Real-world datasets are frequently ambiguous or comprise mixed formats, requiring adaptive parsing strategies and heuristic-driven processing. MuleSoft allows embedding decision logic within parsers to detect payload types at runtime. For example, a preliminary check of initial characters or document-type declarations may identify whether a payload is JSON, XML, or other.

In certain cases, hybrid payloads embed multiple formats (e.g., XML containers with inner JSON fields). DataWeave transformations can sequentially parse nested formats, applying format-specific interpreters in a layered processing approach. Employing MuleSoft's metadata capabilities, the system tracks the provenance and transformations applied, facilitating debugging and auditability.

When data sources are unstructured beyond recognition by conventional parsers, Natural Language Processing (NLP) or machine learning models may be invoked externally via connectors to classification or entity extraction services. The annotations returned from such services can be introduced into MuleSoft flows, converted into structured formats, and integrated into the canonical data pipeline.

Practical Example: Parsing and Normalizing a Multi-format Input

Consider an integration scenario where an inbound payload may arrive as JSON or CSV representing customer orders. The target system requires a unified XML format with specific field mappings and enriched with validation status.

A DataWeave script fragment demonstrates conditional parsing and normalization:

```
%dw 2.0
output application/xml
var isJson = __payload as String startsWith "{"
var parsedPayload =
  if (isJson)
    read(payload, "application/json")
  else
    read(payload, "application/csv")
```

```
---
order: {
  id: parsedPayload.orderId default parsedPayload."Order ID",
  customer: {
    name: parsedPayload.customerName default parsedPayload."
    Customer Name",
    email: parsedPayload.customerEmail default parsedPayload."
    Customer Email"
  },
  items: parsedPayload.items map (item) -> {
    productId: item.productId default item."Product ID",
    quantity: item.quantity as Number default item."Quantity" as
    Number
  },
  validationStatus: if ((parsedPayload.customerEmail default "")
    contains "@")
                    "Validated" else "Invalid Email"
}
```

The above script evaluates the payload type at runtime (JSON or CSV) and leverages default alternatives to normalize fields with varying names. It also enriches the output by performing a simple validation on the customer email. The generated XML structure conforms to an agreed canonical schema ready for downstream consumption.

Best Practices and Performance Considerations

Dealing with unstructured and semi-structured data demands careful attention to performance and error handling. Streaming parsers should be preferred for large payloads to avoid excessive memory consumption. Breakpoints, retry policies, and exception strategies must be configured meticulously to recover gracefully from parsing errors induced by malformed inputs.

Caching frequently accessed reference data during enrichment phases reduces latency and external dependency bottlenecks. Employing MuleSoft's DataSense and schema metadata inspection capabilities enhances the correctness and automation of transformations.

Finally, comprehensive logging and observability integrated at each stage of parsing, normalization, and routing are essential to maintain operational transparency in complex integration pipelines managing heterogeneous data sources.

6.6. Data Lineage, Quality, and Provenance

The effective management of an enterprise's data assets hinges critically on the ability to track and understand the complete lifecycle of data, from its origin through transformation and consumption. Data lineage, quality, and provenance collectively underpin governance frameworks that ensure data integrity, compliance, and trustworthiness across varied integration environments. This section elucidates methods to establish and maintain comprehensive data lineage, enforce rigorous data quality standards, and leverage data provenance to support auditable and accountable data ecosystems.

Data lineage represents the end-to-end documentation of a data element's flow through diverse systems, processes, and transformation logic. It provides visibility into the sequence of steps that raw data undergoes as it evolves into actionable insights within business intelligence or analytic applications. Tracking lineage throughout an integration landscape requires capturing metadata about data sources, intermediate processing stages, and downstream targets.

A robust lineage model consists of four principal components: data sources, transformation processes, movement channels, and data targets. Each component is annotated with metadata describing origin identifiers, timestamps, transformation rules or algorithms, and change histories. Systems often employ directed acyclic graphs (DAGs) to represent lineage, where nodes symbolize data artifacts and edges denote transformations or data flows.

Operationally, lineage can be captured through multiple approaches: intrinsic capture by integration platforms that

automatically trace data flow at runtime, extraction from ETL
scripts and workflow definitions, or manual annotation supported
by metadata management tools.   Instrumenting pipelines
to emit lineage metadata facilitates reproducible audits and
impact analyses, enabling stakeholders to assess how changes to
upstream data affect downstream reports or machine learning
features.

Ensuring data quality involves the systematic validation, cleansing,
and profiling of data as it traverses through integration processes.
Quality dimensions relevant in integration contexts include accuracy, completeness, consistency, timeliness, and conformity to predefined schemas or business rules.

A layered approach to quality enforcement optimizes effectiveness.
Initial source-level validation identifies errors immediately upon
ingestion, minimizing error propagation. Subsequently, intermediate data staging zones apply cleansing routines and standardization methods such as deduplication, format normalization, and
outlier detection using automated scripts or data quality software
modules.   Finally, target systems execute validation constraints
and referential integrity checks tailored to business requirements.

Quality metrics are both operational and analytical. Operational
metrics track error rates, correction frequencies, and latency in
processing, often exposed via data quality dashboards. Analytical
metrics, including statistical profiling and anomaly detection, inform continuous improvement by revealing systemic issues. Automation can incorporate rejection policies, rerouting of suspect
data for remediation, and feedback loops into source systems.

Quality controls must also align with the complexity of data
schemas and heterogeneity of sources in the integration
landscape. Schema evolution and versioning must be managed
carefully to avoid quality degradation due to incompatible input.
Coupling lineage metadata with quality metrics offers a powerful
instrument to pinpoint exact pipeline stages or source systems

responsible for quality deviations.

Provenance extends beyond lineage by specifically documenting the origin, ownership, and custodianship details of data artifacts. Its primary function is to establish a verifiable chain of custody enabling trust and regulatory compliance, especially under stringent data protection regimes such as GDPR, HIPAA, or financial regulatory frameworks.

Provenance metadata captures when and how data was created, modified, or accessed, including identities of responsible agents and contextual information about system states or environmental conditions. This provenance trail must be immutable and tamper-evident to serve as reliable evidence during audits or forensic investigations.

Enterprise provenance systems generally integrate with identity and access management (IAM) infrastructures to associate user credentials with data operations. Cryptographic methods, such as digital signatures and blockchain-inspired ledger technologies, can augment the immutability and non-repudiation features of provenance records. Provenance repositories may utilize specialized provenance-aware databases or extend existing metadata catalogs.

Compliance mandates necessitate that provenance data is readily queryable and interoperable across heterogeneous platforms. Standardization efforts such as the W3C PROV model provide formal ontologies and serialization formats to represent provenance statements in a machine-readable manner, facilitating interoperability and integration into governance processes.

Integrating data lineage, quality, and provenance into a unified governance framework enhances data stewardship and operational transparency. A strategic approach entails:

- **Metadata Unification:** Consolidating lineage, quality,

and provenance metadata into a centralized repository or federated catalog enables coherent visibility and reduces fragmentation. This repository forms the focal point for analysis, reporting, and decision-making.

- **Automated Capture and Instrumentation:** Instrumenting data pipelines, ETL workflows, and streaming platforms to generate standardized metadata continuously minimizes manual intervention and error susceptibility.

- **Policy-driven Enforcement:** Defining explicit data governance policies that embed quality thresholds, lineage tracking requirements, and provenance documentation ensures compliance by design. These policies can be enforced through automated workflows, alerting mechanisms, and workflow gating conditions.

- **Visualization and Impact Analysis:** Providing graphical lineage maps coupled with quality dashboards allows technical and business users to understand data dependencies, assess risk exposure from upstream changes, and prioritize remediation efforts.

- **Audit and Compliance Reporting:** Generating comprehensive, tamper-resistant audit trails demonstrating provenance and quality adherence supports regulatory inspections and internal risk assessments.

Implementing effective data lineage, quality, and provenance solutions involves leveraging an ecosystem of complementary technologies:

- **Metadata Management Platforms:** Tools such as Apache Atlas, Collibra, and Informatica MDM facilitate metadata capture, lineage visualization, policy management, and repository functions.

- **Data Quality Engines:** Solutions like Great Expectations, Talend Data Quality, and Trifacta provide rule-based profiling, validation, and cleaning capabilities that integrate into batch or real-time pipelines.

- **Workflow Orchestration Frameworks:** Apache Airflow or Azure Data Factory can be extended with custom lineage capture hooks and quality enforcement steps within their DAG executions.

- **Provenance Frameworks:** W3C PROV compliant implementations and blockchain ledger platforms can track immutable audit trails, leveraging cryptographic guarantees.

A simplified example of capturing lineage within an ETL script is illustrated below using pseudocode embedded with metadata annotations:

```
# Source data extraction step with lineage metadata
source_data = extract_data(source='Customer_DB',
                           timestamp=current_time(),
                           source_id='cust_db_01')

# Transformation step with lineage links to source
cleaned_data = transform(source_data,
                         operations=['remove_nulls', '
    normalize_names'],
                         parent_id=source_data.metadata_id)

# Load step with propagated lineage information
load_data(target='Analytics_Warehouse',
          data=cleaned_data,
          lineage_info=cleaned_data.metadata)
```

The associated lineage graph constructed from these metadata elements allows tracing each downstream dataset back to the exact source extraction and transformation steps, supporting error diagnosis and data provenance validation.

Despite its critical importance, establishing comprehensive data lineage, quality, and provenance faces several challenges:

- **Complexity and Scale:** Large, distributed environments

with numerous data sources, variable schemas, and heterogeneous transformation technologies complicate unified lineage capture.

- **Performance Overheads:** Automatic metadata instrumentation and quality checks introduce computational overhead, potentially impacting pipeline throughput and latency.

- **Data Privacy and Security:** Capturing detailed provenance may expose sensitive information or conflict with data minimization principles; governance policies must balance transparency with confidentiality.

- **Evolving Systems and Schema Drift:** Lineage and quality frameworks must adapt dynamically to accommodate changing data pipelines and schema versions without loss of traceability.

- **Standards Adoption:** Inconsistent use of provenance and metadata standards across tooling hinders interoperability and requires mediation layers or extensions.

Addressing these challenges demands strategic investments in metadata management capabilities, cross-team collaboration between data engineering and governance teams, and adoption of emerging standards and best practices.

Data lineage, quality, and provenance collectively form the backbone of trustworthy data ecosystems in modern enterprises. Tracking data origins and transformations comprehensively, enforcing rigorous quality standards, and establishing immutable provenance records empower organizations to comply with regulatory requirements, mitigate operational risks, and build confidence among stakeholders. The continuous integration of these elements into enterprise data architectures leverages automated metadata capture, standardized representations, and policy enforcement to ensure consistent and auditable data governance.

Chapter 7

Performance, Observability, and Reliability Engineering

When integrations underpin mission-critical operations, performance and reliability aren't just aspirations—they're architectural imperatives. This chapter guides you through fine-tuning your MuleSoft deployments for maximum throughput, rapid diagnostics, and bulletproof resilience. Journey into the world of distributed tracing, autoscaling, caching, and intelligent error handling, and discover the engineering secrets behind seamless, always-on integration ecosystems.

7.1. Capacity Planning and Vertical/Horizontal Scaling

Effective capacity planning constitutes a fundamental aspect of designing resilient and scalable MuleSoft applications. It enables anticipation of load patterns, optimal resource allocation, and structured growth strategies, ensuring system performance remains robust under varying operational demands. Two primary scaling paradigms underpin the elasticity of application infrastructure: vertical and horizontal scaling. Each approach carries distinct considerations affecting cost, complexity, and fault tolerance, which must be aligned with anticipated usage patterns and long-term architectural goals.

Anticipating Load and Demand Fluctuations

The starting point for capacity planning is an accurate projection of workload characteristics, which includes throughput, request complexity, concurrency levels, and peak load intervals. MuleSoft applications often integrate heterogeneous systems, each contributing to variable latency, processing time, and resource consumption. It is critical to utilize historical telemetry data along with predictive analytics to model workloads under both typical and stress conditions.

Key performance indicators (KPIs) such as CPU utilization, memory footprint, thread counts, and network I/O provide granularity necessary for precise capacity modeling. Monitoring tools integrated with Mule runtime, such as Anypoint Monitoring combined with external observability platforms, facilitate detailed insights into these metrics. This data-driven approach enables the construction of capacity planning models that correlate load increases to resource consumption trends, thus informing scaling thresholds and policies.

Resource Allocation Strategies

196

Resource allocation in MuleSoft environments involves provisioning compute, memory, storage, and network bandwidth in a manner congruent with expected load. Within cloud deployments, this translates to selecting instance types, sizes, and network configurations that balance cost and performance. On-premises systems require careful hardware capacity and resource reservation to avoid contention and bottlenecks.

A typical Mule runtime engine (Mule worker) configuration entails sizing JVM heap memory, configuring thread pools, and tuning connector parameters based on the anticipated concurrency and transaction complexity. For example, increasing the upper bounds of the CPU cores and heap size accommodates vertical scaling, whereas augmenting the number of Mule workers addresses horizontal scaling demands.

```
JAVA_OPTS="-Xms4g -Xmx8g -XX:MaxPermSize=512m -XX:+UseG1GC"
export JAVA_OPTS
```

Optimizing thread pool sizes for processing-intensive or I/O-bound tasks can significantly influence throughput. MuleSoft allows configuring the `defaultServiceThreadPoolMaxSize` in the `mule-artifact.json` or via API Gateway policies to tune concurrency safely within each Mule instance.

Vertical Scaling: Enhancing Existing Resources

Vertical scaling, or scaling up, involves augmenting the capacity of a single Mule worker instance by increasing its allocated CPU, memory, storage, or network capacity. This approach leverages enhanced host capabilities to accommodate more transactions or heavier payload processing without distributing the workload across multiple nodes.

Advantages of vertical scaling include simpler architecture management and reduced inter-instance synchronization overhead, as all processes execute within a single runtime environment. However, vertical scaling encounters limits imposed by the underlying hardware or cloud provider instance sizes. Furthermore, increasing resources on one node may yield diminishing returns due to application-level bottlenecks or JVM garbage collection inefficiencies.

Effective vertical scaling requires careful JVM tuning to handle increased heap sizes, mitigate garbage collection pause times, and ensure thread management remains efficient. The following formula approximates ideal thread pool sizing in vertically scaled Mule runtimes:

$$T_{\text{optimal}} = N_{\text{cores}} \times U_{\text{target}} \times \left(1 + \frac{W}{C}\right)$$

where T_{optimal} is the optimal thread count, N_{cores} is the number of processor cores, U_{target} is the target core utilization (fraction), and $\frac{W}{C}$ is the ratio of wait time to compute time per thread.

Due consideration must also be given to the Mule application's architecture-particularly the deployment of flows and connectors-to prevent resource contention under amplified workloads.

Horizontal Scaling: Distributing Load Across Instances

Horizontal scaling, or scaling out, entails adding more Mule worker instances or servers to handle increased load. This approach is especially suited for cloud-native, containerized Mule deployments or cluster environments where multiple workers operate concurrently behind load balancers.

Load distribution mechanisms such as round-robin, least connections, or weighted algorithms enable efficient request routing to horizontally scaled instances. Horizontal scaling improves fault tolerance and availability since failures in one instance do not incapacitate the entire system. It also permits incremental capacity expansion aligned with traffic growth.

When horizontally scaling Mule applications, state management becomes pivotal. Stateless or loosely stateful flows simplify scaling by avoiding complex session replication. For stateful components, externalizing session state to shared caches or persistent stores (e.g., Redis, database systems) is necessary to maintain consistency and session affinity.

Cloud orchestration platforms such as Kubernetes automate horizontal scaling using metrics-based triggers like CPU load, memory utilization, or custom business KPIs. Configurations defining minimum and maximum worker counts, coupled with scaling thresholds, enable responsive elasticity to fluctuating demands.

```
apiVersion: autoscaling/v2
kind: HorizontalPodAutoscaler
metadata:
  name: mule-app-hpa
spec:
  scaleTargetRef:
    apiVersion: apps/v1
    kind: Deployment
    name: mule-app-deployment
  minReplicas: 2
  maxReplicas: 10
  metrics:
  - type: Resource
    resource:
      name: cpu
      target:
        type: Utilization
        averageUtilization: 70
```

Application design must consider eventual consistency and idempotency in order to safely handle scenarios where requests might be routed to different instances on retries or after failover. Employing a distributed message queue or event-driven architecture supports horizontal scalability by decoupling components and smoothing load spikes.

Architectural Considerations for Growth and Future-Proofing

Beyond immediate scaling needs, capacity planning extends to long-term architectural decisions that accommodate evolving business requirements and technology landscapes. MuleSoft applications should be architected with modularity, reuse, and abstraction layers to facilitate incremental scaling with minimal refactoring.

A strategic combination of vertical and horizontal scaling often delivers optimal results-initial vertical scaling to fully utilize host resources and maintain simplicity, then incremental horizontal scaling to distribute load and improve fault tolerance. Load testing and chaos engineering validate these strategies under controlled stress conditions, revealing performance bottlenecks and failure modes.

Integration designers must exploit MuleSoft's API-led connectivity model to modularize interfaces and orchestrations, enabling deployment units that can be independently scaled. Internal microservices or integration layers may be hosted in containerized environments, while API gateways route external requests dynamically to scaled backends.

Resource quotas, environment segregation (development, testing, production), and deployment pipelines with continuous integration and delivery (CI/CD) enable rapid provisioning and scaling aligned with business cycles. Usage of Infrastructure as Code (IaC) tools automates repeatable capacity adjustments, facilitating on-demand scalability while minimizing manual intervention.

Cost and Performance Trade-offs

Capacity planning inherently involves balancing the trade-offs between cost, performance, and operational complexity. Vertical scaling may incur higher costs per compute unit but reduces internode communication overhead. Horizontal scaling distributes load and enhances resilience but increases the operational footprint and complexity of state management.

Quantitative modeling based on key metrics such as cost per transaction, average response time, and availability SLAs guides decision-making. Cloud providers often offer spot or reserved instances which can further optimize cost in scaling strategies. Monitoring and alerting should be configured to detect underutilization or performance degradation preemptively, allowing dynamic scaling adjustments that align with economic efficiency.

A synthesis of methodologies to support capacity planning and scaling includes:

- **Load Modeling**: Employ statistical analysis and telemetry-driven predictions to characterize demand profiles.

- **Resource Profiling**: Benchmark Mule runtime configurations under target workloads to guide JVM and thread pool tuning.

- **Scaling Policies**: Define thresholds and policies based on CPU, memory, and application-layer metrics for automated scaling triggers.

- **Stateless Design**: Architect flows for minimal state dependence and externalize session/state management for horizontal scaling compatibility.

- **Redundancy and Failover**: Implement clustering and load balancing to ensure high availability and resilience.

- **Automation**: Utilize orchestration and IaC tools for reproducible, audited capacity changes.

- **Continuous Validation**: Conduct capacity and stress testing to validate assumptions and refine scaling models.

These integrated approaches underpin the ability of MuleSoft-based architectures to not only meet current load requirements but adapt fluidly to future demands while maintaining predictable performance and operational integrity.

7.2. Performance Tuning of Mule Applications

Performance tuning of Mule applications is essential for achieving efficient processing and consistent, low-latency responses, especially in environments with high throughput or stringent latency requirements. This process involves systematically profiling Mule flows, identifying performance bottlenecks, optimizing resource consumption, and applying advanced runtime configurations. Effective tuning ensures the platform's resilience and scalability while maintaining acceptable operational costs.

Profiling Mule flows begins with establishing a clear baseline of application performance metrics. MuleSoft provides various tools such as Anypoint Visualizer, Runtime Manager, and the embedded Profiler, which collectively allow comprehensive monitoring of flows and components. Central to profiling is the measurement of latency, throughput, CPU utilization, memory usage, and external system response times. Granular logging and the use of Mule's built-in metrics exporters (compatible with Prometheus and JMX) facilitate detailed capture of flow execution statistics. Instrumentation of specific processors and connectors can pinpoint stages with disproportionate resource consumption or delays.

A common initial focus is on identifying bottlenecks, which may be caused by inefficient transformations, network latency, thread starvation, or suboptimal connector configurations. The Mule debugger can isolate slow-running components, while Thread Profiler and JVM-level tools (e.g., JVisualVM, YourKit) provide visibility on thread pool saturation and garbage collection impact. For instance, detecting excessive backpressure from a connector interacting with a remote service under high load often directs tuning efforts to connection pool sizing and timeout parameters. Similarly, inefficient DataWeave expressions or redundant transformation cycles can be revealed through CPU profiling and transaction tracing.

Resource utilization optimization targets both the Mule runtime and the underlying Java Virtual Machine (JVM). Thread pool configuration is critical-the default settings for processing threads might require adjustment depending on the flow design and the nature of invoked APIs or services. For example, asynchronous processing patterns, using Mule's `Async` scope and queues, can relieve synchronous threads and improve throughput but demand careful sizing of thread pools and queue lengths to prevent memory pressure. The distinction between CPU-bound and I/O-bound tasks informs allocation strategies: CPU-intensive tasks should be parallelized without overwhelming CPU cores, while I/O-bound tasks benefit from increased concurrency due to idle wait times on external calls.

Memory management also plays a significant role. Mule applications that handle large payloads or complex data structures may encounter increased garbage collection (GC) overhead, leading to latency spikes. JVM tuning parameters such as heap size, garbage collector type (G1GC is often preferred for low-latency workloads), and pause time goals must be calibrated in accordance with Mule runtime expectations and deployment environment constraints. Monitoring heap usage and GC pause metrics over time guides iterative refinement of these settings.

Advanced runtime tuning encompasses several Mule-specific configurations. Adjusting the `maxConcurrency` and `maxBufferSize` in HTTP connectors influences the degree of concurrent request handling and buffering behavior, directly impacting flow throughput and backpressure management. Similarly, the configuration of connection pools (e.g., in database and HTTP connectors) in terms of maximum active and idle connections prevents resource exhaustion and connection leaks. Fine-tuning retry policies and circuit breakers modifies system tolerance to transient failures without introducing cascading delays.

Leveraging Mule's asynchronous event-driven architecture facilitates decoupling of slow or blocking operations through queues and durable stores. Persistent queues ensure message durability and enable smoother handling of workload spikes, effectively controlling flow pressure. However, queue configurations require balancing throughput with latency since message persistence, especially with distributed queues, can introduce delays. Monitoring queue metrics like enqueue/dequeue rates, queue depth, and processing lag assists in optimizing these parameters.

Load distribution strategies, such as employing multiple, scaled Mule runtime instances behind load balancers, distribute processing load to maintain performance under high concurrency. Horizontal scaling paired with sticky sessions or session replication reduces contention and preserves stateful interactions. Additionally, the use of caching mechanisms, both within Mule (object stores, caching scopes) and at the infrastructure level (CDNs, distributed caches), reduces redundant processing and external calls, significantly improving flow responsiveness.

Profiling should be an iterative, continuous activity, integrating with CI/CD pipelines and monitoring frameworks for proactive performance management. Automated load testing and stress testing simulate production conditions and reveal latent performance issues before deployment. Synthetic monitoring, combined with real-time alerting on latency and error rate thresholds, enables rapid response to degradation.

The following configuration snippet illustrates tuning an HTTP request connector with adjusted concurrency, timeouts, and connection pool sizing:

```
<http:request-config name="HTTP_Request_Config" protocol="HTTPS"
    host="api.example.com" port="443">
    <http:connection maxConnections="100" maxIdleTime="60000" />
    <http:request-connection-timeout>5000</http:request-
    connection-timeout>
    <http:response-timeout>10000</http:response-timeout>
    <http:max-concurrency>50</http:max-concurrency>
    <reconnect freq="5000" count="3" />
</http:request-config>
```

In practice, tuning extends beyond connector configurations. DataWeave transformations merit optimization through pre-compilation and expression simplification, as complex operations can significantly contribute to CPU load and processing latency. Avoiding unnecessary payload copies and leveraging streaming capabilities during data manipulation reduces memory pressure.

Furthermore, the judicious use of persistent object stores versus in-memory caching impacts both scalability and fault tolerance. Persistent stores guarantee data survivability across application restarts but incur I/O overhead, while in-memory caching provides speed at the risk of data loss on failure. Understanding workload patterns informs selection and configuration of object store types and expiration policies.

Threading models within Mule can also affect performance. By default, Mule processes events synchronously in a single-threaded context per flow instance, but introducing asynchronous processing points-via Async scopes, queued message processors, or Scatter-Gather routing-can enhance concurrency. However, increased parallelism must be balanced against thread pool sizes, JVM heap constraints, and connector limitations to avoid thread contention and context-switching overhead.

Runtime logging levels constitute another performance consideration. Excessive logging at DEBUG or TRACE levels can induce significant overhead and I/O bottlenecks. It is advisable to maintain INFO or WARN levels during normal operations and use fine-grained logging selectively during profile-driven diagnostics.

Integration with the Java ecosystem allows Mule applications to benefit from JVM features such as Just-In-Time (JIT) compilation optimizations and native memory tracking. Profiling with native JVM tools helps correlate Mule-specific metrics with system-level resource behaviors, providing a holistic view of performance.

In distributed deployment scenarios, network latency and serialization costs between Mule runtime instances or external systems become non-negligible factors. Employing efficient serialization formats (e.g., binary formats instead of verbose JSON/XML when feasible), compressing messages, and minimizing network round-trips reduces cumulative delay. Additionally, considering Mule's SOA orchestration capabilities to minimize synchronous call chains helps prevent latency amplification.

Collectively, these profiling and tuning practices require a thorough understanding of both Mule's architecture and the deployed environment. Data-driven identification of bottlenecks, followed by precise resource allocation and tailored runtime parameter adjustments, forms the foundation of maintaining optimal Mule application performance under varied and challenging operational conditions.

7.3. Caching and State Management for Low Latency

Achieving low latency in modern distributed systems fundamentally depends on effective caching and state management strategies. The ever-increasing demand for real-time responsiveness, coupled with the massive growth of data and simultaneous users, necessitates architectures capable of delivering lightning-fast response times while balancing consistency and reliability. This balance is particularly challenging when systems span multiple geographic regions, data centers, or cloud services, where communication delays and partial failures are inherent.

Caching is the primary technique to reduce data access latency by storing frequently accessed or computationally expensive data closer to the point of use. The design of a cache layer involves choices regarding cache location, granularity, eviction policies, and coherence mechanisms.

Cache Location and Granularity Caches can be implemented at various levels: client-side, server-side, or in an intermediary layer such as Content Delivery Networks (CDNs). Client-side caches reduce round-trips to servers for frequently read data, although their use is limited by device memory constraints and security considerations. Server-side caches, often embedded within application servers or proximate databases, enable shared access and refresh control. Large-scale distributed applications increasingly leverage multi-tier caching hierarchies, where edge caches handle global user populations while centralized caches provide authoritative data.

Granularity can range from caching entire objects (e.g., database rows or JSON documents) to fragments (e.g., web page elements or computed query results). Fine-grained caching enables higher cache hit ratios and tailored updates but increases coherence complexity. Coarse-grained caching simplifies consistency management but may lead to stale or redundant data.

Cache Eviction Policies Given limited cache storage, eviction policies govern which entries are discarded to make room for new data. Common policies include Least Recently Used (LRU), Least Frequently Used (LFU), and time-to-live (TTL)-based expiration. Though simple, TTL offers a balance between freshness and performance, preventing indefinite staleness at the cost of suboptimal cache utilization. Adaptive policies that dynamically adjust eviction thresholds based on workload patterns can enhance cache efficiency.

Cache Coherence and Invalidation Maintaining cache coherence is critical to prevent stale or inconsistent data from degrading system correctness. Coherence strategies vary by application requirements and available infrastructure:

- *Write-through Caches*: Synchronously propagate all writes to the backing store. This approach simplifies coherence but adds write latency.

- *Write-back Caches*: Accumulate writes locally and persist in batches. This reduces write latency but risks data loss on failure and complicates consistency.

- *Cache Invalidation*: Explicitly invalidate cache entries when upstream data changes, either via push notifications or polling mechanisms.

Real-time invalidation ensures data freshness but increases communication overhead and complexity. In contrast, periodic refresh reduces overhead but allows transient staleness. Applications with stringent consistency demands often lean towards strong coherence protocols, while those prioritizing speed may accept eventual consistency.

Distributed in-memory data grids (IMDGs) provide scalable, high-throughput, and low-latency data storage by distributing state across clusters of nodes, typically using RAM rather than disk. IMDGs combine caching with distributed data structures and processing capabilities, offering rich APIs, transactional support, and event-driven mechanisms.

Key characteristics of IMDGs include:

- *Partitioning and Replication*: Data is partitioned to distribute storage and computation load, while replication ensures availability and fault tolerance.

- *Consistency Models*: Support ranges from strong consistency (linearizability) to eventual consistency, configurable per application needs.

- *Elasticity*: Capability to dynamically add or remove nodes, balancing load and maintaining state synchronization.

- *Query and Processing*: Integration of SQL-like querying, continuous queries, and distributed computing frameworks (e.g., MapReduce, streaming).

By co-locating state and computation within memory on multiple nodes, IMDGs dramatically reduce network hops and disk I/O latency. Applications such as session management, real-time analytics, and transaction processing benefit from this approach. However, operational complexity increases: the system must address partition tolerance, node failures, and consistency trade-offs.

In systems that require globally consistent and available state, distributed state management frameworks and consensus protocols play a pivotal role. Common patterns to manage distributed state with low latency involve:

Consensus Protocols Protocols like Paxos, Raft, and Zab underpin consistent replication across nodes by ensuring a majority of replicas agree on the order and content of updates. Although these protocols guarantee strong consistency, their latency depends on the number of participating nodes and failure conditions. Practical deployments often optimize leader election, batching, and pipelining to reduce latency.

Conflict-free Replicated Data Types (CRDTs) CRDTs enable low-latency, eventually consistent updates by allowing concurrent modifications and automatic conflict resolution without coordination. These data types (e.g., counters, sets, maps) propagate changes asynchronously, which suits geo-distributed applications where immediate consistency is impossible or too expensive.

Stateful Stream Processing Modern stream processing engines incorporate state management by checkpointing operator state with durable storage and recovering from failures. State is partitioned and local to processing tasks, minimizing latency for time-critical operations. Integration with external state stores (e.g., key-value databases, IMDGs) expands scalability and fault tolerance.

Transactional State Stores To balance speed and correctness, some systems implement highly optimized, distributed transactional stores supporting ACID semantics. Leveraging techniques such as multi-version concurrency control (MVCC), lightweight locking, and hardware acceleration, these stores minimize latency impacts of locking and validation.

The interplay between consistency, speed, and reliability defines the choice of caching and state management techniques. The Brewer's CAP theorem asserts that in presence of network partitions, systems can only guarantee two of Consistency, Availability, or Partition tolerance simultaneously. Thus, practical systems select a balance tailored to application semantics.

Strong Consistency with High Latency Guaranteeing strong consistency typically incurs blocking during write operations, higher coordination overhead, and increased failure recovery costs. Write-through caching, synchronous replication, and consensus protocols impose additional latencies but are essential for financial, inventory, or mission-critical applications.

Eventual Consistency for High Availability and Speed Accepting eventual consistency enables cheaper coordination through asynchronous replication and local writes. This allows caches and data grids to respond quickly at the cost of temporary data divergence. Use cases suited to this model include social feeds, user preference caching, and telemetry.

Hybrid and Tunable Consistency Modern distributed systems increasingly offer tunable consistency levels, allowing developers to dynamically select per operation or data type the appropriate consistency guarantee. For instance, read-your-writes consistency ensures a client always sees their latest writes, while other reads may be stale but fast. This nuanced layering mitigates latency without sacrificing correctness where it is critical.

Trade-offs in Reliability Caching and in-memory solutions inherently introduce volatility risk: data stored in RAM can be lost on node failure. Replication and persistent checkpoints mitigate this risk but introduce write amplification and latency costs. Balancing durability guarantees with latency objectives is a core design challenge, often addressed by multi-tier architectures wherein ephemeral caches accelerate reads backed by durable stores.

Industry implementations illustrate the complexity of these trade-offs. For example, large-scale e-commerce platforms employ edge caches for static content delivery and session caches backed by in-memory grids, combining TTL-based invalidation with persistent database synchronization. Real-time bidding systems in advertising maintain distributed state using CRDT-based counters to reconcile bids at microsecond speeds. Financial trading platforms require strong consistency on trades and positions, leveraging consensus protocols and transaction logs optimized for low latency.

```
public class WriteThroughCache<K, V> {
    private final Map<K, V> cache = new ConcurrentHashMap<>();
    private final DataStore<K, V> backingStore;

    public WriteThroughCache(DataStore<K, V> store) {
        this.backingStore = store;
    }

    public V get(K key) {
        return cache.computeIfAbsent(key, k -> backingStore.read(
    k));
    }

    public void put(K key, V value) {
        backingStore.write(key, value);
        cache.put(key, value);
    }

    public void invalidate(K key) {
        cache.remove(key);
    }
}
```

This straightforward design writes data synchronously to the backing store, ensuring consistency at the cost of increased write latency. Cache invalidation can be triggered by notifications or time-based policies to keep data fresh.

The following considerations guide the deployment of caching and distributed state management:

- **Access Patterns**: Read-heavy workloads benefit more from caching, while write-heavy systems may require more sophisticated invalidation and consistency controls.

- **Latency Budgets**: Applications with stringent latency targets may favor eventual consistency and replicate state locally, accepting complexity in conflict resolution.

- **Fault Model**: Tolerance to node failures influences replication factor and checkpointing frequency, impacting latency.

- **Data Freshness Requirements**: The tolerance for stale data mitigates the need for strict coherence.

- **Operational Complexity**: Systems requiring minimal operational overhead may prefer simpler caching layers to complex distributed state stores.

Understanding these dimensions allows architects to tailor caching and state management approaches, optimizing real-world systems for rapid responsiveness without compromising correctness and availability.

7.4. Monitoring, Telemetry, and Distributed Tracing

Complex integration landscapes, characterized by heterogeneous systems, microservices, and dynamic infrastructures, demand a rigorous approach to observability-one that extends well beyond traditional monitoring. The modern paradigm for mastering observability rests on three intertwined pillars: comprehensive monitoring, standardized telemetry data collection through frameworks such as OpenTelemetry, and distributed tracing. Together, these techniques enable rapid diagnostics, root cause analysis, and proactive incident prevention, forming the backbone for operational excellence in contemporary software ecosystems.

Advanced Monitoring in Multi-Component Environments

Monitoring in complex integration scenarios requires capturing multidimensional data from disparate sources including applications, infrastructure, middleware, and network components. Traditional monitoring paradigms-primarily reliant on static thresholds and periodic health checks-are insufficient in environments where dynamic scaling, ephemeral instances, and asynchronous communication abound.

Key to advanced monitoring is the adoption of metric aggregation with rich dimensionality and contextual tagging. Time series data collected from components such as CPU utilization, memory usage, request latency, error rates, and custom business metrics must be enriched with metadata (e.g., service version, deployment zone, instance identifiers). This indexing enables flexible querying and correlation across services. Additionally, the incorporation of health status and event logs alongside metrics allows for a more holistic understanding of system behavior.

Adaptive alerting mechanisms based on anomaly detection, machine learning models, or baseline deviations supplant rigid threshold alerts, mitigating alert fatigue and improving signal-to-noise ratio. Techniques such as dynamic baselining inspect metric patterns in real-time and generate alerts when statistically significant anomalies occur. Monitoring frameworks must support high cardinality data without compromising performance, ensuring scalability across hundreds or thousands of services.

OpenTelemetry: The Standard for Telemetry Instrumentation

OpenTelemetry has emerged as the de facto open-source standard for instrumenting, generating, collecting, and exporting telemetry data in distributed systems. It consolidates the functionality of multiple legacy projects into a unified, vendor-neutral framework, supporting three primary data sources: metrics, logs, and traces.

At its core, OpenTelemetry provides language-specific SDKs and APIs for seamless instrumentation of code, as well as auto-instrumentation agents that minimize manual overhead. This unification fosters interoperability and prevents vendor lock-in by decoupling data collection from backend storage and analysis systems.

The telemetry data captured by OpenTelemetry follows standardized semantic conventions, ensuring consistent attribute naming, span relationships, and metric labels across heterogeneous services. This common vocabulary is critical in complex landscapes where services may evolve independently or be sourced from multiple teams and vendors.

A typical OpenTelemetry pipeline consists of the following components:

1. **Instrumentation:** Automatic or manual code-level hooks capture runtime events, metric increments, and trace spans.

2. **Collection:** SDKs or agents aggregate telemetry data locally, often performing batching, sampling, and buffering to optimize throughput.

3. **Export:** Telemetry is transmitted to backends using protocols such as OTLP (OpenTelemetry Protocol), enabling downstream analysis.

Effective use of OpenTelemetry requires configuring adaptive sampling strategies. Sampling balances fidelity and overhead by selecting a representative subset of traces and metrics for export. Tail-based sampling, which evaluates traces after initial collection, allows focusing on anomalous or error-prone requests, enhancing the efficiency of observability pipelines.

The integration of OpenTelemetry across services encourages a composable telemetry ecosystem where multiple observability tools and databases can be employed simultaneously-a concept known as telemetry federation. This architecture facilitates redundancy, longitudinal analysis, and multi-tenant service monitoring within complex organizational structures.

Enabling Distributed Tracing for Cross-Service Visibility

Distributed tracing extends observability by reconstructing the end-to-end flow of individual requests as they propagate through interconnected services. This approach addresses the limitations of isolated metrics and logs, which often provide only partial insights into complex workflows.

A trace is composed of spans that represent timed operations within services, including RPC calls, database queries, or internal processing steps. Each span contains context identifiers such as trace ID, span ID, parent span ID, timestamp, duration, tags, and logs. Distributed tracing propagates this context across process and network boundaries, enabling the reconstruction of causal relationships.

Tracing aids in several crucial operational tasks:

- **Latency Breakdown:** Pinpointing slow components within a chain of service invocations clarifies latency contributors, guiding optimization efforts.

- **Error Attribution:** Identifying the precise service and operation responsible for failures enables rapid root cause analysis.

- **Bottleneck Detection:** Visual patterns of traces highlight bottlenecks caused by resource contention, synchronous waits, or repeated retries.

- **Service Dependency Mapping:** Tracing data facilitates automated topologies depicting real-time dependencies, critical for understanding systemic impacts of failures.

Implementing distributed tracing mandates meticulous context propagation at every network call boundary. This is frequently achieved via standardized headers, such as W3C Trace Context, carried along HTTP, messaging, or gRPC transports. Middleware and proxies must be configured or instrumented to preserve and forward these headers correctly to avoid trace fragmentation.

The volume and granularity of trace data necessitate efficient storage and visualization platforms that support filtering, aggregation, and query capabilities. Advanced tracing backends apply indexing on attributes such as service names, operation types, and error codes to rapidly surface relevant traces during incidents.

Synergies Between Monitoring, Telemetry, and Tracing

While monitoring provides continuous health signals and anomaly detection, telemetry standardization via OpenTelemetry enables interoperability and large-scale data aggregation, and distributed tracing furnishes causal request-level insight. The synergy of these elements is essential in modern integration landscapes to achieve actionable observability.

For example, an anomalous spike detected by a monitoring system can trigger queries for recent traces tied to the impacted service or operation. Combined with contextual logs, this enables teams to interpret the anomaly's origin in the context of complex workflows. Similarly, metrics derived from tracing data can feed back into adaptive alerting thresholds, creating a virtuous cycle of observability refinement.

Furthermore, the integration of telemetry with incident management and automated remediation systems allows predictive and preventive actions. Patterns extracted from historical traces and metrics can identify early signals of cascading failures, enabling throttling, failover, or resource scaling preemptively.

Challenges and Best Practices

Navigating observability within complex integration ecosystems presents security, privacy, and performance challenges. Telemetry data often includes sensitive information embedded in traces or logs, requiring strict access controls, data masking, and compliance adherence throughout the observability pipeline.

Performance overhead induced by instrumentation must be minimized to avoid perturbing system behavior. This involves selective instrumentation, sampling strategies, and lightweight SDK implementations. Ensuring consistent tracing context propagation across heterogeneous frameworks and languages often requires customized instrumentation bridges and cross-team collaboration.

Best practices include:

- Embedding observability requirements into design and development lifecycles, not as afterthoughts.

- Adopting open standards such as OpenTelemetry for future-proof instrumentation and vendor flexibility.

- Implementing unified telemetry storage architectures capable of multi-modal data handling.

- Leveraging correlation identifiers ubiquitously to bridge metrics, logs, and traces.

- Regularly reviewing monitoring rules and sampling policies to balance visibility and resource consumption.

Examples of OpenTelemetry Instrumentation

217

The following code snippet illustrates a minimal example of manually instrumenting a Python HTTP server with OpenTelemetry for tracing and metrics collection.

```python
from opentelemetry import trace, metrics
from opentelemetry.sdk.resources import Resource
from opentelemetry.sdk.trace import TracerProvider
from opentelemetry.sdk.metrics import MeterProvider
from opentelemetry.sdk.trace.export import BatchSpanProcessor,
    ConsoleSpanExporter
from opentelemetry.sdk.metrics.export import
    ConsoleMetricExporter, PeriodicExportingMetricReader
from opentelemetry.instrumentation.flask import FlaskInstrumentor
from flask import Flask, request

# Resource attributes to identify service
resource = Resource(attributes={
    "service.name": "order-service",
    "service.version": "1.2.3"
})

trace.set_tracer_provider(TracerProvider(resource=resource))
tracer = trace.get_tracer(__name__)

span_processor = BatchSpanProcessor(ConsoleSpanExporter())
trace.get_tracer_provider().add_span_processor(span_processor)

metrics.set_meter_provider(MeterProvider(resource=resource))
meter = metrics.get_meter(__name__)
metric_exporter = ConsoleMetricExporter()
metric_reader = PeriodicExportingMetricReader(metric_exporter)
metrics.get_meter_provider().register_metric_reader(metric_reader
    )

request_counter = meter.create_counter(
    "http_requests_total", description="Total HTTP requests"
)

app = Flask(__name__)
FlaskInstrumentor().instrument_app(app)

@app.route("/orders", methods=["POST"])
def create_order():
    with tracer.start_as_current_span("create_order"):
        request_counter.add(1, {"method": "POST", "endpoint": "/
        orders"})
        # business logic processing here
        return "Order created", 201

if __name__ == "__main__":
    app.run(port=8080)
```

The instrumentation above integrates both tracing and metrics within a Flask application. The spans generated allow visibility into request handling latency and behavior, while the counter metric aggregates the total number of HTTP calls. This data, when exported to suitable backends, enables comprehensive observability and facilitates downstream analysis.

Visualization and Analysis

The observability data collected through monitoring, telemetry, and tracing must be ingested into platforms capable of real-time correlation and visualization. Tools such as Jaeger, Zipkin, Prometheus, and Grafana support trace viewing, metric alerting, and multi-dimensional dashboards.

Distributed tracing visualizes trace trees identifying service calls and execution timelines:

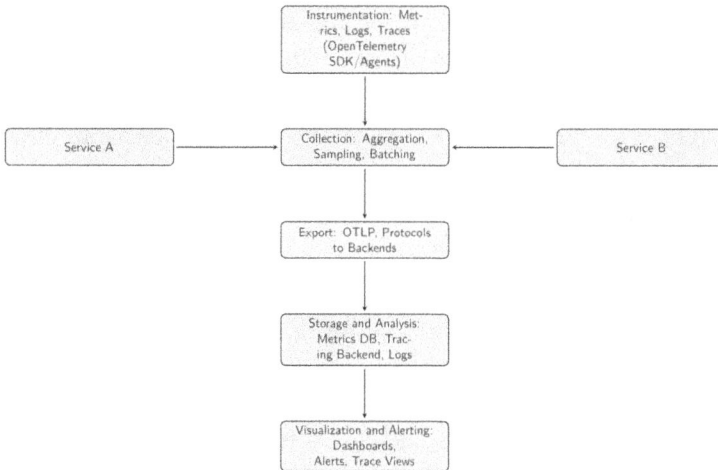

Correlating this visualization with metrics and logs aids in pinpointing latency hotspots and error propagation paths essential for root cause analysis.

Mastering observability in complex integration environments requires a systematic approach combining adaptive monitoring, standardized telemetry collection through OpenTelemetry, and trace-driven diagnostics. These capabilities empower engineering teams to maintain high availability, reduce mean time to resolution, and proactively manage system health in fast-evolving distributed architectures.

7.5. Resilience and Fault Tolerance Patterns

Modern distributed systems face numerous challenges stemming from network unreliability, service failures, resource exhaustion, and cascading errors. Ensuring that applications continue to operate gracefully in the presence of such faults requires deliberate engineering grounded in resilience and fault tolerance. Several well-established design patterns underpin self-healing architectures, offering systematic means to detect, contain, and recover from failures. Among the most prominent are circuit breakers, retries, bulkheads, and fallback logic. These patterns enable integration flows to degrade gracefully, maintaining functionality and user experience even under duress.

Circuit Breakers

The circuit breaker pattern is derived from electrical engineering principles, adapted to software communication pathways. Its primary function is to prevent an application from repeatedly invoking requests to a downstream service that is currently failing or exhibiting high latency, thereby avoiding wasted resources and potential cascading failures.

Conceptually, a circuit breaker maintains state in one of three modes: *closed*, *open*, or *half-open*. In the closed state, calls to the service proceed normally. Upon detecting a threshold of failures-such as a configured number of consecutive errors or a failure rate over a sliding window-the circuit transitions to the open state, where further calls are immediately failed or short-circuited without invoking the downstream service. After a timeout, the breaker enters the half-open state, allowing a limited number of test requests to determine if the service has recovered. Successes during this period heal the breaker back to the closed state, while failures return it to open, ensuring the system does not prematurely resume operations against a still-unhealthy service.

Effective implementation requires careful tuning of thresholds and time intervals. Too sensitive settings may lead to unnecessary failfast behavior, while overly lax configurations risk exacerbating cascading failures. The circuit breaker also serves as an essential component in overall system observability, signaling systemic degradation.

Retries

Retries represent a fundamental error recovery approach, attempting to mitigate transient faults by reissuing failed requests. In distributed environments, many errors-such as intermittent network failures, temporary rate limiting, or resource throttling-are nonpermanent and resolvable after short delays.

However, retries carry risks if not implemented judiciously. Blind, instant retries can amplify system load and provoke resource exhaustion, particularly during already strained conditions. Introducing exponential backoff, jitter, or capped retry counts modulates retry behavior, balancing responsiveness against the need to avoid overload. Exponential backoff increases the delay between attempts, typically doubling the wait time after each failure, while jitter randomizes retry patterns to prevent synchronized retries from multiple clients. Rate limiting the frequency of retry attempts prevents excessive pressure on recovering services.

Retries are especially effective when combined with circuit breakers; if the circuit is open, retries can be suspended to avoid futile attempts. Furthermore, retries should respect idempotency constraints, since non-idempotent operations may yield incorrect states on repeated invocation.

Bulkheads

Inspired by shipbuilding, the bulkhead pattern partitions a system's resources into isolated compartments, preventing failures in one from propagating to others. Within software architectures, this translates to segregating critical components, connections, or resource pools.

Common implementations include dedicating bounded thread pools, connection pools, or processing queues for particular external dependencies or service types. By isolating resource consumption per integration flow or feature domain, bulkheads ensure that overload or failure in one segment does not cause widespread exhaustion.

For example, if a slow or failing downstream service monopolizes all available threads or connections, bulkheads prevent this exhaustion from impacting unrelated service calls, preserving availability and responsiveness elsewhere. A well-architected system provides appropriately sized bulkheads based on workload characteristics and priority, allowing graceful degradation of lower-impact functions under heavy stress while preserving critical paths.

The bulkhead approach encourages robust resource accounting, actively monitoring utilization to trigger preventive measures before depletion. It is particularly valuable in microservices or polyglot stacks where varied dependencies exhibit diverse reliability and performance profiles.

Fallback Logic

Fallback logic complements detection and containment patterns by specifying alternative execution paths when primary interactions fail. These alternatives may range from serving cached or stale data, invoking secondary or degraded service implementations, to returning default responses expressly designed to maintain partial functionality.

Fallback strategies differ depending on domain semantics and integration context. For example, an e-commerce checkout service may provide a simplified offline mode if the payment gateway is unreachable, whereas a recommendation engine may fall back to basic popularity-based suggestions if personalized data retrieval times out.

Incorporating fallback logic requires explicit design of acceptable degraded behaviors, error classification, and functional requirements under failure conditions. This often necessitates comprehensive domain knowledge and close collaboration between system designers and business stakeholders to ensure fallbacks maintain user trust and avoid data corruption.

From an implementation perspective, fallback logic is tightly coupled with circuit breakers and retries. When the breaker opens or retries are exhausted, fallback logic supplies controlled and predictable responses rather than unbounded error propagation.

Engineering Integration Flows for Resilience

Combining these patterns enables construction of integration flows with multi-layered defense mechanisms against faults. A typical resilient flow begins by enclosing critical outbound calls in a circuit breaker, backed by retries with carefully designed backoff and jitter. Each external dependency is isolated behind bulkheads to safeguard resource partitioning. Upon exhaustive failure detection, fallback logic activates to provide controlled alternatives.

For example, a RESTful client service calling an external search API might apply the following architecture:

- *Retry policy*: On transient HTTP 429 (Too Many Requests) or 503 (Service Unavailable) status codes, retry with exponential backoff capped at a maximum number of attempts.

- *Circuit breaker*: Transition to open upon a configurable failure ratio threshold within a time window, short-circuiting subsequent requests and thus reducing pressure.

- *Bulkhead*: Use dedicated connection pools and thread pools per external service, preventing resource starvation due to upstream slowness.

- *Fallback*: When the breaker is open or retries fail, serve cached results or return minimal placeholder data to maintain user experience.

This layered approach provides both preventative and corrective capabilities, significantly improving system availability under adverse conditions. Instrumentation and monitoring of each pattern's health indicators enable adaptive tuning and incident diagnosis.

Interaction Considerations and Caveats

While each pattern offers significant benefits, their combined deployment carries complexity. For instance, retries with aggressive backoff absent a circuit breaker can exacerbate outages, as failing calls pile up. Bulkheads need capacity estimation to avoid underutilization or wasting resources. Fallback correctness hinges on understanding data staleness, eventual consistency implications, and business logic constraints.

Moreover, resilience patterns do not obviate the need for thorough fault injection testing and chaos engineering. Validation under realistic failure scenarios is essential to uncover emergent issues such as deadlocks, resource leaks, or incorrect state transitions.

Integration flows designed for resilience also require clear visibility into state transitions-for example, exposing circuit breaker status and retry attempts through metrics and health endpoints. This enables effective incident management and informed automatic scaling or throttling.

Summary of Pattern Benefits

- **Circuit Breakers**: Reduce cascading failures by fast failing calls to unresponsive services.

- **Retries**: Mitigate transient faults with controlled repeated attempts.

- **Bulkheads**: Contain resource exhaustion by isolating integration paths.

- **Fallback Logic**: Allow graceful degradation with alternative responses.

Together, these patterns enable robust, fault-tolerant integration flows with predictable behaviors under failure, increasing overall reliability and user satisfaction. Their careful orchestration in system architecture forms the foundation of self-healing distributed applications.

7.6. Global Exception Handling and Diagnostics

Robust and centralized error management is fundamental to ensuring platform stability, maintainability, and operational insight. Achieving an effective global exception handling strategy involves unifying disparate sources of runtime errors, enabling coherent propagation paths, and integrating comprehensive diagnostic capabilities that facilitate rapid fault isolation and recovery. This approach mitigates the risks associated with uncaught exceptions, disparate error semantics, and fragmented logging, which are common obstacles in complex, distributed systems.

At the core of global exception handling is the concept of a *cross-cutting concern* that transcends the individual components, modules, or services comprising the platform. Rather than embedding localized error handling ad hoc within each segment, a centralized mechanism intercepts and processes exceptional conditions consistently across the entire application landscape. This unification promotes uniform error classification, systematic remediation workflows, and structured health monitoring.

Architectural Principles for Centralized Exception Management

Centralized exception handling necessitates a design that integrates at multiple layers:

- **Middleware-level interception**: Application frameworks supporting middleware pipelines provide natural interception points such as HTTP request handlers, message bus consumers, or RPC endpoints where exceptions can be caught globally. Middleware enforces global policies on error logging, response shaping, and downstream notification.

- **Asynchronous boundary management**: Many modern architectures employ asynchronous programming models. Integrating global exception handlers with task schedulers, futures/promises, or reactive streams is essential to avoid silent failures and to propagate errors back into the global handling chain.

- **Domain-specific exceptions mapping**: A hierarchy of domain exceptions defined in the platform enables semantic consistency. Global handlers interpret these mapped exceptions to decide on retry strategies, user-visible error messages, or escalation procedures.

- **Fail-fast and fallback strategies**: Central management allows classification of exceptions into recoverable and non-

226

recoverable categories, enabling targeted fail-fast tactics or graceful degradation through fallback components.

Exception Propagation and Handling Patterns

Exception propagation should follow predictable and documented paths to maintain transparency and traceability. Common established patterns include:

- **Bubble-up propagation**: Exceptions percolate upward from the lowest level where they originate until caught and processed by the global handler. This preserves the original context while minimizing localized catch blocks.

- **Exception wrapping**: When crossing subsystem boundaries, exceptions are transformed or wrapped into domain-specific exceptions preserving critical metadata such as error codes, correlation identifiers, or root causes.

- **Exception translation**: Translating low-level errors (e.g., database timeouts, network failures) into high-level domain errors standardizes the error semantics exposed to the rest of the platform and end users.

Implementation of Centralized Handlers

Consider an event-driven platform implemented in a language with native exception support, such as Java or C#. A typical global handler can be implemented as a middleware component that:

```
public class GlobalExceptionMiddleware
{
    private readonly RequestDelegate _next;
    private readonly ILogger<GlobalExceptionMiddleware> _logger;

    public GlobalExceptionMiddleware(RequestDelegate next,
     ILogger<GlobalExceptionMiddleware> logger)
    {
        _next = next;
        _logger = logger;
    }
```

227

```
public async Task InvokeAsync(HttpContext context)
{
    try
    {
        await _next(context);
    }
    catch (Exception ex)
    {
        await HandleExceptionAsync(context, ex);
    }
}

private Task HandleExceptionAsync(HttpContext context,
 Exception exception)
{
    var correlationId = GetCorrelationId(context);
    var errorDetails = MapExceptionToErrorResponse(exception,
  correlationId);

    _logger.LogError(exception, "Unhandled exception occurred
. CorrelationId: {CorrelationId}", correlationId);

    context.Response.ContentType = "application/json";
    context.Response.StatusCode = errorDetails.StatusCode;

    return context.Response.WriteAsync(System.Text.Json.
JsonSerializer.Serialize(errorDetails));
}

private string GetCorrelationId(HttpContext context)
{
    // Extract or generate correlation ID for tracing
    if (context.Request.Headers.TryGetValue("X-Correlation-ID
", out var correlationId))
    {
        return correlationId;
    }
    return Guid.NewGuid().ToString();
}

private ErrorResponse MapExceptionToErrorResponse(Exception
 ex, string correlationId)
{
    // Map to domain-aware and client-appropriate error
 responses
    if (ex is ValidationException validationEx)
    {
        return new ErrorResponse
        {
            StatusCode = StatusCodes.Status400BadRequest,
            Message = validationEx.Message,
```

```
                    CorrelationId = correlationId
            };
        }
        return new ErrorResponse
        {
            StatusCode = StatusCodes.Status500InternalServerError
        ,
            Message = "An unexpected error occurred.",
            CorrelationId = correlationId
        };
    }

    private class ErrorResponse
    {
        public int StatusCode { get; set; }
        public string Message { get; set; }
        public string CorrelationId { get; set; }
    }
}
```

This middleware pattern enables all uncaught exceptions to be logged with a unique correlation ID, converted into a structured error response, and propagated appropriately to the client or upstream consumers. The correlation ID provides an essential linkage for tracing the error journey across distributed components.

Actionable Diagnostics and Health Reporting

Global exception handling extends naturally into diagnostics and health reporting, transforming raw exception data into actionable insights used by monitoring and alerting systems. Four essential facets are:

- **Structured error logging**: Employ structured logs with consistent fields such as timestamps, correlation IDs, error types, stack traces, and contextual metadata. These logs are more amenable to ingestion by log aggregators and analytics platforms.

- **Error classification and aggregation**: Grouping exceptions by root cause or component allows identification of systemic issues or frequently recurring faults, enabling prioritized remediation.

- **Metrics and alerting**: Instrumentation exposes exception rates, error categories, and failure latencies as metrics. Threshold-based alerts on these metrics drive rapid response to emerging incidents.

- **Health checks integration**: Embedding exception status data into health check endpoints reports service health in real-time, supporting automated orchestration and failover decisions.

Correlation and Context Propagation

Successful diagnostics depend on preserving a continuity of context across asynchronous calls and distributed transactions. Implementations typically propagate correlation IDs or tracing headers through service calls, message queues, and logs. The industry standard OpenTelemetry specification facilitates injecting and extracting tracing information across platform boundaries. This propagation allows reconstruction of failure scenarios spanning multiple services and time periods.

Recovery and Resilience Considerations

Error handling and diagnostics are tightly coupled with recovery mechanisms:

- **Retry policies**: Differentiation between transient and permanent exceptions guides configurable automatic retries with exponential backoff, jitter, or circuit breakers.

- **Bulkhead isolation**: Exceptions triggering degradation in one subsystem do not cascade; that is isolated via resource or execution boundary containment strategies.

- **Fallback implementations**: Alternative code paths (e.g., default responses, cached data) maintain partial system availability during component failures.

Integrating these recovery patterns within the centralized exception management framework enhances fault tolerance without scattering recovery code across the platform.

Cross-cutting Tooling and Framework Support

Modern development ecosystems provide tools and frameworks to simplify global exception handling and diagnostics:

- **Logging frameworks**: Libraries such as Serilog, Log4j, or NLog enable structured, extensible logging pipelines.

- **Monitoring platforms**: Prometheus, Grafana, ELK stack, and commercial APMs ingest logs and metrics for visualization and alerting.

- **Tracing libraries**: OpenTelemetry SDKs provide standardized tracing and context propagation capabilities.

- **Error reporting services**: Platforms like Sentry or Rollbar capture detailed exception data along with breadcrumbs and user interactions.

Alignment with these standardized tools permits seamless operational visibility and reduced implementation effort.

Summary of Best Practices

- Define a comprehensive exception hierarchy reflecting platform-specific domain errors.

- Establish global middleware or listener components that catch and process every unhandled exception.

- Use correlation identifiers consistently for end-to-end traceability.

- Emit structured logs and enrich error data with contextual metadata.

- Integrate exception metrics and error states into health checks and observability pipelines.

- Differentiate error types for targeted retry, fail-fast, or fall-back mechanisms.

- Employ external monitoring and tracing frameworks aligned with open standards.

Adhering to these principles ensures error handling is not merely reactive but a proactive foundation supporting platform resilience, operational insight, and maintainability in complex software ecosystems.

Chapter 8

DevOps, Automation, and Continuous Delivery

High-performing integration teams don't just build APIs—they automate, orchestrate, and deliver them with speed and confidence. This chapter is your blueprint for applying DevOps principles in the MuleSoft ecosystem, revealing how to streamline workflows, enforce quality, and achieve continuous integration and delivery at scale. Explore the intersection of infrastructure-as-code, pipeline automation, and operational excellence to transform how your integration solutions evolve and run in production.

8.1. Infrastructure as Code for Integration Platforms

The evolution of integration platforms toward cloud-native and hybrid architectures necessitates automated, consistent, and auditable environment management. Infrastructure as Code (IaC) emerges as a critical paradigm to address these needs by codifying environment provisioning and configuration into declarative, version-controlled artifacts. Within the context of MuleSoft's Anypoint Platform, IaC enables seamless orchestration of deployment topologies and runtime environments, ensuring repeatability and scalability across complex integration landscapes.

IaC leverages tools that transform environment definitions-ranging from cloud infrastructure to platform-specific resources-into machine-interpretable templates. This approach eliminates manual steps prone to error and drift, fosters transparency through version control, and supports Continuous Integration/Continuous Deployment (CI/CD) pipelines for accelerated delivery cycles. For MuleSoft environments, adopting IaC optimizes the management of Anypoint Runtime Manager configurations, API gateway policies, application deployment targets, and associated platform artifacts.

Terraform for MuleSoft Environment Automation

Terraform, a widely used open-source IaC tool developed by HashiCorp, provides a declarative language and execution engine to manage infrastructure across multiple service providers. Its extensibility through providers makes it possible to automate resources both in cloud infrastructures (such as AWS, Azure, or Google Cloud) and within MuleSoft platform components.

The Anypoint Terraform Provider acts as an interface to the MuleSoft Anypoint Platform APIs, allowing programmatic control over key entities including environments, applications, policies, and

234

connectors. Utilizing Terraform to define these platform elements as code allows for the encapsulation of configuration logic, simplifying promotion and replication of environments from development to production.

A fundamental building block in Terraform is the `resource`, which represents a manageable entity. For example, creating an Anypoint environment involves declaring an `anypoint_environment` resource with pertinent attributes such as organization ID and environment label:

```
resource "anypoint_environment" "dev" {
  organization_id = var.organization_id
  label           = "Development"
  name            = "dev"
}
```

In addition to environment creation, Terraform supports the deployment of Mule applications via the `anypoint_application` resource. This resource defines parameters such as the application name, runtime version, target environment, and deployment configurations, encapsulating complex deployment steps into repeatable recipes:

```
resource "anypoint_application" "app" {
  name            = "order-service"
  region          = "us-east-1"
  runtime_version = "4.4.0"
  environment_id  = anypoint_environment.dev.id
  worker_size     = "Medium"
  workers         = 2
  file            = "${path.module}/order-service-mule-app.zip"
}
```

Terraform's modularity further facilitates environment reuse and parameterization, enabling teams to build composable templates that accommodate varying requirements across projects or organizations. State management ensures synchronization between the declared infrastructure and actual platform state, allowing Terraform to detect drifts and enforce consistency.

Beyond basic resource provisioning, Terraform allows for embedding lifecycle rules, dependency graphs, and data sources. This capability is especially valuable in integration platforms where dependencies between APIs, shared resources, and gateways are common. Templates can include variable-driven policy attachments to APIs, ensuring security and governance policies propagate alongside application deployments.

Anypoint CLI and Automation Scripting

Alongside Terraform, the Anypoint Command Line Interface (CLI) provides programmatic control for Anypoint Platform management within automation workflows. The CLI enables scripting of environment interactions, providing granular control of platform artifacts difficult to express declaratively in Terraform.

Using Anypoint CLI, administrators and DevOps teams can automate tasks such as environment creation, organization management, API deployment, and runtime diagnostics directly from command scripts or CI/CD pipelines. For example, to deploy a Mule application to a specified environment, a typical CLI command sequence includes login, selection of the target environment, and deployment invocation:

```
anypoint-cli login --username user@example.com --password
    ********
anypoint-cli select environment dev
anypoint-cli runtime-mgr deploy --file ./order-service-mule-app.
    zip --name order-service
```

The CLI's integration with scripting environments allows conditional execution, parameter handling, and output parsing, which are fundamental for building automated release pipelines and compliance checks. When combined with Terraform, the CLI complements declarative specifications by providing operational commands to address dynamic aspects such as artifact promotion or runtime adjustments.

Repeatability, Auditability, and Scalability

IaC's core advantages for MuleSoft integration platform management are manifest in the properties of repeatability, auditability, and scalability. Repeatability is ensured by codifying the entirety of environment setup into version-controlled templates or scripts. This guarantees identical environment states upon each application of the code, eradicating configuration drift and environment inconsistencies that often cause regressions or failures.

Auditability is provided through the combined use of source control and execution logs from IaC tools. Every change to environment configurations, policy applications, or deployment parameters passes through code review processes, with a persistent trace of modifications and rollbacks. This aligns with governance frameworks requiring change management and traceability for critical integration deployments.

Scalability is addressed by the inherent automation and modularity of IaC constructs. Environments can be provisioned on-demand or replicated rapidly to accommodate workload peaks, new project onboarding, or cross-geographical deployments. Terraform's infrastructure graph enables parallelized resource creation where dependencies allow, enhancing speed and efficiency. Moreover, parameterization of environment attributes supports templated environment variants, catering to different deployment profiles-development, testing, staging, and production.

When integrated with orchestration layers such as Jenkins, GitLab CI/CD, or Azure DevOps pipelines, MuleSoft platform IaC methodologies enable fully automated deployment lifecycles. Validation, compliance enforcement, and rollback procedures can be encoded as pipeline stages, transforming environment and application management into a seamless part of the software delivery process.

Best Practices and Considerations

- **State Management:** Managing Terraform state securely and consistently is crucial to prevent corruption or unauthorized alterations. Remote state backends with encryption, locking, and versioning (e.g., Terraform Cloud, S3 with DynamoDB locking) are recommended to enable team collaboration.

- **Credentials and Secrets:** Sensitive data such as Anypoint access credentials and API tokens must be integrated securely, leveraging secrets management tools or environment variables rather than hardcoding within IaC files.

- **Modularization:** Structure reusable components as Terraform modules or CLI script libraries encapsulating common deployment patterns to avoid duplication and improve maintainability.

- **Testing and Validation:** Employ automated validation tools (e.g., `terraform validate` and `terraform plan`), along with platform API readiness checks to detect misconfigurations before applying changes.

- **Version Synchronization:** Coordinate Mule runtime, connector versions, and Anypoint platform template versions in IaC artifacts to avoid incompatibility issues during deployment.

- **Resource Dependencies:** Explicitly declare dependencies between resources to ensure ordered provisioning, particularly when policies or API gateways depend on underlying applications or environment configurations.

Infrastructure as Code practices, realized through Terraform and Anypoint CLI, provide a robust framework for automating MuleSoft environment lifecycle management with unparalleled control and agility. This approach solidifies integration platform operations, enabling organizations to handle increasing complexity while maintaining high standards of consistency, governance, and operational excellence.

8.2. CI/CD Pipelines for Mule Applications

Continuous Integration and Continuous Delivery (CI/CD) pipelines are fundamental to ensuring the quality, reliability, and rapid delivery of Mule applications. The unique architectural style and deployment paradigms of Mule applications necessitate a tailored approach to automation-one that integrates smoothly with MuleSoft's Anypoint Platform and leverages industry-standard DevOps tools. The core objectives in building robust pipelines encompass automating application builds, executing comprehensive test suites, managing versioned artifacts consistently, and orchestrating deployments seamlessly across development, staging, and production environments.

Automating Builds for Mule Applications

At the heart of CI/CD pipelines lies the automation of the build process. For Mule applications, Maven remains the most widely adopted build tool due to MuleSoft's native Maven plugins designed specifically for packaging and validating Mule projects. The typical build lifecycle includes compilation of Mule configurations, resource packaging, execution of code-generated tests, and validation against Mule runtime constraints.

A well-defined `pom.xml` file includes configurations for the Mule Maven Plugin enabling commands such as `mvn clean package` to produce deployable `.jar` or `.zip` Mule application artifacts. This plugin also allows customization of deployment descriptors, manifest files, and configuration property files dynamically during the build. Integration with repository management systems like Nexus or Artifactory is critical for storing and versioning these artifacts.

```
mvn clean install mule-maven-plugin:package
```

This command ensures source code compilation, validation, and packaging into a deployable artifact, suitable for subsequent test-

239

ing or deployment phases.

Running Tests in CI Pipelines

Automated testing is crucial for maintaining Mule application quality through multiple pipeline stages. Test categories typically incorporated are unit tests (validated through MUnit), integration tests against mocked endpoints, and performance or load tests as needed. MUnit, MuleSoft's testing framework, integrates naturally with Maven, enabling tests to be executed during the `test` phase of the lifecycle.

The invocation of MUnit tests within the pipeline uses Maven goals:

```
mvn test mule-maven-plugin:munit
```

Test reports, typically generated in JUnit XML format, can be consumed by Continuous Integration tools such as Jenkins or GitLab CI to display results, enable test failure gating, and enforce quality gates.

Mocking external dependencies and APIs during tests is essential to isolate Mule flows and ensure deterministic outcomes. Within the pipeline, environment variables or Mule application properties controlling mock endpoints can be dynamically manipulated to switch between mock and real services.

Artifact Management and Versioning

Robust artifact management systems play an indispensable role in Mule-based CI/CD pipelines. Once built and tested, Mule application artifacts need to be stored securely with consistent versioning to allow traceability and rollbacks if necessary.

Conventions for semantic versioning (SemVer) prove effective in Mule projects. Incrementing major, minor, or patch versions depending on the nature of changes enables straightforward artifact

lifecycle management. In automated pipelines, semantic versioning can be dynamically updated based on commit messages or tags
via CI scripts.

Artifacts are typically pushed to enterprise-grade repositories such
as Sonatype Nexus or JFrog Artifactory. These systems support
meta-information tagging, retention policies, and access control
mechanisms, ensuring that only verified artifacts advance to deployment stages.

```
mvn deploy
```

The deploy phase uploads the packaged Mule application to configured remote repositories, tightly integrating with CI tools.

Orchestrating Multi-Environment Deployments

Mule applications usually require deployment across multiple
environments-development, testing, staging, and production-
with each environment having distinct configuration settings
and resource requirements.   CI/CD pipelines orchestrate
this progression efficiently by employing parameterization,
environment-specific profiles, and externalized configuration.

Anypoint Platform's Runtime Manager provides REST APIs and
CLI tools enabling automated deployment of Mule applications.
Pipeline stages leverage these programmatic interfaces to deploy,
update, or rollback Mule applications programmatically.

Deployment commands use Mule Maven Plugin:

```
mvn mule-maven-plugin:deploy -Danypoint.username=user@example.com
    -Danypoint.password=secret -Danypoint.environment=
    Production -Dmule.application=sample-app-1.0.0.zip
```

Here, credentials and environment identifiers are parameterized
and injected securely at runtime. Environment-specific properties
such as endpoints, credentials, or feature toggles are typically managed through Anypoint Runtime Manager properties or external
configuration management tools integrated into the pipeline.

Integration with configuration management and secrets vaults (for example, HashiCorp Vault or CyberArk) is advisable to avoid hard-coding sensitive data in pipeline scripts. Additionally, pipelines can exploit Anypoint Exchange's capabilities for versioned asset sharing and policy enforcement across environments.

Integrating with Industry-Standard CI/CD Tools

Industry-standard CI/CD platforms such as Jenkins, GitLab CI/CD, CircleCI, and Azure DevOps are frequently used to orchestrate the pipeline workflows for Mule applications. These tools provide built-in capabilities for event-driven automation, parallel execution, artifact storage, and pipeline visualization.

A representative Jenkins pipeline for a Mule application might encompass these stages:

- **Checkout**: Pull the latest Mule project source code from Git repositories.

- **Build**: Execute Maven build and packaging goals.

- **Test**: Run MUnit tests and publish test reports.

- **Static Analysis**: Optionally run tools like SonarQube for code quality assessment.

- **Artifact Upload**: Deploy built artifacts to a repository manager.

- **Deploy**: Automatically deploy to a target Anypoint environment.

- **Notification**: Notify relevant stakeholders of pipeline results.

Pipeline orchestration scripts employ declarative syntax (for example, Jenkinsfile) with environment variables, credential bindings, and error handling constructs. Parallel job execution and pipeline stages enhance feedback cycles and optimize resource utilization.

Handling Rollbacks and Blue-Green Deployments

Ensuring minimal disruption during deployments in production requires advanced strategies such as blue-green or canary deployments. While MuleSoft's native platform supports seamless application versioning and swapping, CI/CD pipelines automate the promotion and rollback processes.

Blue-green deployment involves maintaining two identical production environments (blue and green). The pipeline deploys the new Mule application version to the inactive environment, runs validation tests, and switches the traffic routing once validated. Rollbacks, if necessary, simply involve reconnection to the previously active environment.

Scripts leveraging Anypoint Platform's APIs automate these traffic switches and validations:

```
curl -X POST "https://anypoint.mulesoft.com/runtime-manager/api/
    v1/environments/{envId}/applications/{appId}/switch" \
-H "Authorization: Bearer <access_token>"
```

Integrating health checks, automated smoke tests, and monitoring hooks within pipelines further reinforces deployment reliability.

Security and Compliance within CI/CD Pipelines

Security considerations must permeate each stage of the Mule application pipeline. Secure storage of credentials, minimal privilege granted to deployment agents, encryption of artifacts at rest and in transit, and audit logging of all deployment actions are mandatory.

Automated security scanning tools can be incorporated into pipelines, including static code analyzers for Mule XML configurations and dependency vulnerability scanners. Compliance with organizational policies or standards (e.g., SOC2,

ISO27001) often requires embedding approval gates and manual intervention steps in delivery pipelines.

Best Practices and Optimization

- **Granular Environment Profiles:** Define fine-grained Mule environment configurations stored centrally, ensuring that pipeline stages do not require code modifications for environment changes.

- **Incremental Builds and Caching:** Leverage Maven and CI tools' caching mechanisms to accelerate build times, avoiding recompilation or repackaging unnecessarily.

- **Pipeline as Code:** Maintain pipeline definitions in version control, enabling traceability and collaboration on CI/CD workflow evolution.

- **Monitoring and Alerts:** Integrate deployment and test outcomes with dashboards and alerting systems to provide immediate feedback to development and operations teams.

Establishing comprehensive CI/CD pipelines for Mule applications demands a deep understanding of MuleSoft's runtime characteristics and the flexible application of DevOps tooling. Such pipelines deliver continuous feedback, repeatable deployment processes, and accelerate time-to-market while maintaining application stability and security.

8.3. Release Orchestration and Rollback Strategies

Effective release orchestration is a cornerstone of modern software deployment, enabling organizations to deliver new features rapidly while minimizing operational risks. The deployment strategies—phased releases, blue-green deployments, and canary rollouts—are pivotal in achieving reliable production releases and ensuring system stability. Complementing these approaches, rigorous version control practices and robust rollback mechanisms form an integrated framework to address deployment failures and accelerate recovery.

Phased Releases

Phased releases, also known as staged or incremental deployments, distribute the rollout process over a sequence of user cohorts or system environments. Instead of a full-scale production deployment, changes are incrementally exposed to increasing proportions of the user base or target infrastructure segments. Phased releases enable teams to monitor system behavior and user responses closely, rapidly identifying regressions or performance anomalies while limiting the blast radius.

Implementation of phased releases typically utilizes feature toggles or flags that activate new functionality for designated subsets of users. Dynamic configuration management platforms often control these toggles, allowing rapid adjustments without code redeployment. For example, an initial phase may target internal stakeholders or beta users, followed by limited geographic regions or customer segments, before achieving full production exposure.

Phased releases require comprehensive telemetry and real-time monitoring to validate each incremental stage effectively. Metrics such as error rates, latency, and user engagement allow objective assessment. Automated gating mechanisms, integrated with continuous deployment pipelines, can enforce release progression criteria or trigger abort and rollback upon detecting anomalies.

Blue-Green Deployments

The blue-green deployment model mitigates downtime and rollback complexity by maintaining two identical production environments: the *blue* environment, which serves live traffic, and the *green* environment, reserved for the new version deployment. After validating the new release in the green environment, traffic is switched atomically via load balancers or DNS updates, redirecting users from blue to green.

This approach offers several advantages:

- *Zero-downtime deployments:* Since the green environment is provisioned and verified before traffic cutover, service availability remains uninterrupted.

- *Instant rollback:* If the new version exhibits defects, traffic can be redirected back to the blue environment immediately, enabling rapid recovery.

- *Simplified testing under production conditions:* The green environment mirrors production exactly, allowing thorough validation before exposure.

However, blue-green deployments face challenges such as infrastructure cost due to duplicate environments and state synchronization complexities for data stores that require live migration or consistent replication across both environments. To mitigate these, teams often employ versioned APIs, database migration strategies that support backward compatibility, and automated environment provisioning tools.

Canary Rollouts

Canary deployments represent a sophisticated release strategy where new software versions are gradually exposed to a small, controlled subset of users or instances, with traffic progressively increased upon validation. This technique draws its name from the "canary in a coal mine" analogy, serving as an early warning system for potential issues.

Unlike phased releases that segment users based on predefined groups, canary rollouts often use automated traffic routing controlled by deployment orchestration systems. Metrics are continuously evaluated to measure service health, error rates, and user experience indicators during the canary phase. If metrics remain within acceptable thresholds, traffic allocation to the new version increases in configurable increments until full deployment is achieved.

One key benefit of canary rollouts is the ability to detect and contain regressions at a granular level, minimizing impact and facilitating confidence before full deployment. Canary releases integrate seamlessly with feature flagging, allowing rollback of specific features without redeployment, providing additional release agility.

Engineering teams typically leverage distributed tracing, synthetic transactions, and user feedback mechanisms to augment canary assessment. Automated rollbacks or roll-forward decisions are often codified as part of deployment pipelines, minimizing human intervention delays.

Version Control Best Practices

Robust version control underpins effective release orchestration and rollback strategies. Source code management systems must be employed with discipline, incorporating practices that support traceability, reproducibility, and collaboration.

Key best practices include:

- *Semantic versioning:* Use a consistent versioning scheme (e.g., MAJOR.MINOR.PATCH) to communicate release intent, compatibility, and scope of changes clearly to stakeholders.

- *Branching models:* Adopt branching strategies such as Git Flow or trunk-based development to manage feature integration, releases, and hotfixes. Branch protection rules and pull request reviews enforce quality barriers.

- *Commit hygiene:* Maintain atomic, well-documented commits to facilitate code review, bisecting, and auditing.

- *Tagging releases:* Tag commits corresponding to released versions for immutable reference points, enabling precise deployment and rollback targets.

Complementing these, integration with Continuous Integration/-Continuous Deployment (CI/CD) pipelines automates build, test, and deployment steps triggered by version control events, ensuring traceable and repeatable workflows.

Rollback Techniques and Rapid Recovery

Rollback strategies must be as thoughtfully engineered as deployment techniques to minimize recovery time and impact. The goal is to revert the system state to a stable baseline swiftly after deployment anomalies, ensuring continued service reliability.

Several rollback methodologies are common, aligned with the deployment pattern:

For Phased Releases Rollbacks often involve disabling feature toggles, effectively hiding or disabling new functionality without rolling back code. This minimizes disruption and accelerates recovery since the underlying infrastructure remains intact.

For Blue-Green Deployments Rollbacks are straightforward—traffic routing shifts back to the blue environment. Because the blue environment remains untouched during the green deployment, a rollback does not require code or configuration reversion.

For Canary Rollouts Rollbacks are typically partial traffic reversions, reducing traffic to the canary version incrementally back to zero. If the canary version is deployed on distinct infrastructure, terminating those instances suffices. Alternatively, feature flags can disable problematic features without complete rollback.

Database Considerations One of the most challenging aspects of rollback is the database state. Deployments often include schema migrations or data transformations, potentially incompatible with previous versions. Strategies to mitigate rollback complexity include:

- *Backward-compatible schema changes:* Applying additive or non-destructive schema modifications during deployment prevents rollback conflicts.

- *Versioned APIs and data formats:* Decoupling application version from data structure allows coexistence of old and new schemas.

- *Migration automation and verification:* Automated, reversible migration scripts embedded in deployment pipelines facilitate controlled rollbacks.

Integrating Monitoring and Automation for Reliable Releases

Continuous monitoring is indispensable for informed release orchestration and rollback decisions. Deployment health metrics must feed into automated gating mechanisms that can pause, abort, or revert releases without manual intervention. These automated safeguards rely on predefined Service Level Objectives (SLOs) and error budgets, embedding reliability thresholds into deployment orchestration.

Infrastructure-as-Code (IaC) and configuration-as-code tools complement these strategies by enabling consistent, repeatable environment provisioning and deployment configuration rollback. This reduces human error and accelerates recovery workflows.

Ultimately, effective release orchestration and rollback require a holistic approach combining strategic deployment techniques, disciplined version control, automated monitoring, and well-defined recovery processes. This integrated framework ensures that releases are both rapid and resilient, balancing innovation velocity with operational stability.

8.4. Quality Gates and Automated Validation

Automated quality gates are essential components within Continuous Integration and Continuous Deployment (CI/CD) pipelines, particularly for MuleSoft development environments. They serve as automated checkpoints that validate code quality, compliance with security policies, and functional correctness before permitting progression through the pipeline stages. Implementing these gates enforces adherence to organizational standards and ensures releases fulfill both technical and business requirements prior to production deployment.

Quality gates systematically integrate three complementary validation categories: policy-as-code enforcement, static and dynamic code analysis, and test automation. Each category targets distinct dimensions of software assurance, collectively minimizing risks related to defects, vulnerabilities, and functional regressions.

- **Policy-as-Code Enforcement**: This approach expresses organizational rules, security controls, and compliance requirements as executable code artifacts. By codifying policies, validation becomes automated, repeatable, and consistent within the pipeline. MuleSoft APIs and integrations are governed by policies such as authentication, rate limiting, data masking, logging standards, and access control. Encoding these policies as universal, machine-readable artifacts enables early detection of non-conformities.

  Frameworks and tools that support policy-as-code enable validation against defined specifications prior to deployment. This can include tools such as Open Policy Agent (OPA) integrated with CI/CD workflows, which evaluate attributes of MuleSoft configurations and enforce constraints embedded within Rego policies. For example, an OPA policy can validate that all APIs are configured with mutual TLS enforcement or contain required audit logging.

Integrating policy validation early prevents policy violations from advancing through pipeline stages, embedding governance directly within development and release workflows. Automated gates may trigger failure notifications and block pipeline progression upon policy infractions, requiring remediation before further integration.

- **Static Analysis**: Static analysis inspects MuleSoft source code, configuration files, and descriptors without executing the program. For Mule applications, this includes analyzing XML configurations, DataWeave scripts, Java components, and API specifications such as RAML or OAS (OpenAPI Specification). Static analysis tools detect architectural violations, security anti-patterns, code smells, and deviations from coding standards. These analyses improve code maintainability, reduce defect rates, and harden security posture.

Tools specialized for MuleSoft, as well as general-purpose static analyzers, can be integrated into the CI/CD pipeline. Such tools scan for issues like:

- Invalid or incomplete API specifications.

- Exposure of sensitive data within logs or message payloads.

- Use of deprecated components or connectors.

- Hardcoded secrets embedded in configuration files.

- Performance antipatterns such as unbounded loops or inefficient transformations.

- The results of static analysis are aggregated to produce detailed reports highlighting violations with severity levels. Automated quality gates examine these reports and fail the build or deployment if thresholds for critical issues are crossed. This proactive stance catches violations before functional testing or production deployment, reducing expensive post-release remediation.

- **Dynamic Analysis**: Dynamic analysis complements static methods by executing MuleSoft applications within controlled environments to observe runtime behaviors. It focuses on uncovering issues such as memory leaks, runtime security vulnerabilities, transactional inconsistencies, and integration failures. Dynamic testing can include load testing, penetration testing, and behavioral anomaly detection.

  Within CI/CD pipelines, dynamic analysis is frequently realized through functional test suites executed against deployed instances in ephemeral or isolated test environments. Additionally, runtime instrumentation tools monitor resource consumption, error rates, and adherence to service-level objectives (SLOs). Automated quality gates evaluate dynamic test outcomes and runtime metrics to determine readiness.

  Emphasizing dynamic validation ensures that applications perform as expected under realistic conditions, respecting performance, reliability, and security criteria. Failures found in dynamic analysis trigger rollback or pipeline halts, preventing flawed releases.

- **Test Automation**: Test automation is the backbone of validating functional correctness in continuous delivery environments. MuleSoft releases are often subject to multiple layers of testing, including unit tests, integration tests, contract tests, and end-to-end tests that simulate real user workflows and backend interactions. Proper integration of automated test execution into CI/CD pipelines enforces that any regressions or defects are identified instantaneously.

Unit testing validates small logical components such as DataWeave transformations or custom Java classes in isolation. Integration testing, executed against Mule runtime instances, verifies service interactions and message flows across connectors and external endpoints. Contract testing asserts that API interfaces adhere strictly to their RAML or OAS definition, providing confidence in backward compatibility and consumer expectations.

Sophisticated test automation frameworks allow the definition of test suites that can be parameterized and run in parallel for speeding feedback cycles. Test reports are submitted to pipeline orchestrators where test pass rates are assessed as part of quality gates. Thresholds on minimum pass percentages or zero tolerance for critical failures can be established, automatically rejecting code changes that degrade quality.

Integrating these automated validations within MuleSoft CI/CD pipelines involves orchestrating tooling, environment provisioning, and result aggregation into unified quality gates. Typical pipeline stages include source checkout, build and dependency resolution, static code analysis, policy validation, automated testing, dynamic analysis, and finally deployment.

A representative pipeline for MuleSoft might follow this sequence:

- **Code Quality and Policy Validation Stage**: Execute static analyzers and policy-as-code evaluation tools on the Mule project. Fail if forbidden patterns or policy violations are detected.

- **Build and Unit Tests Stage**: Compile code artifacts, run unit tests, and generate reports. Fail pipeline on test failures or insufficient coverage.

- **Integration and Contract Tests Stage**: Deploy to test environment and run integration and contract tests. Collect metrics and fail if functional regressions occur.

- **Dynamic Analysis and Security Assessment Stage**: Run automated security scans, load tests, and runtime instrumentation. Fail deployments with critical vulnerabilities or performance anomalies.

- **Release Stage**: Conditional upon all preceding gates passing, promote artifacts to staging or production.

Pipeline configurations include leveraging containerized test environments, storing artifacts in secure registries, and integrating with version control and issue tracking systems. Code quality dashboards consolidate static and dynamic analysis results for developer visibility.

Establishing effective quality gates requires setting achievable, measurable criteria aligned with organizational goals. Overly stringent gates risk slowing delivery cadence, while lenient gates may permit quality regressions. Incremental adoption starting with static analysis and policy-as-code enforcement is recommended, progressing gradually to full automation of dynamic analysis and comprehensive test suites.

Versioning of validation artifacts such as policy definitions and test scripts ensures reproducibility and traceability across releases. Automated notification mechanisms alert development teams immediately upon quality gate failures, facilitating prompt investigation and remediation.

Finally, continuous monitoring and refinement of the quality gates and validation tooling help maintain relevance amid evolving MuleSoft platforms, dependency updates, and emerging security standards. Sustained investment in automation infrastructure delivers increased confidence, higher software quality, and accelerated release cycles.

```
pipeline {
    agent any
    stages {
        stage('Checkout') {
            steps {
                checkout scm
            }
        }
        stage('Static Analysis') {
            steps {
                sh './run-static-analysis.sh'
            }
            post {
                always {
                    junit 'reports/static-analysis-results.xml'
                    script {
                        def issues = readFile('reports/static-
issues-count.txt').trim()
                        if (issues.toInteger() > 0) {
                            error("Static analysis detected
issues; aborting pipeline.")
                        }
                    }
                }
            }
        }
        stage('Policy Validation') {
            steps {
                sh 'opa eval --fail-defined "data.mulesoft.
policies.deny" -i config/api-config.json -d policies/'
            }
        }
        stage('Unit Tests') {
            steps {
                sh './mvnw test'
            }
            post {
                always {
                    junit 'target/surefire-reports/*.xml'
                }
            }
        }
        stage('Integration Tests') {
            steps {
                sh './run-integration-tests.sh'
            }
            post {
                always {
                    junit 'reports/integration-tests.xml'
                }
            }
```

```
            }
    stage('Dynamic Analysis') {
        steps {
            sh './run-security-scans.sh'
        }
        post {
            always {
                archiveArtifacts 'reports/security-scan-
report.html'
            }
        }
    }
}
post {
    failure {
        mail to: 'dev-team@example.com',
        subject: "Pipeline Failure: ${env.JOB_NAME} #${env.
BUILD_NUMBER}",
        body: "Build failed. Please check Jenkins console
output."
    }
}
}
```

Example output snippet from static analysis tool:

```
[INFO] Analyzing Mule XML configurations...
[WARNING] Detected hardcoded credentials in mule-config.xml line 42.
[ERROR] API RAML specification incomplete: Missing response schema at /users
GET.
[INFO] Deprecated connector version 1.5 detected.
[SUMMARY] 1 ERROR, 1 WARNING, 2 INFO messages found.
```

Build failed due to static analysis violations.

8.5. Operational Monitoring and Incident Response

Ensuring the high availability of integration workloads within MuleSoft environments demands a comprehensive approach to operational monitoring and incident response. The development of robust operational playbooks, dynamic dashboards, and automated monitoring frameworks is central to maintaining service continuity and achieving rapid incident resolution. These mechanisms collectively enable teams to detect, diagnose, and remediate anomalies before they impact business-critical processes.

At the foundation of effective operational monitoring lies the construction of detailed operational playbooks that codify institutional knowledge and prescribe precise workflows for incident detection and resolution. These playbooks encapsulate typical failure modes, diagnostic commands, escalation paths, and recovery steps specific to MuleSoft components such as Anypoint Platform, Mule runtimes, and API gateways. By formalizing response strategies tailored to integration scenarios involving orchestrations, transformations, and connectivity issues, playbooks reduce the cognitive load on on-call engineers during high-pressure situations and contribute to consistent incident handling practices.

Dashboards serve as the pivotal interface for real-time visibility into the health and performance of integration workloads. These dashboards consolidate metrics, logs, and alerts from distributed Mule applications and middleware into unified, customizable visualizations. Key performance indicators (KPIs) include API response times, transaction volumes, error rates, CPU and memory utilization of Mule runtimes, and queue depths in messaging systems. Visual elements such as heat maps, sparklines, and trend curves aid in quickly identifying deviations from baseline operational patterns. Furthermore, integrating MuleSoft's out-of-the-box monitoring data with external Application Performance Management (APM) tools via REST APIs or event streaming enhances situational awareness across hybrid cloud architectures.

Automated monitoring extends beyond static threshold-based alerts to incorporate anomaly detection techniques designed to identify subtle and emerging deviations in integration workloads. Statistical methods, such as moving averages and exponential smoothing, provide baseline estimates of expected behavior, while machine learning models-including unsupervised clustering and time-series forecasting-detect patterns indicative of performance degradation or security threats. For example, sudden spikes in payload size or unusual latencies in API calls can be flagged automatically, triggering alert workflows. Anomaly detection algorithms are trained on historical telemetry data collected from MuleSoft environments, adapting continuously to evolving traffic patterns and operational changes.

Real-time alerting systems form the backbone of incident response workflows. Alerts are generated according to predefined conditions and severity levels, prioritized to avoid alert fatigue while ensuring critical events receive immediate attention. These alerts are dispatched via multiple communication channels such as email, SMS, mobile push notifications, and messaging platforms like Slack or Microsoft Teams, enabling rapid dissemination to on-call personnel. Integrating alerting mechanisms with incident management solutions (e.g., PagerDuty, Opsgenie) facilitates automated incident creation, assignment, and escalation, streamlining operational workflows tailored for MuleSoft runtimes and APIs.

Effective on-call management is a critical dimension, particularly in organizations operating 24/7 global integration services. On-call rotations, shift handovers, and knowledge transfer are orchestrated through well-defined schedules that balance workload and prevent burnout. Coupling these schedules with integrated alert routing ensures the right responder is notified promptly based on expertise and availability. Playbooks embedded within incident response platforms provide contextual information alongside alerts, including recent deployment changes, known issues, and diagnostic commands. This contextual enrichment shortens mean time to recovery (MTTR) and fosters continuous improvement in operational resilience.

The instrumentation of MuleSoft environments with comprehensive logging facilities supports post-incident analysis and forensic investigations. Structured logging, enhanced with correlation identifiers propagating through API calls and message flows, facilitates end-to-end traceability of transactions. Log aggregation and indexing via centralized platforms such as Elasticsearch or Splunk augment searchability and pattern detection. Combined with monitored metrics and alert histories, these logs enable root cause analysis workflows embedded within operational playbooks.

A representative operational playbook for an API latency spike scenario in MuleSoft might contain the following sequence:

```
# Step 1: Check Mule runtime CPU and memory usage
curl -X GET "http://mule-runtime.api/actuator/metrics/system.cpu.
    usage" | jq .
curl -X GET "http://mule-runtime.api/actuator/metrics/jvm.memory.
    used" | jq .

# Step 2: Inspect active flows and thread pool utilization
curl -X GET "http://mule-runtime.api/actuator/metrics/flow.active
    .count" | jq .
curl -X GET "http://mule-runtime.api/actuator/metrics/threadpool.
    active.count" | jq .

# Step 3: Query message queue depth and latency
rabbitmqctl list_queues name messages_ready
    messages_unacknowledged

# Step 4: Examine recent deployment or configuration changes
git log -1 --pretty=oneline

# Step 5: Check API Manager logs for errors or throttling events
tail -n 100 /var/log/mule/apimanager.log | grep ERROR
```

Output from these diagnostics is typically examined within centralized logging and dashboard tools to correlate observations:

```
{
  "measurements": [
    {
      "statistic": "VALUE",
      "value": 0.85
    }
  ],
  "availableTags": []
}
{
  "measurements": [
    {
      "statistic": "VALUE",
      "value": 72345678
```

259

```
    }
  ],
  "availableTags": []
}
```

Queue Name	Messages Ready	Messages Unacknowledged
integration-q1	150	12
deployment-q2	0	0

```
ERROR 2024-05-12 14:23:15 [api-throttle] Throttling limit exceeded for API: P
aymentService
```

Dashboards monitoring latency across APIs will represent these internal system metrics alongside business transaction KPIs, highlighting bottlenecks and enabling operators to initiate defined remediation steps such as scaling Mule runtime instances, adjusting thread pools, or rolling back recent deployments.

The continuous evolution of monitoring and incident response capabilities in MuleSoft environments benefits from integration with DevOps pipelines and infrastructure-as-code paradigms. Automated deployment of monitoring agents, configuration of alert rules, and updates to playbook content through version-controlled repositories ensure alignment with the fast-paced lifecycle of integration workloads. Furthermore, synthetic transaction monitoring simulating end-user API requests provides proactive verification of service health and functionality.

In sum, operational monitoring and incident response for MuleSoft integrations require a systematic synthesis of playbooks, dashboards, automated alerting, anomaly detection, and on-call coordination. This integrated approach minimizes downtime, enhances fault diagnosis precision, and strengthens organizational readiness to maintain seamless integration services critical to enterprise digital ecosystems.

8.6. Cost Analytics and Resource Optimization

Cost management is a fundamental requirement for maintaining sustainable automation workflows in modern hybrid environments. Achieving operational efficiency necessitates embedding cost control mechanisms directly into orchestration pipelines to enable continuous visibility and proactive adjustments. This integration hinges on implementing robust monitoring of resource consumption, automating cost-aware scaling strategies, and optimizing the allocation of both cloud-based and on-premises assets. Together, these capabilities empower organizations to balance performance demands with financial constraints, thereby eliminating unexpected expenditures while maintaining seamless service levels.

Monitoring Resource Consumption

The foundation of cost-aware automation begins with comprehensive and granular monitoring of resource utilization across all infrastructure components involved in integration workflows. Traditional monitoring systems focus primarily on availability and performance metrics; however, sophisticated cost analytics extend these capabilities to include consumption patterns directly tied to financial impact.

Key metrics include CPU and memory usage, network bandwidth, storage I/O, and instance uptime, all annotated with their associated billing rates or amortized cost models. Establishing a unified telemetry pipeline, often leveraging cloud provider cost APIs in conjunction with on-premises performance counters, provides a single pane of glass for cross-environment cost visibility. Such integration ensures that cost drivers are correlated with workload behaviors, facilitating accurate attribution and trend analysis.

Resource consumption data must be captured at high temporal resolution to detect transient spikes or bursts, which often contribute disproportionately to overall cost. By applying time-series analysis and anomaly detection algorithms within cost analytics platforms, organizations can proactively identify inefficiencies such as idle resources or over-provisioned components before they escalate into budget overruns.

Automating Cost-Aware Scaling

Dynamic scaling of resources is a well-established practice for optimizing performance and availability. Embedding cost-awareness into scaling logic represents an evolution that not only reacts to workload demands but also actively minimizes expenditure.

Cost-aware scaling algorithms incorporate real-time pricing models-including spot market fluctuations, reserved instance discounts, and tiered volume pricing-to determine the optimal scale levels that meet service-level objectives (SLOs) at minimal cost. This requires the integration of pricing and usage data sources, with scaling triggers adjusted from purely technical thresholds (e.g., CPU utilization > 70%) to multidimensional criteria reflecting cost-efficiency.

For example, during off-peak periods, scaling policies may leverage lower-cost instance types or spot instances with automatic evictions handled gracefully within the workflow. In contrast, critical workloads might prioritize availability by temporarily suspending cost-saving modes, highlighting the necessity to balance financial and operational priorities explicitly.

Advanced implementations embed machine learning models that predict workload patterns and associated costs, enabling preemptive scaling decisions that avoid unnecessary resource provisioning. These models continuously refine their accuracy by analyzing historical consumption and pricing data, adapting to changes in demand and market conditions.

The following illustrates a cost-aware scaling decision pseudo-code that factors in utilization, cost per unit time, and market pricing signals:

```
def should_scale(current_util, cost_rate, spot_price,
    sla_threshold):
    # Determine if scaling is needed based on utilization and SLA
    if current_util > sla_threshold:
        # Calculate cost if on-demand vs spot instance
        cost_on_demand = cost_rate
        cost_spot = spot_price if spot_price < cost_rate else
    cost_rate
        # Select instance type minimizing cost while meeting SLA
        if cost_spot < cost_on_demand:
            instance_type = 'spot'
        else:
            instance_type = 'on-demand'
        return True, instance_type
    else:
        return False, None
```

Optimizing Cloud and On-Prem Resource Allocation

Hybrid integration architectures introduce unique challenges in cost optimization due to differing cost structures between cloud and on-premises environments. Effective resource allocation requires a detailed understanding of workload characteristics, latency constraints, security policies, and cost implications across these domains.

Cost models for cloud resources are transparent and often granular, enabling straightforward chargeback calculations. Conversely, on-premises costs are generally fixed capital and operational expenses amortized over extended periods, complicating direct cost attribution on a per-integration basis. Overcoming this requires adopting activity-based costing techniques that allocate on-prem resource usage proportionally based on consumption metrics such as CPU hours, memory consumption, and storage use.

Optimization strategies include workload placement heuristics that assign integration tasks to the environment yielding the lowest total cost of ownership (TCO) while satisfying functional requirements. For instance, burstable or ephemeral workloads with unpredictable scaling needs usually benefit from cloud deployment to leverage elasticity and avoid over-provisioning on-premises hardware. Conversely, steady-state, compliance-sensitive processes may realize cost efficiencies by executing on-premises where infrastructure is fully depreciated.

Implementing intelligent orchestration layers capable of evaluating cost-performance trade-offs dynamically is crucial. These layers incorporate constraints including data transfer costs, cross-environment latency, availability zones, and contractual pricing terms. Optimization algorithms can leverage linear programming or heuristics to solve multi-objective resource allocation problems, balancing operational efficiency with cost minimization.

A representative mathematical formulation for resource allocation optimization is expressed as:

$$\min_{\mathbf{x}} \quad \sum_{i \in \{\text{cloud,on-prem}\}} \sum_{j} c_{ij} x_{ij}$$

$$\text{subject to} \quad \sum_{i} x_{ij} = d_j, \quad \forall j$$

$$x_{ij} \geq 0, \quad \forall i, j$$

$$\text{latency}_j(\mathbf{x_j}) \leq L_j^{\max}, \quad \forall j$$

$$\text{security}_j(\mathbf{x_j}) \geq S_j^{\min}, \quad \forall j$$

where x_{ij} denotes the resource allocation for workload j on environment i, c_{ij} the associated cost, and d_j the demand requirements. The latency and security constraints enforce operational thresholds.

Integrating Cost Analytics into Continuous Workflow Management

Embedding cost control as a continuous feedback loop within automation workflows enables sustained optimization rather than one-off adjustments. This integration involves augmenting pipelines with cost checkpoints and remediation triggers that

264

respond automatically to budget anomalies.

Cost analytics outputs feed into orchestration decision modules, which may halt, scale down, or reconfigure tasks based on predefined cost budgets or anomaly detection alerts. These policies are codified using infrastructure-as-code or workflow definition languages enriched with cost-awareness primitives.

For example, a workflow segment can include conditional execution steps triggered if forecasted cumulative costs exceed thresholds, enabling proactive throttling or queued execution to smooth expenditure over time. Real-time dashboards and alerting mechanisms provide operational teams with visibility into cost impact, facilitating timely interventions when manual review or strategic decisions are necessary.

Cost Metrics and Reporting

Consistent measurement and reporting of cost-related metrics are vital for transparency and governance. Metrics should aggregate across hierarchical levels, from individual integration tasks to entire pipeline executions and organizational units.

Useful metrics include:

- **Cost per Integration Operation**: Cost incurred per message or transaction processed.

- **Cost Efficiency Ratio**: Comparison of cost against workload units, such as cost per API call.

- **Resource Utilization Efficiency**: Captures ratio of active usage versus allocated capacity.

- **Budget Variance**: Difference between actual spend and allocated budget over periods.

Automated reporting tools generate periodic summaries and anomaly alerts, enabling data-driven governance. Integration with financial management systems supports chargebacks and showbacks, fostering accountability across technical and business teams.

Challenges and Best Practices

Effective cost analytics and optimization are impeded by complexities such as multi-cloud heterogeneity, dynamic pricing models, and unpredictable workload spikes. Achieving reliable cost control requires:

- **Consolidated Data Integration**: Harmonizing cost and usage data from disparate sources.

- **Accurate Cost Attribution**: Employing tagging and metadata strategies to map costs to specific integration activities.

- **Automation and Orchestration Integration**: Embedding cost considerations directly within automated scaling and deployment workflows.

- **Regular Model Tuning**: Continuously refining predictive models and optimization algorithms to adapt to evolving usage patterns and pricing.

- **Cross-Functional Collaboration**: Aligning technical, financial, and operational teams to establish shared understanding and governance frameworks.

Adhering to these practices ensures that cost optimization efforts become an integral, sustainable component of automation lifecycle management rather than an afterthought.

Embedding cost analytics and resource optimization into integration workflows transforms the approach to automation from reactive expenditure control to proactive financial governance. Continuous, automated monitoring combined with intelligent scaling and hybrid resource allocation guarantees alignment of operational performance with economic objectives, enabling organizations to confidently scale and innovate without fiscal surprises.

Chapter 9

Security, Compliance, and Data Protection

Protecting sensitive data and maintaining compliance isn't just a technical checkbox—it's the foundation of digital trust and business continuity. In this chapter, you'll unravel the layers of robust security controls, automated compliance enforcement, and advanced data privacy measures that fortify enterprise MuleSoft integrations. From API authentication protocols to incident response frameworks, explore battle-tested strategies that keep your data and applications safe—and your organization ahead of emerging threats.

9.1. Authentication, Authorization, and Identity Federation

Enterprise-grade integration solutions demand robust mechanisms for authentication, authorization, and identity federation to safeguard APIs and applications. MuleSoft, a prominent integration platform, offers diverse methods to enforce secure identity management by interfacing seamlessly with OAuth2, SAML, LDAP, and a variety of external identity providers. These protocols and technologies serve as pillars for implementing flexible, scalable, and fine-grained access control across heterogeneous environments.

A foundational element of secure API management is *authentication*, the process by which users or systems prove their identity. MuleSoft's API Manager facilitates integration with authentication frameworks such as OAuth 2.0, a widely adopted authorization framework designed to delegate limited access to resources without exposing user credentials. OAuth 2.0 externalizes authentication to trusted authorization servers, issuing access tokens that APIs consume to enforce access policies. Within MuleSoft, OAuth 2.0's use can be architected via several grant types, including the `authorization_code`, `client_credentials`, and `password` grants, adapting to diverse client capabilities and trust boundaries. The API Manager validates these bearer tokens through introspection endpoints or JWT (JSON Web Token) validation to authenticate incoming requests robustly.

Complementing OAuth 2.0, Security Assertion Markup Language (SAML) provides a mature XML-based framework for exchanging authentication and authorization data between identity providers and service providers. SAML facilitates Single Sign-On (SSO) by transmitting digitally signed assertions that confirm a user's identity and entitlements. MuleSoft supports SAML 2.0 by acting as a service provider through connectors or custom policies, enabling enterprises to leverage corporate identity infrastructures and federated identity arrangements. SAML's strengths lie in federating identities across organizational boundaries with strong cryptographic assurances and rich attribute statements that contribute to authorization decisions.

The Lightweight Directory Access Protocol (LDAP) remains central to enterprise identity management, offering a hierarchical, highly optimized directory access protocol for user and group information stored in directory services such as Microsoft Active Directory or OpenLDAP. MuleSoft's connectors for LDAP enable direct authentication against directory stores and allow retrieval of user attributes for context-aware authorization. LDAP integration is particularly beneficial in legacy or on-premises environments where directory stores govern user lifecycle and role assignments. By combining LDAP queries with MuleSoft access policies, applications enforce granular role-based access control (RBAC) consistent with organizational governance.

Identity federation is the umbrella that enables users to access multiple systems across trust domains based on authentication managed by external identity providers (IdPs). This paradigm significantly simplifies user experience while centralizing identity administration. MuleSoft capitalizes on federation standards like OAuth2 and SAML to delegate authentication to widespread providers-including enterprise IdPs such as Okta, Azure Active Directory, and Ping Identity. By doing so, MuleSoft APIs ensure that authentication aligns with enterprise Single Sign-On strategies, reducing password sprawl and strengthening security postures through consistent policies and multi-factor authentication.

Beyond authentication, *authorization* determines whether an authenticated entity has the right privileges to perform requested actions on resources. MuleSoft enables fine-grained authorization policies through Access Management capabilities, combining token scopes, user roles, and custom attributes obtained via external identity providers. Policies can be crafted to inspect claims embedded within OAuth tokens or SAML assertions to validate permissions dynamically, allowing complex rules such as resource ownership, temporal constraints, or location-based access. This is critical in microservices architectures and multi-tenant systems where permissive or overly coarse-grained access could lead to data exposure or privilege escalation.

A common pattern in MuleSoft security configurations is the use of OAuth 2.0 JWT token validation policy, which parses and validates JSON Web Tokens issued by trusted authorization servers. JWT tokens encode user identity and privileges in a signed, compact format, permitting stateless validation without centralized token introspection overhead. MuleSoft responses can extract claims such as user roles, tenant identifiers, and custom attributes to tailor backend service behavior accordingly. For example, an API may enforce that only users with the admin role in the token scopes can invoke sensitive operations, enhancing separation of duties within a single API surface.

The orchestration of identity-related flows within the Mule runtime is frequently accomplished by leveraging dedicated security connectors and gateway policies. The OAuth 2.0 Provider module within Mule enables the platform to function as an OAuth authorization server if necessary, issuing tokens as per enterprise requirements and incorporating corporate identity workflows. This capability extends to issuing refresh tokens, implementing token revocation, and conforming to best practices such as Proof Key for Code Exchange (PKCE) to mitigate authorization code interception attacks. On the consumer side, Mule applications consume access tokens from external IdPs and enforce validation at both gateway and individual API endpoints.

LDAP integration in MuleSoft.js or Mule runtime typically involves executing bind operations to authenticate credentials against the directory, followed by search queries to retrieve user attributes or group memberships. These attributes can be decoded and mapped into application roles and permissions through Mule's DataWeave transformations. For example, a simple LDAP filter retrieving group membership could be constructed as:

```
(&(objectClass=groupOfNames)(member=uid=${username},ou=users,dc=
    example,dc=com))
```

This query checks whether a user identified by username belongs to a particular group, enabling role-based authorization upon successful authentication.

SAML integration requires handling XML-based assertions, parsing their cryptographically signed elements, and verifying the issuer's authenticity and assertion validity periods. MuleSoft's policies process these assertions, extracting claims such as `NameID` for user identity and `AttributeStatements` describing roles or permissions. Ensuring time synchronization (via NTP) between IdP and Mule processing runtime is essential to avoid assertion replay or expiration errors.

Identity federation enhances enterprise security by centralizing user identities and enabling seamless access across diverse applications. MuleSoft acts as a service provider relying on Identity Provider (IdP)-initiated or Service Provider (SP)-initiated SSO flows, where HTTP redirection exchanges enable assertion and token flows. Federation reduces redundancy in credential management, improving auditability and policy enforcement over broad application ecosystems.

In scenarios demanding combined authentication strategies, MuleSoft supports chaining different authentication methods, such as validating client certificates, performing LDAP authentication, and consuming OAuth tokens simultaneously. This layered approach increases assurance levels and fits multi-factor authentication requirements. Combined with MuleSoft's rate limiting and threat protection policies, integrated authentication and authorization form a comprehensive defense-in-depth posture.

MuleSoft's integration with identity and access protocols-OAuth2, SAML, LDAP, and external identity providers-enables enterprises to implement secure, scalable, and federated identity management. These integrations support the enforcement of rigorous authentication and nuanced authorization policies, essential to safeguarding API access within complex, distributed, and hybrid IT landscapes. By leveraging these technologies, architects design resilient sys-

273

tems that comply with organizational security mandates while providing streamlined, user-centric access experiences.

9.2. API Security Controls and Secure Design

API security is a fundamental aspect of modern software architectures, especially as systems increasingly rely on service-oriented and microservice-based designs. Secure API design requires a rigorous approach that addresses potential threats throughout the API lifecycle, from initial design to deployment and operation. The core principles and practices to build resilient and trustworthy interfaces include comprehensive input validation, rate limiting, API firewalling, and robust mitigation techniques against common vulnerabilities such as injection attacks, broken authentication, and excessive data exposure. This section delineates security blueprints that align with these principles, emphasizing both conceptual underpinnings and practical controls.

Input Validation and Sanitization

Input validation stands as the first line of defense against injection flaws and malformed requests, which are among the most pervasive sources of vulnerabilities. Robust APIs must treat all incoming data as untrusted, irrespective of the source, applying strict validation rules tailored to the expected input semantics.

There are multiple dimensions to effective input validation:

- **Type Checking and Constraint Enforcement:** Input values should be verified to conform to defined data types, length constraints, formats (e.g., email or UUID), and enumeration sets where applicable. For example, numeric parameters must reject non-numeric characters; date fields must follow strict ISO-8601 formatting.

- **Whitelist Over Blacklist Approaches:** Whitelisting defines allowable patterns and rejects all else, as opposed to blacklisting suspicious tokens. For instance, a username field might allow only alphanumeric characters and underscores, rejecting anything not explicitly permitted.

- **Context-Aware Sanitization:** Input destined for different contexts (SQL queries, HTML outputs, JSON encodings) requires context-specific escaping or encoding to mitigate injection attacks like SQL injection or Cross-Site Scripting (XSS).

A common mistake is relying solely on client-side validation; all checks must be enforced server-side to prevent bypass by malicious clients. Furthermore, input validation must be tightly integrated with the schema definition, using standards such as JSON Schema or OpenAPI specifications to enforce constraints uniformly across implementations.

Rate Limiting and Throttling

Rate limiting is essential to prevent abuse of APIs through excessive or automated requests that may lead to denial-of-service (DoS) conditions or resource exhaustion. Fine-grained throttling policies can both improve availability and protect backend systems.

Key rate limiting strategies include:

- **Quota-based Limits:** Define maximum allowable requests over defined time windows (e.g., 1000 requests per user per hour). Quotas can vary by API endpoint based on criticality and expected traffic.

- **Burst Control:** Allow short bursts above the normal rate but enforce strict limits over longer time intervals to accommodate legitimate traffic spikes without compromising stability.

- **Differentiated Limits per Client or Role:** Privileged

users or internal services may have higher limits than anonymous users, implemented using API keys or OAuth scopes.

- **Dynamic and Adaptive Thresholds:** Incorporate real-time analytics to adjust limits adaptively under unusual load patterns or detected attack attempts.

Rate limiting is usually implemented at the API gateway or reverse proxy level, providing a centralized enforcement point. It must be coordinated with authentication mechanisms to correctly identify clients. Denied requests should return appropriate HTTP status codes (e.g., 429 Too Many Requests) along with informative headers indicating retry windows.

API Firewalling and Advanced Filtering

API firewalls function as specialized intermediaries that analyze request attributes and enforce security policies to block malicious traffic. Unlike traditional web application firewalls (WAFs), API-focused firewalls incorporate semantic understanding of API protocols, payload structures, and authentication schemes.

Features of effective API firewalls include:

- **Protocol and Payload Validation:** Enforce strict conformance to API specifications, rejecting calls that violate expected methods, headers, or payload formats.

- **Behavioral Analysis:** Monitor request patterns to detect abnormal sequences such as parameter tampering, replay attacks, or credential stuffing attempts.

- **Threat Intelligence Integration:** Utilize updated signatures and heuristics to block known attack vectors, such as injection payloads, malformed JSON, or excessive enumeration of resources.

- **Granular Access Control:** Apply rules based on user identity, IP reputation, geolocation, and custom attributes to restrict unauthorized access dynamically.

API firewalls often combine static rules with machine learning models to improve detection accuracy and reduce false positives. They should be integrated tightly with logging and monitoring systems to enable fast incident response and forensic analysis.

Defending Against Common API Vulnerabilities

Secure API design must address prevalent vulnerability classes detailed in industry standards such as the OWASP API Security Top 10. Several mitigations pertain to the most frequent and damaging attack types:

Injection Attacks

Injection flaws, including SQL, NoSQL, command, and XPath injection, exploit unsanitized input to execute unintended commands on backend systems. Defenses include:

- Parameterized queries and prepared statements avoid concatenating user input into command strings.

- Input validation and encoding block injection payloads.

- Use of Object-Relational Mappers (ORMs) or API abstraction layers reduces direct query construction.

Broken Authentication and Authorization

Compromised authentication or insufficient authorization checks lead to unauthorized data access or privilege escalation. Mitigation measures:

- Enforce strong authentication mechanisms (e.g., OAuth 2.0, OpenID Connect).

- Employ multi-factor authentication for sensitive endpoints.

- Implement fine-grained access control using scopes, roles, and claims.

- Consistently validate authorization for every API call; never trust client-supplied context.

Excessive Data Exposure

APIs should avoid returning unnecessary or sensitive data in responses. Techniques to minimize data exposure include:

- Strict output filtering based on user roles and permissions.

- Designing APIs around data minimization principles.

- Applying response schema validation to exclude non-required fields.

Lack of Rate Limiting and Throttling

As described previously, missing rate limiting can facilitate brute force, scraping, and DoS attacks.

Mass Assignment

Mass assignment vulnerabilities arise when clients are able to modify object properties that should be immutable or protected. Defenses include:

- Whitelisting permissible fields explicitly for update operations.

- Employing separate Data Transfer Objects (DTOs) that expose only intended properties.

Security-by-Design and Secure Development Lifecycle

278

Embedding security considerations early in the API design process reduces risks and technical debt. Building APIs with security by design involves:

- Threat modeling to identify assets, attack vectors, and risk mitigation strategies.

- Defining and enforcing strict API schema contracts using tools such as OpenAPI to ensure consistent input/output validation and documentation.

- Adopting secure coding standards and regular code reviews focused on security.

- Automated security testing, including static and dynamic analysis, fuzz testing, and penetration testing against API endpoints.

Cryptographic Controls and Transport Security

Ensuring confidentiality and integrity of API communication channels is critical. Common practices include:

- Enforcing TLS (Transport Layer Security) for all API communications.

- Using digital signatures and message authentication codes (MACs) for messages requiring end-to-end integrity.

- Proper key management and rotation policies.

Authentication tokens such as JWTs must be securely generated, transmitted, and validated, including validation of signature, expiration, and audience claims.

Logging, Monitoring, and Incident Response

Even with rigorous preventive controls, APIs must maintain comprehensive observability:

- Detailed logging of authentication attempts, rate limit violations, and suspicious payloads.

- Real-time monitoring and alerting for anomalous usage patterns.

- Integration with Security Information and Event Management (SIEM) for correlation and forensic investigation.

This continuous feedback loop enables rapid identification of exploitation attempts and supports proactive defense measures.

Summary of Best Practices for Secure API Design

- **Validate all inputs rigorously,** leveraging schema definitions and whitelisting techniques.

- **Apply rate limiting** contextually to mitigate abuse and ensure availability.

- **Utilize API firewalls and semantic filtering** to block malicious and malformed requests.

- **Design with the OWASP API Security Top 10** as a baseline security checklist.

- **Enforce strong authentication and authorization** on every request.

- **Practice least privilege and minimize data exposure** in responses.

- **Ensure transport security and safe token management.**

- **Implement audit logging and monitoring** to detect and respond to threats quickly.

Adhering to these principles enables the construction of API ecosystems that not only provide functional excellence but also resilient security postures against evolving threats.

9.3. Message Encryption and Key Management

End-to-end message encryption serves as a fundamental pillar in securing data communication by ensuring that messages remain confidential and unaltered from sender to recipient, regardless of intermediary systems. The effectiveness of this security model critically depends on robust cryptographic key management and secret handling procedures throughout the data lifecycle-including data in transit, at rest, and within distributed environments.

At the cryptographic core lies the principle that only the intended parties possess the keys necessary to encrypt and decrypt the transmitted information. Message encryption typically employs a combination of symmetric and asymmetric cryptographic techniques. Symmetric encryption algorithms (e.g., AES) offer efficient bulk data protection with shared secret keys, while asymmetric algorithms (e.g., RSA, elliptic curve cryptography) facilitate secure key exchange and digital authentication without the prior sharing of secrets.

End-to-End Encryption Mechanics

End-to-end encryption (E2EE) restricts access such that plaintext messages are never exposed outside of the communicating endpoints. The sender encrypts the message with a symmetric session key, which is itself encrypted using the receiver's public key. Only the receiver can then decrypt the session key with their private key and use it to recover the original message. This hybrid encryption approach balances performance and security.

$$\text{ciphertext} = \text{Enc}_{K_{\text{session}}}(\text{message}) \quad ; \quad K_{\text{session}} = \text{Enc}_{K_{\text{receiver}}^{\text{pub}}}(K_{\text{session}})$$

Such constructions necessitate secure generation, storage, and distribution of keys, as any compromise can lead to catastrophic breaches. Key management thus focuses on safeguarding private keys and session keys, controlling access to them, and orchestrating their lifecycle-including creation, distribution, rotation, revocation, and destruction.

Secure Secret Storage and Access Control

Secrets such as private keys and symmetric encryption keys must reside within hardened environments to prevent unauthorized extraction. Hardware Security Modules (HSMs), Trusted Platform Modules (TPMs), or secure enclaves enforce strict access restrictions and tamper resistance. When hardware-based solutions are unavailable, secrets should be stored encrypted with keys derived from secure credentials or key hierarchies protected by access control policies.

Access to secret material must incorporate multifactor authentication and strong role-based access controls (RBAC), minimizing insider threats. Logging and auditing of all key usage and secret access are indispensable for forensic traceability and proactive security monitoring.

Key Lifecycle Management

Effective key lifecycle management mitigates risks arising from key compromise, algorithm obsolescence, and operational mishaps. Key management practices include:

- **Key Generation:** Keys must be generated with cryptographically strong random number generators (CSPRNGs) conforming to standards such as NIST SP 800-90A. Key strength should meet or exceed current security recommendations (e.g., 256-bit symmetric keys, 2048-bit RSA keys or stronger ECC curves).

- **Key Distribution:** Secure transmission of keys to authorized endpoints requires authenticated channels and confidentiality mechanisms. Protocols such as TLS, alongside key agreement algorithms (e.g., Diffie-Hellman or ECDH), provide cryptographically sound distribution of ephemeral or long-term keys.

- **Key Storage:** Once received, keys must be securely stored. For symmetric keys supporting message encryption, ephemeral session keys are often generated per message or session. Long-term keys, such as asymmetric private keys, demand persistent protection mechanisms as previously described.

- **Key Rotation and Renewal:** Keys must be periodically rotated to limit exposure from potential compromise and to adhere to security compliance requirements. The rotation interval balances operational overhead with risk reduction and is influenced by key usage patterns and threat models.

- **Key Revocation and Destruction:** Compromised keys must be promptly revoked to prevent unauthorized use. Revocation mechanisms should propagate swiftly within the system. Secure destruction involving cryptographic erasure ensures no residual data remains in any medium or backup.

Handling of Keys in Distributed Systems

In distributed environments where message exchanges occur asynchronously and across heterogeneous nodes, secure key management must account for replication, synchronization, and platform diversity. Strategies utilize hierarchical key management, where master keys secure subordinate keys specific to services or message channels, allowing compartmentalization and limiting exposure from individual node compromises.

Decentralized key management protocols, including blockchain-based registries or threshold cryptography, facilitate distributed trust models that mitigate single points of failure. In threshold schemes, a private key can be split among multiple parties, each holding a share such that a minimum quorum is required for decryption or signing, thus improving resilience and operational security.

Protocols and Standards Supporting Secure Key Management

Standardized protocols and frameworks enable interoperability and have been designed to embed robust cryptographic practices in key management. These include:

- **PKCS (Public-Key Cryptography Standards):** A set of standards for secure generation, exchange, and storage of keys and certificates.

- **KMIP (Key Management Interoperability Protocol):** Defines communication between key management systems and clients for lifecycle management operations.

- **X.509 Certificates:** Facilitate authenticated public key binding to identities, essential for public key distribution.

- **OAuth and OpenID Connect:** Standards often combined with encryption to manage authorization tokens securely.

Adherence to these standards ensures cryptographic agility, allowing systems to adopt newer algorithms or key sizes in response to evolving threats without redesigning key management infrastructure.

Cryptographic Algorithm Considerations

Careful selection of encryption algorithms and key sizes is paramount. While symmetric encryption algorithms like AES (Advanced Encryption Standard) in modes such as GCM (Galois/Counter Mode) provide authenticated encryption with associated data (AEAD), asymmetric schemes should leverage elliptic curve algorithms (e.g., Curve25519) over classical RSA for better security per bit length and performance in constrained environments.

Algorithms must be selected according to threat assessments, with planned transitions to quantum-resistant algorithms imminent given advancements in quantum computing. Hybrid post-quantum solutions start combining classical and quantum-safe algorithms for key exchange as part of the key management lifecycle.

Practical Example: Secure Message Encryption Workflow

```python
from cryptography.hazmat.primitives.asymmetric import rsa,
    padding
from cryptography.hazmat.primitives import hashes, serialization
from cryptography.hazmat.primitives.ciphers import Cipher,
    algorithms, modes
import os

# Generate ephemeral AES session key
session_key = os.urandom(32)  # 256-bit symmetric key

# Load recipient's public RSA key (PEM format)
with open("recipient_public_key.pem", "rb") as key_file:
    public_key = serialization.load_pem_public_key(key_file.read
    ())

# Encrypt the session key using the recipient's public RSA key
encrypted_session_key = public_key.encrypt(
    session_key,
    padding.OAEP(
        mgf=padding.MGF1(algorithm=hashes.SHA256()),
        algorithm=hashes.SHA256(),
        label=None
    )
)

# Encrypt the message using AES-GCM
message = b"Confidential message payload"
iv = os.urandom(12)  # GCM standard IV length
encryptor = Cipher(
    algorithms.AES(session_key),
    modes.GCM(iv)
).encryptor()

ciphertext = encryptor.update(message) + encryptor.finalize()

# Output includes ciphertext, encrypted session key, iv, and tag
```

285

Output:

- encrypted session key: binary blob encrypted asymmetrically

- ciphertext: AES-GCM encrypted message payload

- iv: Initialization vector used for AES encryption

- tag: Authentication tag from AES-GCM to verify integrity

This code fragment demonstrates encrypting a message with a session key and then protecting the session key through an asymmetric cipher, encapsulating the essence of secure key usage and message confidentiality.

Protecting Data at Rest and in Transit

Message encryption must also seamlessly integrate protection for data at rest and in transit:

- **Data in Transit:** Transport Layer Security (TLS) or Datagram TLS (DTLS) provide channel encryption but do not guarantee end-to-end security if intermediaries can access plaintext. Overlaying application-layer end-to-end encryption ensures confidentiality independent of channel security.

- **Data at Rest:** Encrypted storage solutions complement message encryption by safeguarding stored messages and keys. Transparent data encryption (TDE) and file-level encryption rely on key management solutions to govern access control and key rotation policies consistently.

Mitigating Key Compromise Risks

A critical security challenge arises when keys are compromised. Effective measures include:

- **Forward Secrecy:** Session keys are ephemeral and not

derivable from long-term keys, limiting exposure if a private key is compromised after message transmission.

- **Backward Secrecy:** New keys replace old ones frequently, preventing attackers from decrypting previously captured traffic.

- **Multi-Factor Key Access:** Control who can use or distribute keys by requiring multiple independent authorizations.

- **Anomaly Detection:** Employ monitoring tools to detect unusual key usage patterns suggesting compromise.

Each mitigation step strengthens the overall integrity and confidentiality assurances that end-to-end encryption promises.

Key management and message encryption necessitate a holistic approach encompassing secure algorithm selection, hardware- or software-enforced secret handling, rigorous lifecycle management, and integration of standard protocols. Combining hybrid encryption schemes, hierarchical and distributed key management techniques, and strong operational policies forms a resilient system architecture capable of defending sensitive communications from diverse modern threats.

Robust message encryption paired with exacting key controls thus remains indispensable in safeguarding digital information, particularly in distributed and cloud-native infrastructures where attack surfaces and complexity continue to expand.

9.4. GDPR, HIPAA, and Compliance Automation

Ensuring compliance with regulatory frameworks such as the General Data Protection Regulation (GDPR) and the Health Insurance

Portability and Accountability Act (HIPAA) demands a meticulous approach to data governance, privacy, and security within integration architectures. The complexity of these regulations necessitates automation frameworks capable of consistently enforcing policies, collecting runtime evidence, and supporting audit requirements. MuleSoft's tooling offers a comprehensive ecosystem for building such automated compliance controls directly within enterprise integration lifecycles.

A fundamental aspect of compliance automation involves *runtime evidence collection*, which encompasses the systematic logging and capturing of data processing events relevant to regulatory mandates. Within MuleSoft, the runtime environment provides native support for capturing detailed message metadata, transformation activities, and endpoint interactions. This granular telemetry can be configured via custom loggers and enhanced with standardized metadata schemas to encapsulate critical fields such as data subject identifiers, consent flags, and purpose of processing. By aligning the logged information with GDPR Article 30 for records of processing activities or HIPAA's audit controls under 45 CFR §164.312(b), organizations establish a verifiable trail of data subject interactions and operational compliance.

Complementing runtime evidence is the enforcement of *audit logging*, which secures immutable and tamper-evident records of system activities. MuleSoft's Anypoint Platform enables integration with external Security Information and Event Management (SIEM) systems, employing syslog forwarding or API-based ingestion of consolidated audit logs. These logs facilitate near-real-time monitoring for anomalous activity, supporting compliance with GDPR's data breach notification requirements and HIPAA's audit logging standards. Best practice dictates the implementation of role-based access controls (RBAC) at the logging infrastructure level to prevent unauthorized access or modification, preserving the integrity and confidentiality of audit records. Additionally, hashing or digital signatures can be applied for cryptographic validation of log contents.

Automated policy checks form a critical layer of compliance assurance by embedding regulatory controls within integration flows. MuleSoft's policy framework supports the declarative definition and enforcement of security and privacy constraints at the API gateway level. For instance, data masking policies can leverage DataWeave scripting to obfuscate personally identifiable information (PII) or protected health information (PHI) during data transit and at rest. Authentication policies such as OAuth 2.0 and Mutual TLS enforce access restrictions and ensure only authorized entities can interact with sensitive endpoints. Further, rate limiting, quota, and payload validation policies guard against denial-of-service attacks and data exfiltration risks. By integrating compliance policies into CI/CD pipelines, these checks become automated gatekeepers that prevent deployment of flows violating regulatory mandates.

Building *compliant integration architectures* on MuleSoft entails aligning design principles with regulatory requirements from the outset. Segregation of data processing environments for development, testing, and production ensures that sensitive data is shielded during nonproduction stages. Moreover, data minimization principles advocate for processing only the strictly necessary fields, achievable through transform components that selectively filter and redact data. Encryption at transit and at rest is implemented through TLS protocols in transport layers and encrypted connectors accessing databases or cloud stores. Architectures leveraging API-led connectivity foster modularity and traceability, allowing individual components to be audited and verified separately. Such modularization simplifies breach impact assessments and streamlines revocation or modification of access privileges in compliance with GDPR's data subject rights and HIPAA's minimum necessary standard.

Integration testing and monitoring are inseparable components of a compliant automation lifecycle. MuleSoft supports runtime alerts and anomaly detection via integrated monitoring dashboards. These monitoring systems are often extended with business activity monitoring (BAM) tools and external governance platforms to correlate operational metrics with compliance KPIs. Test automation frameworks incorporate regulatory validation scripts ensuring, for example, that data masking is correctly applied or that consent flags are properly propagated through microservices. The use of MUnit tests, combined with mocks for sensitive data elements, enforces policy adherence before deployment, reducing the risk of noncompliance in production environments.

Advanced compliance automation leverages MuleSoft's support for *policy-as-code* and infrastructure as code (IaC) methodologies. By encoding compliance requirements as reusable policy templates and versioned code artifacts, teams can enforce consistency across distributed environments and accelerate audit readiness. Continuous compliance scanning tools may integrate directly with Anypoint Exchange APIs to catalog deployed assets against regulatory baselines, flagging deviations for remediation. Additionally, MuleSoft's extensibility enables the creation of custom connectors and processors that implement organization-specific compliance logic, such as consent management or data subject access request (DSAR) fulfillment workflows. This extensible architecture ensures that evolving regulatory landscapes can be accommodated without wholesale redesign.

Within the broader compliance ecosystem, integration automation acts as the nexus bridging data producers, consumers, and regulatory oversight. MuleSoft's ability to centralize logging, policy enforcement, and evidence gathering reduces operational silos and creates a unified framework for regulatory adherence. When combined with organizational governance practices such as appointing Data Protection Officers (DPOs), conducting Data Protection Impact Assessments (DPIAs), and maintaining up-to-date docu-

mentation, automation in MuleSoft provides the technical foundation necessary for sustained compliance. Continuous evaluation
against regulatory updates and industry best practices forms an
essential feedback loop that ensures MuleSoft-based integrations
remain robust against emerging compliance risks.

```
<http:listener-config name="HTTP_Listener_config" host="0.0.0.0"
    port="8081" />
<policy name="DataMaskingPolicy" descriptor="dataMasking">
    <config>
        <masking>
            <fields>
                <field>ssn</field>
                <field>email</field>
            </fields>
            <maskCharacter>*</maskCharacter>
        </masking>
    </config>
    <apply>
        <expression><![CDATA[
            %dw 2.0
            output application/json
            ---
            payload map ((item) -> {
                ssn: item.ssn replace /./ with "*",
                email: (item.email splitAt "@")[0] ++ "@****.com
    ",
                otherFields: item.otherFields
            })
        ]]></expression>
    </apply>
</policy>
```

Sample Audit Log Output

2024-04-15T14:32:45.123Z | INFO | API-Gateway | UserID: 12345 | Endpoint: /p
atientRecords | Operation: Retrieve | GDPR-Consent: true | Masking-Applied: t
rue
2024-04-15T14:33:10.456Z | WARN | API-Gateway | UserID: 67890 | Endpoint: /p
atientRecords | Operation: Retrieve | GDPR-Consent: false | Access-Denied: tr
ue

The above example demonstrates a declarative policy applying
data masking to personally identifiable fields such as Social Security Numbers and Emails before data is transmitted through
the API gateway. This approach satisfies data minimization and
pseudonymization mandates within GDPR. The accompanying au-

dit log excerpts reveal how runtime events record user identifiers, consent status, endpoint interactions, and security actions, providing a robust evidentiary basis for compliance assessment.

The convergence of runtime evidence collection, audit logging, automated policy enforcement, and architected integration designs within MuleSoft's environment significantly reduces manual overhead for sustaining compliance with GDPR, HIPAA, and similar frameworks. The modular and programmable nature of Mule-Soft's platform enables scalable and auditable integration workflows, ensuring that compliance is not a one-time effort but an integral, continuous characteristic of enterprise integration operations.

9.5. Secure Deployment Topologies

MuleSoft deployments, whether hosted on-premises or in cloud environments, demand careful architectural planning to maintain robust security postures. The fundamental principles guiding secure deployment topologies encompass network segmentation, enforcement of least-privilege access, and stringent protection of communication boundaries. These principles enable organizations to minimize attack surfaces, prevent lateral movement of threats, and uphold compliance requirements in complex integration landscapes.

Network Segmentation and Isolation

Network segmentation is the cornerstone of secure system architecture. By dividing the deployment environment into discrete, isolated zones, it becomes possible to control data flows and restrict unauthorized access. In MuleSoft architectures, this typically involves separating API gateways, runtime manager consoles, application runtimes, and backend service endpoints into distinct network segments or virtual private clouds (VPCs). The objective is to prevent compromise in one segment from cascading into others.

Cloud deployments leverage native virtual networking constructs, such as AWS VPCs, Azure Virtual Networks, or Google Cloud VPCs, to establish isolated subnets for Mule runtime engines and their supporting services. Security groups or network access control lists (ACLs) govern ingress and egress traffic, only permitting communications essential for service functionality. On-premises deployments achieve analogous segmentation using VLANs, firewalls, and physically demarcated network zones classified by sensitivity or function.

Logical segmentation is further enhanced by deploying multiple API gateways-each scoped to a particular business domain or data sensitivity level. These API gateways act as bastions, exposing only the necessary services to particular client populations while isolating internal runtime engines and backend resources. This pattern achieves granular control over invocation paths and reduces exposure of critical assets to untrusted networks.

Enforcement of Least-Privilege Access

A critical security control within secure topologies is the adherence to the principle of least privilege. Each Mule runtime instance, API manager, or support tooling component must operate using identities and permissions scoped strictly to the minimal privileges necessary for their function. Overprivileged access increases risk by broadening attack vectors and escalation opportunities.

Identity and access management (IAM) systems play a pivotal role in implementing least-privilege models across both cloud and on-premises deployments. Cloud platforms provide integrated identity services (e.g., AWS IAM, Azure AD) enabling fine-grained role-based access control (RBAC) for MuleSoft components. Roles are carefully defined to separate duties such as deployment, administration, monitoring, and runtime execution.

Within MuleSoft itself, granular role assignments restrict user capabilities in Anypoint Platform dashboards and runtime controls. Runtime credentials, including keystores and encrypted environment variables, must be protected and retrieved dynamically where feasible, avoiding static embedding of sensitive data in configuration files.

Service-to-service authentication must leverage short-lived credentials or mutual TLS to ensure that each Mule runtime instance and backend service authenticates only with explicit authorization and context-aware credentials. This approach prevents unauthorized lateral movement and aids in forensic auditing.

Securing Communication Boundaries

Securing communication boundaries encompasses protecting data in transit, validating service identities, and ensuring message integrity. Considering the distributed nature of MuleSoft deployments, traffic often traverses multiple network segments, cloud environments, or hybrid connections, making boundary security essential.

Encrypting all internal and external communication using TLS (Transport Layer Security) is mandatory. TLS certificates should stem from trusted certificate authorities (CAs) or internally managed public key infrastructures (PKIs) with appropriate certificate lifecycle management policies. Enabling mutual TLS (mTLS) enforces two-way authentication between API gateways, Mule runtime engines, and backend services, significantly enhancing trust verification and eliminating risk of impersonation.

API gateways enforce policy-driven security controls such as OAuth 2.0, JWT validation, and rate limiting to further protect exposed interfaces. Leveraging MuleSoft's API Manager, each API endpoint can be configured to require strict authentication tokens and scope validations consistent with organizational access policies.

In hybrid deployments, network tunnels or private connectivity (e.g., AWS PrivateLink, Azure ExpressRoute) provide secure channels between on-premises systems and cloud-hosted Mule run-times. VPNs incorporating strong encryption and mutual authentication add layers of protection when private connectivity is unavailable or impractical.

Cloud-Native Versus On-Premises Deployment Considerations

Architecting secure deployment topologies diverges partly based on whether the MuleSoft runtime is hosted in the cloud or on-premises, though many security principles remain consistent.

Cloud-Native Deployments

Cloud-native deployments exploit provider-native security capabilities to automate and enforce secure topologies. The placement of Mule runtime engines in private subnets, use of auto-scaling groups with instance roles, integration with cloud-native secrets managers, and deployment via container orchestration platforms (e.g., Kubernetes on AWS EKS, Azure AKS) allow dynamic, policy-driven security enforcement.

Separation of environments (development, staging, production) leverages distinct VPCs or subscriptions to avoid cross-environment data leakage. Cloud services enable comprehensive logging and distributed tracing integrated with SIEM systems, facilitating real-time detection and incident response.

On-Premises Deployments

On-premises deployments require explicit implementation of network and physical security controls. Hardware firewalls, intrusion detection systems (IDS), regular network audits, and strict patch management policies are essential. Deployment topologies often incorporate DMZ zones to segregate external access points from sensitive internal systems.

Integration with enterprise identity providers (e.g., LDAP, Kerberos) ensures consistent authentication across the organization's asset base. Hardware security modules (HSMs) or equivalent secure cryptographic modules may be deployed to safeguard private keys and root certificates used by Mule runtimes.

Automation tools applied to on-premises environments, such as configuration management frameworks and container orchestration platforms, aid in maintaining consistent secure configurations and enforcing compliance across all runtime nodes.

Patterns for Resilience and Defense in Depth

A defense-in-depth model is achieved through layered security controls within the deployment topology. This includes perimeter security via network segmentation and firewalls; application-level security through API gateways and identity verifications; host-level hardening of runtime environments; and data security controls with encryption both in transit and at rest.

Resilience patterns, such as multi-region deployments and failover clustering, not only improve availability but also limit the impact of attacks localized to single data centers or cloud zones. Logging, audit trails, and alerting integrated at every layer enable rapid threat detection and response.

Additional mitigation strategies include employing dedicated management networks isolated from data traffic, integrating runtime anomaly detection, and conducting regular security assessments aligned with frameworks such as NIST or ISO/IEC 27001.

Example Deployment Topology Illustration

Consider a hybrid MuleSoft deployment servicing critical financial applications. The API gateways reside in a cloud provider's isolated VPC subnet, enforcing TLS termination and OAuth policy enforcement. Backend Mule runtimes deploy in private subnets without direct internet access, retrieving secrets dynamically from a managed secrets vault. Communications between API gateways and runtimes occur over mTLS-secured channels.

On-premises backend systems are segmented into secure VLANs, connected to cloud resources over an IPSec VPN with mutual authentication. Firewall rules strictly limit access to required ports, and network ACLs enforce unidirectional traffic flows where applicable. IAM roles granted to cloud resources strictly restrict actions to those required for operation and monitoring.

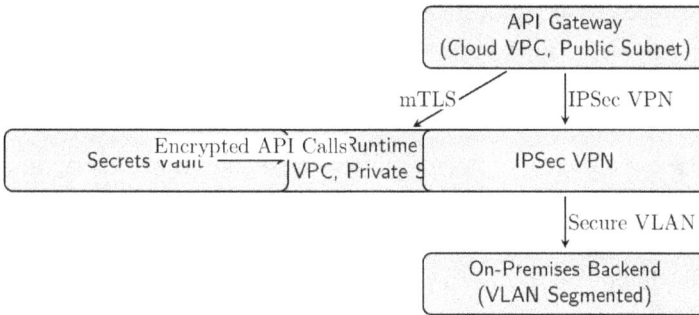

This topology exemplifies layered perimeter, network, and application controls to enforce segmentation, secure communications, and strict access governance-a model aligning to stringent security standards for sensitive enterprise environments.

Achieving secure MuleSoft deployment topologies demands a coherent strategy incorporating network isolation, least-privilege access enforcement, and communication boundary protections. Whether cloud-native or on-premises, these patterns cultivate resilient, defensible environments necessary for trustworthy enterprise integrations.

9.6. Threat Detection and Security Incident Handling

Effective threat detection and security incident handling require a multi-layered, proactive approach to identify potential security breaches and respond with agility. The increasing complexity of modern IT environments and the sophistication of threat actors necessitate continuous monitoring combined with advanced anomaly detection to prevent damage before it occurs.

Proactive Threat Monitoring

Proactive threat monitoring involves the continuous observation of network traffic, system logs, user activities, and application behaviors to uncover potential threats early. Central to this approach is the deployment of Security Information and Event Management (SIEM) systems that aggregate and normalize data from disparate sources in real time. SIEM platforms enable correlation of seemingly innocuous events into actionable intelligence by applying predefined threat models, behavioral baselines, and rule sets.

An essential element of proactive monitoring is integration with Threat Intelligence Feeds that provide external data on emerging vulnerabilities, Indicators of Compromise (IoCs), and threat actors. These feeds enhance detection capabilities by correlating internal observations with global threat landscapes. Automated ingestion and parsing of threat intelligence allow the system to update detection rules and prioritize alerts dynamically.

Behavioral monitoring, leveraging machine learning models, complements signature-based detection by learning standard operational patterns and identifying deviations indicative of novel attack vectors. For instance, a sudden surge in failed authentication attempts or unusual lateral movement within a subnet may trigger alerts even if no known signatures match. These anomaly detection mechanisms rely on robust baselining and adaptive thresholds that minimize false positives while maintaining sensitivity.

Anomaly Detection Techniques

A wide array of anomaly detection algorithms serves in identifying suspicious activities without prior knowledge of specific attack signatures. Statistical methods such as clustering, principal component analysis, and time-series forecasting uncover deviations from historical patterns. More advanced approaches include unsupervised and semi-supervised machine learning models, which learn to distinguish between benign and malicious activities with minimal labeled data.

Network-based anomaly detection typically focuses on unusual traffic volumes, protocol misuse, and unexpected connections. Host-based anomalies involve deviations in process behavior, file system changes, and privilege escalations. Combining these perspectives through data fusion methodologies enhances detection efficacy. For example, correlating increased CPU utilization of a server with rare outbound connections can isolate indicators of a cryptomining malware infection.

The implementation of anomaly detection must take into account the evolving nature of normal behavior in dynamic environments. Periodic retraining of models and context-aware adjustment of sensitivity parameters are necessary to reduce alert fatigue. Confidence scoring and prioritization frameworks assist security operators in focusing on high-impact anomalies.

Incident Response Workflows

The rapid containment and mitigation of security incidents depend on well-defined, repeatable incident response workflows that span detection to recovery. Automated response orchestration platforms facilitate these workflows by integrating monitoring systems, forensic tools, and remediation components.

A typical incident response workflow consists of the following phases:

1. **Identification**: Confirming the presence of a security event through alerts generated by monitoring or detection systems.

2. **Containment**: Applying measures to limit the spread or impact of the threat. This may include network segmentation, account disabling, or process termination.

3. **Eradication**: Removing the root cause, such as deleting malicious files, patching vulnerabilities, or updating firewall rules.

4. **Recovery**: Restoring systems to normal operations, validating integrity, and monitoring for recurrence.

5. **Lessons Learned**: Conducting post-incident analysis to improve detection capabilities and response plans.

Automated playbooks provide step-by-step guidance aligned with organizational policies, ensuring consistent execution under stress. Conditional logic in these playbooks supports dynamic decision-making, adapting responses based on incident severity, asset criticality, and operational context.

Real-Time Detection and Response Integration

Tight integration between threat detection systems and incident response processes enables real-time mitigation, reducing the window of exposure. Event-driven automation platforms subscribe to alerts and trigger scripted responses without manual intervention where appropriate. For example, upon detecting an IoC on a host, the system may automatically isolate the machine, initiate forensic data collection, and notify security teams.

Integration with endpoint detection and response (EDR) technologies enhances real-time capabilities by providing granular visibility into endpoint activities and allowing immediate remediation actions such as process kill or rollback. Similarly, network detection and response (NDR) tools deliver network-wide anomaly insights and support containment strategies at the traffic flow level.

The use of Application Programming Interfaces (APIs) facilitates interoperability among diverse security components, enabling orchestration layers to coordinate detection, analysis, and response. Leveraging centralized dashboards with unified alert triage improves situational awareness and expedites decision-making.

Advanced Techniques: Threat Hunting and Automation

Proactive threat hunting is a complementary approach where analysts search for hidden threats using hypotheses-driven investigation rather than relying solely on automated detection. Threat hunting employs tools such as query languages over log repositories, sandbox environments for malware analysis, and visualization of attack paths within kill chain frameworks.

Automation plays a critical role in scaling threat detection and incident handling efforts. Repetitive tasks including log aggregation, alert enrichment, and initial triage benefit from machine-led workflows, enabling analysts to focus on high-value investigations. Automation frameworks incorporate feedback loops where outcomes inform and refine detection algorithms, continuously enhancing accuracy.

```
import requests

def enrich_alert(alert):
    ioc = alert.get('ioc')
    ti_url = f"https://threatintel.example.com/api/iocs/{ioc}"
    response = requests.get(ti_url)
    if response.status_code == 200:
        data = response.json()
        alert['threat_level'] = data.get('severity')
        alert['associated_campaign'] = data.get('campaign')
    return alert
```

```
# Sample enriched alert output
{
  "ioc": "192.168.1.100",
  "threat_level": "High",
  "associated_campaign": "APT29 Phishing Operation",
```

```
  "timestamp": "2024-05-15T14:23:52Z"
}
```

Performance Metrics and Continuous Improvement

Metrics such as mean time to detect (MTTD), mean time to respond (MTTR), false positive rates, and incident recurrence inform the effectiveness of detection and response strategies. Regular audits and red team exercises simulate attack scenarios, validating system readiness.

A robust feedback mechanism incorporates incident learnings into updated detection rules and response playbooks. Collaboration between security, IT, and business units ensures alignment of security operations with overall organizational risk tolerance.

Embedding threat detection and incident handling as an integral part of security infrastructure demands comprehensive monitoring, sophisticated anomaly detection, and automated response workflows. Continuous adaptation through analytics and human expertise fortifies defenses against evolving threats, minimizing impact and preserving system integrity.

Chapter 10

Future Trends and Advanced Integration Scenarios

Stay ahead of the curve by exploring integration frontiers that are reshaping business and technology landscapes. This chapter navigates the convergence of MuleSoft with AI, edge computing, blockchain, and composable architectures—equipping you to architect for tomorrow's challenges while capitalizing on emerging opportunities today. Dive into real-world scenarios, experiment with no-code strategies, and master the principles required to adapt your integration ecosystem to whatever comes next.

10.1. MuleSoft and Edge Integration

Integrating MuleSoft's Anypoint Platform with edge computing environments necessitates a deliberate architecture designed to achieve resilience, minimal latency, and adaptability in distributed systems. The proliferation of Internet of Things (IoT) devices and the increasing demand for real-time analytics impose stringent requirements on data processing, mandating a shift from purely centralized cloud-based integration toward hybrid models that blend edge and central processing.

Edge deployment architectures with MuleSoft typically fall into three primary categories: *edge-only*, *hybrid edge-cloud*, and *centralized with intelligent edge proxies*.

- **Edge-only deployments** locate integration runtimes directly on edge nodes such as gateways, industrial controllers, or localized servers. These deployments support real-time processing by minimizing data round-trips and enable immediate decision-making. MuleSoft's lightweight runtime components (e.g., Mule Runtime embedded on edge devices) facilitate deployment in resource-constrained environments, although careful profiling of memory and CPU usage is essential.

- **Hybrid edge-cloud deployments** balance processing workloads between the edge and the cloud. Time-sensitive, high-frequency data streams or transformations occur on the edge, while less latency-critical workloads execute in centralized systems. This model optimizes bandwidth utilization and supports offline capabilities by enabling local persistence during connectivity disruptions.

- **Centralized with intelligent edge proxies** involve deploying API gateways or proxy layers near the edge that route data and manage communication with centralized MuleSoft platforms. While primary integration logic remains centralized, these proxies provide caching, protocol translation, and security enforcement close to data sources, effectively reducing latency for edge-originated requests.

Selecting the appropriate deployment model depends on specific use cases, device capabilities, network reliability, and latency requirements inherent to the IoT ecosystem.

A core challenge in edge integration is ensuring data consistency between distributed edge nodes and the central system. This involves selecting appropriate synchronization paradigms and data replication techniques while handling intermittent connectivity and variable network latency.

Event-Driven Synchronization
Event-driven architectures leverage message brokers, event bus technologies, or MuleSoft's CloudHub connectors to asynchronously propagate data changes. At the edge, events such as sensor readings, state changes, or alarms generate messages that are queued locally and relayed to the cloud upon network availability. Conversely, control commands or configuration updates can be broadcast from the cloud to edge nodes, enabling near real-time bidirectional synchronization.

Data Reconciliation and Conflict Resolution
Due to the decentralized nature of edge deployments, conflicting updates may arise when multiple nodes modify the same data offline. MuleSoft's runtime allows incorporation of reconciliation logic implemented through DataWeave scripts or custom flows to detect and resolve conflicts based on timestamps, priorities, or domain-specific rules. Idempotent processing pipelines and compensation transactions further ensure data integrity across distributed systems.

Stateful vs. Stateless Integration Patterns
Stateless integration at the edge simplifies scalability and fault tolerance but constrains local processing to ephemeral data handling. Stateful integration preserves contextual information such as session data or cumulative metrics within the edge runtime, enhancing complex event processing and anomaly detection but increasing demands on device resources and synchronization complexity. Designing effective state management strategies that lever-

age MuleSoft's Object Store and persistent queues ensures reliable message processing and state recovery after failures.

The interplay between centralized control and local edge autonomy defines the scalability, security, and operational agility of the integration solution.

Latency and Bandwidth Optimization

Local processing at the edge reduces dependency on wide-area networks by performing filtering, aggregation, and protocol translation close to data sources. For example, pre-processing telemetry data via MuleSoft flows deployed on gateway devices eliminates unnecessary transmission of raw data to the cloud, conserving bandwidth and reducing operational costs. Conversely, centralization facilitates global analytics, policy enforcement, and data archival but relies on robust network links.

Security and Compliance Considerations

Edge deployments demand rigorous security postures to protect sensitive data and prevent unauthorized access. MuleSoft's platform supports TLS encryption, OAuth 2.0 authentication, and role-based access controls that can be selectively configured at the edge or centralized layers. Implementing mutual TLS for device-to-edge authentication, alongside encrypted data storage and secure logging practices, mitigates attack surfaces. Compliance mandates may also dictate specific data residency or privacy restrictions, influencing the distribution of processing tasks.

Operational Management and Observability

Maintaining visibility into thousands of edge nodes requires leveraging MuleSoft's monitoring tools combined with distributed tracing frameworks adapted to constrained environments. Health metrics, runtime performance, message throughput, and error rates captured locally must be aggregated efficiently. Automated deployment pipelines utilizing CI/CD practices ensure consistent versioning of Mule applications across heterogeneous edge devices. Balancing update frequency and rollback capabilities minimizes dis-

306

ruption to critical IoT operations.

An archetypal MuleSoft edge integration flow commonly ingests IoT data streams via MQTT or HTTP connectors, validates and transforms payloads using DataWeave expressions, and triggers local decision logic through business rules or predictive models embedded within Mule runtime. Processed events may then be forwarded to a cloud-based analytics platform or persisted to local edge storage for short-term retention.

```
<mule xmlns="http://www.mulesoft.org/schema/mule/core" ...>
  <mqtt:listener clientId="edgeClient" topic="sensor/data" ... />
  <flow name="EdgeProcessingFlow">
    <mqtt:listener doc:name="MQTT Listener" />
    <dw:transform-message doc:name="Filter & Transform">
      <dw:set-payload><![CDATA[
        payload.filter((item) -> item.value > threshold)
                map ((item) -> {
                  id: item.id,
                  measurement: item.value,
                  timestamp: now()
                })
      ]]></dw:set-payload>
    </dw:transform-message>
    <choice doc:name="Local Action or Forward">
      <when expression="#[payload.size() > 0]">
        <logger message="Data filtered and transformed for local
processing" level="INFO"/>
        <http:request method="POST" url="https://cloud-
integration/api/ingest" />
      </when>
      <otherwise>
        <logger message="No relevant data to process" level="
DEBUG"/>
      </otherwise>
    </choice>
  </flow>
</mule>
```

In this example, edge runtime listens for MQTT messages from sensors, filters data points exceeding a threshold, transforms and annotates them, and conditionally forwards them to a cloud API endpoint. Such patterns exemplify how MuleSoft enables flexible, event-driven edge logic that integrates seamlessly with broader enterprise systems.

Trade-offs inherent to edge integration include handling limited compute resources versus the benefits of localized autonomy. Careful workload partitioning ensures latency-critical functions reside at the edge, while heavy analytic processing remains centralized. Moreover, selecting appropriate messaging infrastructure and adopting resilient networking strategies, such as store-and-forward queues and circuit breakers implemented via MuleSoft connectors, mitigate transient failures and promote graceful degradation.

Ultimately, designing edge-enabled MuleSoft architectures empowers organizations to harness distributed IoT data streams effectively, delivering responsive and scalable integration solutions tailored to the constraints and demands of edge environments.

10.2. Integrating AI and ML Pipelines

Integrating artificial intelligence (AI) and machine learning (ML) into MuleSoft flows enhances enterprise-grade automation by embedding real-time predictions, adaptive decision-making, and analytics within API-led connectivity architectures. This integration transforms static data pipelines into intelligent services that continually refine operational workflows through inferencing at scale. Achieving this synergy requires thoughtful design that spans model deployment, data orchestration, and the seamless invocation of predictive endpoints from within MuleSoft's Anypoint Platform.

Central to embedding AI/ML capabilities in MuleSoft flows is the orchestration of data preparation and the invocation of trained models. Data science pipelines typically involve data cleansing, feature extraction, and normalization, which must be operationalized as discrete Mule components or reusable sub-flows. These preprocessing steps prepare raw input streams into the structured formats demanded by inference engines. By leveraging Mule-

Soft's rich data transformation components-including DataWeave scripts-developers can execute sophisticated feature engineering inline, reducing latency and eliminating the need for separate batch jobs.

Model integration itself involves invoking AI/ML models hosted either on cloud-based platforms (e.g., AWS SageMaker, Azure ML, Google AI Platform) or on-premise servers equipped with model-serving frameworks such as TensorFlow Serving or TorchServe. MuleSoft connectors or HTTP requestors can interface with REST-ful APIs exposed by these model endpoints. For example, a Mule flow might capture streaming customer transaction data, enrich it with contextual information, and perform an HTTP POST to a prediction endpoint to flag potential fraud cases in near-real time. The lightweight, event-driven architecture of Mule enables concurrent processing of multiple prediction requests, facilitating high throughput and minimal response times.

```
<flow name="FraudDetectionFlow">
    <http:listener config-ref="HTTP_Listener_Configuration" path
    ="/detectFraud"/>
    <json:json-to-object-transformer returnClass="java.util.Map
    "/>
    <dw:transform-message doc:name="Prepare features">
        <dw:set-payload><![CDATA[%dw 2.0
        output application/json
        ---
        {
            transactionAmount: payload.amount,
            merchantId: payload.merchantId,
            userId: payload.userId,
            timestamp: payload.timestamp as String {format: "yyyy
        -MM-dd'T'HH:mm:ssZ"}
        }]]></dw:set-payload>
    </dw:transform-message>
    <http:request method="POST" url="https://ml-api.company.com/
    predict" doc:name="Invoke ML Model">
        <http:request-builder>
            <http:header headerName="Content-Type" value="
        application/json"/>
            <http:header headerName="Authorization" value="#[vars
        .authToken]"/>
        </http:request-builder>
        <http:body><![CDATA[#[payload]]]></http:body>
    </http:request>
```

```
        <json:object-to-json-transformer />
    </flow>
```

Data preparation within Mule flows can also utilize advanced integration with AI model inputs. Batch processing transformations, conditional enrichments, and context-aware parameters form essential parts of feature pipelines. Coupling this capability with MuleSoft's Anypoint Monitoring allows operational teams to track data quality metrics, input distribution drift, and feature integrity-critical indicators when deploying ML models in dynamic environments. For example, a flow ingesting IoT sensor data may normalize readings to a standard scale before prediction requests, thereby ensuring consistent model input.

Operationalizing AI/ML within MuleSoft further extends to incorporating feedback loops that facilitate continuous learning and model retraining. Real-time scoring results, paired with outcome labels or user feedback collected downstream, can be routed back to model management services via Mule flows. This feedback is paramount for supervised learning models requiring periodic updates to maintain accuracy in evolving operational contexts. Mule's connectivity with data lakes, streaming platforms such as Kafka, and databases supports these bi-directional data movements, thus closing the AI/ML model lifecycle within the integration fabric.

Security and governance form foundational considerations when embedding AI/ML pipelines in enterprise integration flows. MuleSoft's policy framework enables securing the data streams exchanged with model endpoints through OAuth, mutual TLS, and IP whitelisting. Additionally, encryption of sensitive payloads and role-based access to the models' invocations ensures compliance with regulatory and organizational requirements. Logging enriched with AI inference metadata, such as prediction scores and confidence intervals, provides auditing capabilities critical for high-stakes decisioning applications like credit approval and fraud prevention.

Realizing intelligent automation at scale also involves handling asynchronous interactions and large volumes of inference requests. MuleSoft's support for non-blocking flows, batch processing modules, and streaming consumption patterns addresses these performance requirements. For instance, a model deployed on a GPU cluster might impose latency constraints that necessitate queuing requests and loading batches of input data. Mule flows can integrate with message brokers or stream processors, managing backpressure and guaranteeing ordered delivery of prediction requests, thus enabling robust, scalable AI/ML services.

Coupling AI/ML pipelines with MuleSoft's API-led connectivity pattern unlocks interoperability across heterogeneous systems ranging from legacy ERP applications to modern SaaS offerings. By exposing ML-powered services as REST or SOAP APIs via Mule gateways, organizations encapsulate complexity and provide easy access to AI capabilities for diverse consumer applications. This approach also fosters reuse: a single Mule API can aggregate multiple predictive models' responses or orchestrate composite logic that combines rule-based systems with ML inferences, thereby creating hybrid intelligence.

An illustrative example is the integration of a natural language processing (NLP) model for sentiment analysis within a customer support platform. Incoming chat messages processed through MuleSoft are parsed, sanitized, then sent to an NLP model endpoint. The predicted sentiment score is fed back into the support ticket workflow, prioritizing urgent cases for human agents. DataWeave scripts transform raw text into model-friendly tokens, while Mule error handling routes malformed messages appropriately.

```
<flow name="SentimentAnalysisFlow">
    <http:listener config-ref="ListenerConfig" path="/
    analyzeSentiment"/>
    <json:json-to-object-transformer returnClass="java.util.Map
    "/>
    <dw:transform-message doc:name="Sanitize input">
```

```
<dw:set-payload><![CDATA[%dw 2.0
output application/json
var sanitizedText = payload.message replace "\\p{Punct}"
with ""
---
{ text: sanitizedText }]]></dw:set-payload>
</dw:transform-message>
<http:request method="POST" url="https://nlp-api.inc.com/
sentiment" doc:name="Call NLP Model">
    <http:request-builder>
        <http:header headerName="Content-Type" value="
application/json"/>
    </http:request-builder>
    <http:body><![CDATA[#[payload]]]></http:body>
</http:request>
<logger message="Sentiment Score: #[payload.score]" level="
INFO"/>
</flow>
```

Beyond invoking external services, a growing trend is the deployment of lightweight ML models directly within Mule runtime. Through Java custom components or embedded Python scripting via external libraries, Mule flows can perform inferencing locally without network overhead. This approach reduces prediction latency and ensures offline capabilities but demands constraint-aware model designs and runtime environment compatibility. Integration with specialized ML inferencing engines such as ONNX Runtime or TensorFlow Lite is possible through native connectors or Java interop, widening the range of supported applications.

Key implementation challenges revolve around managing data schemas, versioning models, and ensuring seamless rollback mechanisms to mitigate erroneous predictions. Data engineers and integration architects must collaborate closely with data scientists to maintain model registry services and structured metadata that enable automated deployment pipelines. MuleSoft's DevOps toolkit supports CI/CD workflows that synchronize API changes with ML model updates, guaranteeing consistent behavior across development, staging, and production environments.

Embedding AI and machine learning pipelines within MuleSoft

flows elevates integration platforms from data conduits to intelligent decision frameworks. This interweaving demands coherent data preparation, robust model invocation strategies, real-time operational monitoring, and secure governance. By constructing modular, reusable components and employing API-led connectivity, organizations build scalable AI-powered systems that seamlessly orchestrate analytics and automation at the core of their digital ecosystems.

10.3. Blockchain, Immutable Ledgers, and Digital Trust

The integration of MuleSoft with blockchain networks and immutable ledgers represents a convergence of API-led connectivity and distributed ledger technology (DLT), enabling enterprises to craft secure, transparent, and trustworthy digital workflows. Critical to this integration are established patterns that address secure messaging, transaction verification, and the orchestration of smart contracts, all of which enhance data integrity and trustworthiness across decentralized systems.

At the core of this integration lies the immutable ledger, a cryptographically secured append-only data structure that guarantees non-repudiation and tamper-evidence of transactions. Blockchain's distributed consensus mechanisms ensure that once a transaction is recorded, it cannot be altered or deleted without network consensus, thereby creating a robust trust anchor for inter-organizational processes. MuleSoft's Anypoint Platform, with its mature API management and integration tooling, acts as a conduit for seamless interaction between enterprise systems and blockchain networks, abstracting complex native blockchain operations into reusable APIs and connectors.

A proven pattern in this context is the use of secure messaging through MuleSoft's native support for enterprise-grade protocols

313

combined with blockchain-specific cryptographic primitives. The process typically involves MuleSoft APIs encapsulating blockchain transaction requests, digitally signing messages using asymmetric key pairs, and transmitting these signed payloads over encrypted channels such as TLS. This approach preserves confidentiality and integrity while fostering non-repudiation by cryptographically binding the sender's identity to the transaction data. For instance, MuleSoft connectors can leverage blockchain node RPC APIs (such as Ethereum JSON-RPC or Hyperledger Fabric SDKs) to push signed transactions efficiently to the ledger while simultaneously validating signature authenticity prior to submission.

Transaction verification is another critical element in bridging MuleSoft and blockchain platforms. The integration pattern involves a two-phase protocol where MuleSoft orchestrates workflows to generate a transaction proposal and subsequently execute a verification step against the blockchain state. For permissioned ledgers, verification entails querying the ledger's endorsement policy and transaction validity logic to confirm consensus compliance before committing state changes. For public chains, the integration verifies transaction inclusion through block confirmation checks. These validations, facilitated by MuleSoft API flows, ensure only accurate and authorized transactions propagate, reducing the risk of replay attacks or unauthorized data manipulation. As an example, MuleSoft orchestration can implement automated webhook event listeners that subscribe to blockchain events, such as the confirmation of a specific transaction hash, triggering downstream business processes only when ledger state changes are finalized and verified.

Smart contracts extend the notion of trust and automation by embedding business logic directly within the blockchain. MuleSoft's integration strategy capitalizes on smart contracts as programmable, self-executing entities that enforce transparent rules and conditions without human intervention. By abstracting smart contract functions as RESTful APIs or GraphQL endpoints via

MuleSoft's runtime, enterprises gain the ability to invoke contract methods remotely while maintaining security controls such as OAuth 2.0, mutual TLS, or API gateways. This abstraction supports end-to-end traceability where each interaction with a smart contract records a verifiable transaction on chain, providing an auditable and tamper-proof trail within distributed systems.

A concrete implementation example involves a supply chain scenario where smart contracts automate asset provenance verification. MuleSoft APIs capture data from IoT sensors or ERP systems, format inputs to match contract parameters, and submit these to a blockchain-based provenance contract responsible for asset history validation. The contract emits events upon successful checkpoints, which MuleSoft listeners detect in near real-time, updating enterprise systems or triggering alerts in case of anomalies. This pattern greatly enhances operational transparency and trust across distributed stakeholders by providing a single source of truth reconciled on the blockchain.

Furthermore, MuleSoft's event-driven architecture complements blockchain's asynchronous transaction confirmation model. By leveraging message queues, event brokers, and streaming platforms like Kafka or Anypoint MQ, MuleSoft enables reactive flows that respond to blockchain events. This design pattern ensures scalability and resilience by decoupling blockchain interactions from enterprise logic, making it possible to handle high transaction volumes while maintaining consistent state synchronization. Additionally, event-driven MuleSoft flows can aggregate multiple blockchain events to derive composite business insights, thus augmenting digital trust not only at the transaction level but also at the analytic level.

Security considerations within these patterns are paramount given the sensitive nature of distributed transactions and cryptographic keys. MuleSoft's secure vault and key management capabilities integrate seamlessly with hardware security modules (HSMs) or cloud key management services (KMS) to safeguard private keys used in transaction signing. This layered security model prevents unauthorized access and supports compliance with industry standards such as FIPS 140-2 or GDPR. Moreover, MuleSoft facilitates role-based access control (RBAC) and fine-grained policy enforcement on blockchain APIs, ensuring that only authorized identities can invoke contract functions or retrieve ledger data.

To optimize interoperability between disparate blockchain platforms and enterprise systems, MuleSoft leverages canonical data models along with transformation policies. This abstraction layer harmonizes heterogeneous data schemas and transaction formats, reducing integration complexity and avoiding vendor lock-in. For instance, a canonical asset token representation can be transformed into Ethereum ERC-721 or Hyperledger Fabric asset model specifications dynamically, allowing a single MuleSoft integration layer to interface with multiple ledgers seamlessly.

The convergence of MuleSoft and blockchain via these proven integration patterns enables enterprises to create digital ecosystems characterized by immutable data integrity, cryptographically enforced identity, and autonomous process automation. Secure messaging ensures confidentiality and non-repudiation; transaction verification upholds consistency and correctness; smart contract utilization boosts transparency and automatic compliance; event-driven architectures provide scalable and reactive solutions; and stringent security practices protect cryptographic assets. Together, these architectural constructs allow for the realization of truly trustworthy digital workflows essential for modern decentralized applications and enterprise digital transformation initiatives.

10.4. Composable Integration and Microservices

Achieving business composability requires an architectural approach that decomposes enterprise functions into discrete, reusable, and independently deployable components, which can be dynamically assembled to fulfill evolving business needs. MuleSoft's integration platform provides a robust foundation for realizing such composability through the application of microservices patterns within its orchestration architecture. This approach demands careful attention to modular integration flows, clear service boundaries, and the automation of end-to-end processes to enable agility and scalability.

At the core of composable integration lies the principle of modularity, which dictates that integration solutions should be segmented into distinct functional units, each responsible for a well-defined business capability. Within MuleSoft environments, these units correspond to microservices-self-contained APIs or integrations that encapsulate specific business logic or data transformation tasks. By isolating integration concerns into microservices, teams gain the ability to develop, test, deploy, and scale components independently, reducing coupling and accelerating time-to-market.

Defining precise service boundaries is crucial to avoid ambiguity and ensure that each microservice provides a clear contract and scope. Service boundaries in MuleSoft architectures often align with domain-driven design principles, where each microservice encapsulates the logic of a single bounded context. These microservices expose standardized APIs, typically RESTful, which support CRUD operations, event consumption, or messaging protocols as needed. Establishing boundaries at this level facilitates loose coupling between services, limits the blast radius of changes, and improves governance by maintaining domain ownership.

Orchestrating integration flows involves composition of microservices in a manner that delivers coherent business processes. MuleSoft's Anypoint Platform supports orchestration through API-led connectivity layers: System APIs for core transactional systems, Process APIs for business logic orchestration, and Experience APIs for user-facing interactions. Process APIs act as the orchestrator of microservices, coordinating calls to multiple System APIs or other Process APIs, aggregating data, and applying business rules. This separation permits reuse of core components while enabling flexible assembly of integration flows tailored to specific use cases.

Reliable orchestration also requires handling asynchronous communication and state management. MuleSoft excels in integrating message queues, event-driven architectures, and API gateways to enable event-based microservices interactions. Patterns such as event sourcing and saga orchestration can be implemented to maintain consistency across distributed transactions or workflows. For instance, a business process spanning order management, inventory, and billing microservices can leverage MuleSoft's orchestration combined with message brokers for event propagation and compensating transactions, thereby achieving eventual consistency without tight coupling.

Automation of end-to-end business processes relies on the combination of API orchestration, rules-driven execution, and automated error handling within MuleSoft. Automation scripts or flows encapsulate standard operating procedures and decision logic, often incorporating frameworks like the Mule Expression Language (MEL) or DataWeave transformations to govern data enrichment and validation. Process automation also extends to CI/CD pipelines for deployment, where MuleSoft's integration with DevOps tools ensures rapid delivery and rollback capabilities for microservices. Automated monitoring and alerting based on MuleSoft's runtime and analytics components provide real-time insights into service health and performance, enabling proactive adjustments and SLA adherence.

Scalability is inherent in MuleSoft's lightweight runtime engine, which supports cloud-native deployments on Kubernetes or Anypoint Runtime Fabric. Microservices designed within this fabric benefit from container orchestration, auto-scaling, and service discovery. Performance optimization is achieved by employing API gateways for rate limiting, caching, and security enforcement, preventing system overloads and ensuring consistent response times. Such infrastructure considerations are integral to supporting business composability at scale.

Security is another cornerstone in the design of composable microservices. MuleSoft enables implementation of fine-grained security policies, including OAuth2, JWT validation, TLS encryption, and IP whitelisting at API gateways. Each microservice enforces its own security context, consistent with the principle of least privilege, and communicates through secured channels. These measures preserve data integrity and confidentiality across distributed integration flows while allowing services to evolve independently.

Reusability forms the backbone of business agility within composable architectures. MuleSoft fosters reuse through the establishment of API specifications as reusable templates, shared connector libraries, and centralized asset repositories available via Anypoint Exchange. Standardizing interfaces accelerates onboarding of new integrations and simplifies maintenance. Moreover, versioning strategies enable backward compatibility, allowing multiple service versions to coexist as consumers transition to updated APIs without disruption.

The alignment of integration patterns with microservices also accentuates fault tolerance and resilience. Circuit breaker patterns implemented in MuleSoft flows prevent cascading failures by isolating malfunctioning microservices, while retry policies and fallback mechanisms ensure graceful degradation of services. Coupled with distributed tracing and logging capabilities inherent in the Anypoint platform, these patterns enable rapid diagnosis and recovery from issues, thereby increasing overall system robustness.

MuleSoft's support for polyglot integration is essential to composability in heterogeneous IT landscapes. Microservices can be developed in multiple runtime environments and languages but integrated seamlessly via standardized APIs managed by MuleSoft. This flexibility enables gradual migration of legacy systems towards more modular architectures, ensuring interoperability while protecting past investments.

Enabling business composability through microservices patterns within MuleSoft architectures revolves around modularizing integration flows, delineating clear service boundaries, and orchestrating automated, scalable processes. These principles empower enterprises to respond swiftly to changing business environments, minimize operational risk, and achieve continuous innovation through reusable, governed, and resilient integration components.

10.5. No-Code/Low-Code Integration Trends

The landscape of software development has undergone a transformative shift with the rise of no-code and low-code platforms. These visual, declarative paradigms enable a wider spectrum of users-including business analysts, domain experts, and citizen developers-to participate in application and integration development, traditionally the domain of professional software engineers. This democratization of software creation has profound implications for integration architectures, software delivery velocity, and maintainability of enterprise systems.

At the core of no-code/low-code platforms lies the abstraction of complexity through visual modeling, drag-and-drop interfaces, and pre-built components that encapsulate common integration patterns. This abstraction accelerates the design and deployment of integrations by reducing the need for hand-coding and deep technical expertise. Key contemporary platforms offer connectors to cloud services, data sources, APIs, and legacy systems, enabling rapid assembly of integration workflows. Enhanced with AI-assisted development features, these platforms further reduce cognitive load by recommending next steps, detecting anomalies, or automating routine tasks.

Despite their advantages, no-code/low-code solutions do not supplant traditional programming entirely but rather complement it by shifting the scope of coding effort. Complex logic, performance optimization, and advanced customization often require pro-code development. The prevailing trend involves hybrid architectures wherein visual integration processes coexist with custom-coded modules, each selected for suitability to their unique tasks. This hybridization demands diligent strategy and governance to preserve code quality, traceability, and security.

Interoperability between no-code/low-code components and pro-code assets emerges as a critical factor for sustaining extensibility and maintainability. Modern integration platforms provide standard interfaces such as RESTful APIs, event-driven hooks, and scripting extensions to facilitate seamless integration with bespoke codebases. Establishing clear boundary definitions, interface contracts, and data transformation schemas between visual workflows and custom modules mitigates integration fragmentation. Furthermore, adopting a service-oriented mindset-with encapsulated microservices or serverless functions-enhances composability and reuse irrespective of development paradigms.

Accelerating delivery cycles is a principal driver behind no-code/low-code adoption. By empowering domain experts to build and iterate integration solutions directly, these platforms shorten feedback loops and reduce dependency bottlenecks on scarce engineering resources. Continuous integration and continuous deployment (CI/CD) pipelines increasingly incorporate automation suited for no-code/low-code artifacts, such as versioning visual workflow definitions and automated environment provisioning. Effective DevOps practices extend to include the management, testing, and monitoring of no-code/low-code components, ensuring they adhere to enterprise standards for reliability and governance.

As no-code/low-code usage expands, maintainability challenges surface, especially when visual workflows become large, complex, or poorly documented. Unlike traditional source code, visual artifacts can suffer from opaque logic and difficulty in code review. Employing best practices such as modularization of workflows, adherence to naming conventions, and use of comments within platform-supported metadata improves readability and transferability. Traceability tools that map visual components to underlying API calls, data schemas, and version histories are essential to understanding system evolution and performing impact analysis during change requests.

Security and compliance considerations require equally rigorous treatment in environments blending no-code/low-code with pro-code. Role-based access control (RBAC), audit trails, and encryption must be embedded at the platform and integration layer. Validation of data inputs, output sanitization, and secure credential management remain critical across the full spectrum of integration components. Organizations invest in integration governance frameworks that encompass policy enforcement, automated compliance checks, and artifact certification to prevent shadow IT and proliferation of unsanctioned workflows.

The adoption of open standards and portable artifact formats further facilitates the integration of no-code/low-code solutions into heterogeneous IT ecosystems. Standards such as BPMN (Business Process Model and Notation), OpenAPI, and AsyncAPI provide common semantics for documenting and exchanging integration designs, enabling interoperability between different tooling vendors and runtime environments. Containerization and infrastructure-as-code approaches accommodate deployment and scaling of integration services, whether visually configured or custom-developed, within cloud-native architectures.

A concrete example of blending no-code/low-code development with pro-code involves event-driven integration architectures. Visual platforms can orchestrate event flows, apply conditional routing, and execute simple transformations, whereas specialized event processing logic or complex data enrichment might be implemented in pro-code microservices. By standardizing on event bus technologies like Apache Kafka or cloud-native messaging services, these hybrid solutions facilitate loose coupling and extensibility while preserving development agility.

Testing and quality assurance practices adapt accordingly. Automated testing frameworks evolve to support hybrid artifacts by combining UI-driven test scenarios for workflows with unit and integration tests for code modules. Mocking APIs or data services empowers iterative validation without reliance on external dependencies. Monitoring solutions integrate observability features such as distributed tracing and metrics dashboards covering both no-code/low-code executions and underlying code, providing holistic operational insights.

The rising influence of no-code and low-code integration paradigms reflects a broader trend toward technology democratization in software development. This trend unlocks faster delivery, greater innovation, and closer alignment with business objectives, but it also introduces complexity in integration management, quality control, and security. Organizations that achieve success typically embrace hybrid development models where no-code/low-code platforms and pro-code assets are thoughtfully integrated through standardized interfaces, governance frameworks, automated tooling, and best practices.

Such an approach fosters sustainable scalability, maintainability, and resilience in the evolving digital enterprise landscape.

10.6. Architecting for Extensibility and Change

The rapid pace of technological advancement, frequent shifts in business requirements, and evolving integration needs demand platform architectures designed from the ground up for extensibility and adaptability. Ensuring that an integration platform remains future-proof involves embracing modular design principles, prioritizing API-centric development, and leveraging adaptive architectural patterns. These strategies collectively empower enterprises to incorporate innovation seamlessly, mitigate risks associated with change, and maintain operational continuity.

Modularization: Building Blocks for Continuous Evolution

Modularization disassembles a complex integration platform into distinct, loosely coupled, and independently deployable components or modules. Each module encapsulates specific functionality or business logic, enabling parallel development, targeted updates, and easier troubleshooting. This separation of concerns fosters enhanced maintainability and scalability.

A module boundary ideally aligns with cohesive, domain-specific concerns or bounded contexts derived from domain-driven design (DDD) principles. This alignment helps prevent tight interdependencies that can create cascading changes when a single module evolves. By exposing well-defined interfaces, modules manage their internal complexities, avoiding leakage of implementation details across boundaries.

For example, consider an integration platform with dedicated modules for protocol adaptation, message transformation, orchestration, and monitoring. Changes in the message transformation module-such as incorporating support for a new data format-can then proceed without necessitating modifications to the protocol adapters or monitoring components, provided the interface contracts remain stable.

Modularization also facilitates incremental refactoring. As new requirements surface, individual modules can be rewritten or optimized without disrupting the entire platform. Moreover, the potential to reuse modules across projects and environments accelerates development cycles and ensures consistency.

API-First Thinking: Enabling Interoperability and Flexibility

An API-first approach positions APIs not as afterthoughts but as primary artifacts that drive platform design, development, and evolution. APIs function as explicit contracts between modules and external consumers, defining expectations for data formats, operations, error handling, and security.

Designing APIs with extensibility in mind involves:

- **Versioning**: Implementing clear versioning strategies allows changes to be introduced without breaking existing consumers. Semantic versioning, combined with backward-compatible enhancements, fosters non-disruptive evolution.

- **Discoverability**: APIs should be self-describing through mechanisms such as OpenAPI specifications or GraphQL schemas, facilitating easy integration and automated tooling.

- **Idempotency and Resilience**: Designing operations that can be safely retried aids recovery in distributed systems, increasing robustness against transient failures.

- **Extensible Data Models**: Employing flexible serialization formats (e.g., JSON with extension fields) permits augmenting payloads with additional information without invalidating consumers.

API gateways and management layers enhance the extensibility framework by enabling policies such as throttling, authentication, and logging to be applied consistently and changed dynamically. These runtime controls enable feature toggling and staged rollouts, allowing new functionality to be introduced gradually and safely.

The API-first approach lays the foundation for integration as a platform service, where internal and external parties can feed back innovations, plug in new capabilities, or consume services without awaiting monolithic releases.

Adaptive Architectural Patterns for Change Absorption

Extensible architectures incorporate adaptive patterns enabling the system to absorb change gracefully while maintaining scalability, reliability, and clarity. Some pivotal adaptive patterns include:

Event-Driven Architectures (EDA)

EDA decouples producers and consumers through asynchronous event messaging. This loose coupling allows new event consumers to be added without affecting producers, and new event types to be introduced side-by-side with legacy ones. Event streams also provide a durable audit trail, enabling temporal replay and state reconstruction.

The use of well-defined event schemas with schema evolution capabilities (e.g., using Apache Avro or Protocol Buffers) supports backward and forward compatibility, allowing event producers and consumers to evolve independently over time.

Service Mesh and Sidecar Proxies

Introducing a service mesh abstracts operational concerns - such as service discovery, traffic routing, retries, and circuit breaking - out of application logic and into an infrastructure layer. Sidecar proxies deployed alongside services manage cross-cutting concerns transparently, enabling developers to focus on feature evolution without worrying about communication complexity.

Dynamic configuration and policy management in the service mesh permit runtime behavior changes, such as shifting traffic patterns for canary deployments or toggling observability features, fostering continuous improvement and safer change introduction.

Feature Toggles and Canary Releases

Feature toggles allow selective activation or deactivation of features at runtime, decoupling feature rollout from code deployment. They support A/B testing, gradual adoption, and rollback capabilities without redeployment cycles.

Canary releases further enhance adaptability by directing a small subset of traffic to new platform versions or modules to validate functionality and performance under real-world conditions before full-scale rollout. This staged approach reduces risk and enables rapid feedback loops.

Domain-Driven Design (DDD) and Bounded Contexts

Mapping the platform architecture to business domains using DDD concepts limits the scope of changes within bounded contexts. Each bounded context maintains its own model and integration contracts, containing complexity and avoiding ripple effects across unrelated domains.

This discipline allows teams to evolve specific contexts independently, adopting new technologies or paradigms within a bounded context while maintaining overall coherence.

Governance for Sustainable Extensibility

Extensibility and adaptability rely not only on technical constructs but also on governance frameworks that balance agility with control. Key governance practices include:

- **API Lifecycle Management**: Establishing processes for API design, review, versioning, deprecation, and documentation ensures quality and stability.

- **Change Management**: Implementing structured change advisory boards (CABs) or automated policy enforcement to validate compatibility and compliance minimizes unintended disruptions.

- **Continuous Integration and Continuous Deployment (CI/CD)**: Automating build, test, and deployment pipelines reduces feedback latency and enables safe progressive delivery.

- **Monitoring and Observability**: Proactive monitoring of module health, API usage patterns, and system metrics enables timely detection and mitigation of issues introduced by changes.

By integrating governance into the architecture lifecycle, enterprises balance rapid innovation with the stability necessary for mission-critical operations.

Infrastructure Considerations for Extensibility

Cloud-native infrastructure paradigms, such as containerization and orchestration platforms (e.g., Kubernetes), augment extensibility by providing elastic, environment-agnostic deployment capabilities. These platforms support:

- **Microservices Deployment**: Independent versioning and scaling of modules.

- **Service Discovery and Load Balancing**: Dynamic routing to evolving components without hardcoded endpoints.

- **Infrastructure as Code (IaC)**: Declarative environment definitions supporting reproducibility and auditability.

Combining these infrastructural enablers with modular and API-first design establishes a robust foundation for platforms capable of continuous evolution.

Case Illustration: Evolving a Payment Integration Platform

A payment platform initially built as a monolithic system underwent modularization to isolate payment protocol adapters, fraud detection, and transaction logging. APIs governing these modules were designed with versioning and extensible data models, enabling introduction of new payment schemes without breaking existing integrations.

Event-driven architecture supported asynchronous notifications to downstream reconciliation services. Service mesh technologies managed secure communication and traffic shaping during feature rollouts.

Governance processes enforced strict API lifecycle management, coordinated canary releases, and monitored operational health, allowing the organization to rapidly incorporate regulatory changes and emerging payment methods with minimal downtime and risk.

The architectural philosophies outlined here do not merely prepare integration platforms for change; they transform change into an enabler of innovation. By structuring platforms for modularity, API-first interoperability, adaptive operation, and governed evolution, enterprises can confidently embrace continuous technological advancement without compromising stability or agility.

www.ingramcontent.com/pod-product-compliance
Lightning Source LLC
Chambersburg PA
CBHW061235220326
41599CB00028B/5431